CU00854610

M-MOTHER

M-MOTHER

DAMBUSTER FLIGHT LIEUTENANT
JOHN 'HOPPY' HOPGOOD

JENNY ELMES

The
History
Press

First published 2015

The History Press
The Mill, Brimscombe Port
Stroud, Gloucestershire, GL5 2QG
www.thehistorypress.co.uk

British Library Cataloguing in Publication Data.
A catalogue record for this book is available from the British Library.

ISBN 978 0 7509 6184 4

Typesetting and origination by The History Press
Printed in Great Britain

M-MOTHER

Jenny Elmes

The night was so bright that it was possible to see the boys flying on each side quite clearly. On the right was John Hopgood in *M-Mother*, that grand Englishman whom we called 'Hoppy'. He was one of the greatest guys in the world. He was devoted to his mother, and devoted to flying; used to go out with us a lot, get drunk – used to go out a lot to Germany, do a wonderful job.

He had no nerves; he loved flying, which he looked upon rather as a highly skilful art, in which one can only become proficient after a lot of experience. He was one of the boys who completely refused to be given a rest, and had done about fifty raids with me in my last squadron.

Perfect at formation was Hoppy too. There he was, his great Lancaster only a few feet from mine, flying perfectly steady, never varying position.

Once when training for this raid we had gone down to Manston in Kent, and had shot up the field with wings inside tail planes, and even the fighter boys had to admit it was the best they had ever seen.

I should say Hoppy was probably the best pilot in the squadron.

Extracted from article in *The Sunday Express* on 3 December 1944, and reproduced in *Enemy Coast Ahead* by Wing Commander Guy Gibson, VC DSO DFC, who commanded 617 Squadron in the raid on the Ruhr Dams on the night of 16/17 May 1943.

Flt Lt John V. Hopgood DFC and Bar

Contents

Foreword

by Shere Fraser

It is a daunting task to name a child, and yet my parents did not have to toil over their decision and draw from a pool of a thousand names. In fact, it was quite the opposite, and neither my brothers, John Hopgood and Guy, nor I, Shere, could comprehend the significance of those names until much later in life. I remember in childhood hearing my parents say I was named after the beautiful village of Shere, which was a special place, especially for my father. He didn't talk much about his heroic wartime service, and for us children, we came to know that Daddy was a hero and he helped to stop the war in Europe. For us, he busted dams in Germany, his plane crashed and he then became a prisoner of war for a very long time. Tragically, my father died in a plane crash in 1962 and those memories of his heroic service died with him.

Fast forward fifty years, after a series of life events and what some may call an epiphany, I began a healing journey of getting to know my father through the lens of his wartime letters and experiences. As I opened each new chapter in this journey, I became very grateful for each new revelation. One of the more rewarding experiences was learning about John Hopgood, the man who saved my father on the night of 16/17 May 1943. On that fateful night prior to their departure from Scampton, the crew sensed they might not return, so much so that the navigator, Earnshaw, told my father that they were not coming home. Hopgood's *M-Mother* was hit by flak some twenty minutes before the dam was reached and yet he pressed on with a serious head wound and a fervent determination to get the job done. Much has been documented about the Dams Raid, but sadly not much has been written or said about the courage and gallantry of John Hopgood. He was made deputy leader of the attack on the Möhne Dam for a very good reason: Guy Gibson knew the character of this man and entrusted this responsibility fully upon him. Hopgood should have at least got a DSO for his courage and sacrifice, and I feel he should have got the Victoria Cross (VC) posthumously. I know that my father never forgot Hopgood's act of heroism and demonstrated this by naming his first son after him. My research brought me full circle and I have come to understand now why I was named after the village of Shere. It was in remembrance of the place where 'Hoppy' grew up, but in my heart Shere is not just a village. It is a name of honour, where I will uphold John Vere Hopgood's memory for the rest of my life.

NB The log books of Shere Fraser's father, John Fraser, bombardier, and Ken Earnshaw, navigator, both crew members of AJ-M, were stolen in 2003. Any help from the public in tracing them would be very much appreciated.

Introduction

John Vere Hopgood died a hero on the night of 16/17 May 1943, a Dambuster, piloting a Lancaster Bomber (AVRO–M) over the Möhne Dam in one of the most iconic bombing missions of the Second World War. This book is drawn on previously unpublished family papers to show how a typical English public school boy and his family responded to the war, particularly through his letters to his mother, Grace, to whom, as Guy Gibson stated, John was devoted.

John's mother, Grace, was Harold Hopgood's second wife. Harold's first wife, Beatrice Walker, had died leaving him with two children, Joan and Oliver Hopgood. Grace and Harold then went on to have three more children, Marna (born June 1920), John (born August 1921) and Elizabeth (Betty), my mother (born December 1923).

John's mother, Grace, aged 45 years, plus a scrap of letter written by her in later life

Grace Fison's father, Lewis, was connected to the Fison seed and fertiliser family of Cambridge, but her mother, Jane Bukely De Vere Hunt, was descended from an Earl of Oxford through the Irish De Vere Hunt lineage. This gave Grace a somewhat exaggerated opinion of her social status, and she passed this on to Marna and John along with the De Vere name. There are some examples of this 'snobbery' in John's early letters, and it is a combination of all John's traits, exemplary or otherwise, which made him the hero he became. It also made him the perfect material to be an officer and possibly Guy Gibson's closest friend: they shared the same background and attitudes and were both a product of their time.

You will see how John fitted in well with squadron life, partly due to, and partly despite of, the prejudices of his upbringing. John was a team player, and he loved the competitive camaraderie of his crew and squadron. His crews were cosmopolitan and with mixed backgrounds but they instantly became a close-nit group, necessarily totally reliant and trusting of each other in the extreme circumstances they were placed. The loss of some of those who shared the training and execution of Operation Chastise (as the Dams Raid was originally termed) on that fateful night of 16/17 May 1943 was like losing family members.

Without understating John's undoubted heroism, this book is a 'warts and all' account of how he metamorphosed from a young, somewhat over-sensitive boy, through his perfectionism and idealism as a teenager and his rebellious youth, to the selfless hero he became. In the twenty-one short years of his life, John was transformed from a gutless goodie to a daredevil Dambuster.

But M is not just for John's mother and the AV-M Lancaster he flew on the Dams Raid; there were other significant Ms in his life, namely his sister Marna and Marlborough College. Marna was only fourteen months older than John and very close to him: 'almost a twin', as Grace wrote. They were both frightfully competitive; however, whereas John was dynamic and forthright, Marna was practical and domesticated. Their mother, Grace, carefully and proudly kept her letters from Marna (in the Auxiliary Territorial Service, or ATS) and John (in the RAF), and their two styles of writing give a balanced and interesting picture of events at home and in service.

My mother, Betty (their sister Elizabeth), who has contributed much to this book in hindsight of those years, was two and a quarter years younger than John and slightly removed from the real horrors of war; she is somewhat embarrassed by her lack of emotion at the time. She admits to living, for the most part, in a bubble of innocence, content with climbing trees and enjoying her little cat, Susan, and the countryside. Now in her nineties and looking back on that time, reliving it through John and Marna's letters, she does feel emotional and adds extra insight and flavour to the accounts in this book. Betty muses that the war was a great leveller, seeing the destruction, to a great extent, of the class divisions under which she, John and Marna had grown up.

Attending Marlborough College, John was well educated, particularly in the arts, and he mixed with many of the sons of the British elite. He experienced a comradeship with his peers which would prepare him almost seamlessly for squadron life. At school, John was in the Officers Training Corps (OTC) and enjoyed team sports, where, despite being very rebellious in the sixth form, he learnt discipline and team responsibility. His regimented education, along with his family's influence, led John to despise anybody with 'no guts', adult or young person alike. This was to be highly significant in the outcome of his all too short life. John volunteered for the RAF, wanting a sense of excitement and challenge, and the RAF automatically led him into Bomber Command. Here he would have wanted to complete the task his uncles had valiantly fought for in the trenches of the First World War, and John would have been full of the knowledge and idealism that it was a just war for Britain against the Nazis.

John fully expected that the targets would be, as Neville Chamberlain had promised, 'purely military objectives', reinforced by Air Commodore Sir John Slessor's promise that 'indiscriminate attack on civilian populations' would 'never form part of our policy'. Once on the treadmill of Bomber Command, there was no way out, except to desert and be classed as LMF (Lacking in Moral Fibre), a term widely used in the RAF to incur shame and deter desertion. This route would of course have been absolute anathema to John. It was probably a blessing that John never knew that the Dams Raid cost more than 1,300 lives, many of them civilian.

However, towards the middle of the war it became clear that precision bombing was not precise: only one in three bombs were landing within 5 miles of their target because of the primitive nature of the navigation aids. Chief of the Air Staff, Charles Portal, decided, in order 'to hasten the end of the war', to abandon previous principles and order more general bombing of German cities. Portal's deputy, and soon-to-be chief of Bomber Command, Arthur 'Bomber' Harris, carried out orders enthusiastically and lobbied the British Prime Minister, Winston Churchill, to increase the size of his bomber force; the Lancaster Bomber was manufactured in large numbers and became 'Harris's Shining Sword'. So Bomber Command soon became responsible for the indiscriminate bombing of Cologne and Hamburg, something that after the war must have preyed on the consciences of many who had served in the RAF. John would have been no exception. (It is interesting to note, however, that despite the general change of tactics, John's 617 Squadron was, even after the Dams Raid, still preserved as a specialist squadron for precision bombing, one of its next major targets being the *Tirpitz*.)

It seems that Portal made some quite radical decisions whilst in the position of Air Chief Marshal; it was, after all, he who approved Wallis's bouncing bomb plan. Bomber Harris, along with Ralph Cochrane, Chief of No. 5 Group Bomber Command, despite thinking it a crackpot idea which would sap his

Lancaster force, obeyed his superior's orders and saw that Operation Chastise was carried through with the highest priority and with all the resources it needed. Operation Chastise, now known as the Dams Raid, became the icon of what was Best of British in the Second World War, and luckily for Portal, it justified the risk he had taken in backing it. The breaching of the dams served as a terrific morale boost to the British people: one and all could wholeheartedly celebrate the skill of invention, the cooperation of industry and the heroism of Bomber Command, for a feat untainted by controversy and executed in an extraordinarily short timescale. John just happened to be one of the cogs which enabled its success.

By then, living on borrowed time, John could have been forgotten, like many of the other unsung heroes of the war, but he lost his life in a raid which is now legendary, so his heroism is celebrated by all who have been inspired by 'The Dambusters'. Through John's letters and diary we can see how his tough upbringing both at home in Shere, Surrey, and through his schooling, especially his public school, had moulded him, along with his church attendance, sport and a strong independent and competitive nature, into the hero he became in his cruelly truncated yet, in the end, celebrated life. John's strength of character and professionalism enabled him, when faced with extreme challenges as he was in Bomber Command, to glorify his country and to serve his fellow comrades with extreme courage ('Courage Beyond Fear') and selflessness.

The mementoes documented and illustrated in this compilation were saved and treasured by John's mother, Grace, who was staunchly proud of her son. She must have been aware of all the pieces that would add to this glorious story, because I even found the following snippet written by Grace in her latter years. It was torn from a letter in her hand and stated:

> It's so sad having to throw away letters from long ago which bring back so many memories, & which I could have kept; they would make human interest for posterity (if any) & often throw quite interesting sidelights on manners, customs, financial expenses, etc, etc, of one's forbears. Of such can good stories be made. It is difficult to find out about the intimate daily life of common folk.

Although Grace Hopgood would never have included herself in the term 'common folk', I know she would have been delighted that the letter writings of her beloved son, John Vere Hopgood, and others have been preserved in this book 'for posterity'.

After Grace's death in 1968, his sister Marna kept the letters and mementoes, just as proudly, in the original old leather case, which I rescued, with her daughter Annabel's blessing, from under her bed at the nursing home in Marlborough. Here, sadly, in the last stages of dementia, Marna's life ended in 2011.

Now, more than seventy years after Operation Chastise, its participants are heralded with more admiration than ever, and the question most frequently asked is 'Why was John Hopgood never awarded the Victoria Cross?' And the probable answer: John was killed in the raid considered to be, along with the coincidental North African success, probably the biggest morale boost of the Second World War and even the turning point of the war; Churchill would have felt that to give posthumous awards would be dwelling on the tragic losses and morbidity of the raid and so diminish its glorious effect. In modern times, as a hero deprived of his just deserts, this seems to have only enhanced the image of Flt Lt John V. 'Hoppy' Hopgood, DFC and Bar. His family can bask in this adulation, his mother Grace would have been justifiably proud, but John himself has missed it all!

Jenny Elmes, John's niece, daughter of Elizabeth (Betty) Dorothea Hopgood

1

Early Years: A Dambuster is Born

John Vere Hopgood was born on 29 August 1921 at Dorndon, in the village of Hurst, Berkshire. A robin appeared on the windowsill as John Vere Hopgood emerged from his long struggle to be born, its fiery orange breast an unlucky omen, as the midwife remarked. Was this to be prophetic of his end in the flaming *M-Mother*?

John was second son to London solicitor Harold Burn Hopgood but first son to Harold's second wife, Grace (née Fison). This notice appeared in *The Times*: 'HOPGOOD, – On Monday, the 29th August 1921, at Dorndon, Hurst, Berks, to GRACE, wife of HAROLD BURN HOPGOOD, of Hurst, and 11, New Square, Lincoln's Inn – a son.'

John's youth was spent in the family home Hurstcote in Shere, near Guildford, Surrey. He attended the Lanesborough Prep School in Guildford, followed by Marlborough College, where he was a good all rounder. In March 1939 he qualified as a school member of the junior division of the OTC. He played football and cricket in school teams and also played a good deal of tennis; he enjoyed entering local tournaments during the holidays. Music was his chief hobby: he played the piano and the oboe quite proficiently and was a member of the school orchestra. Natural history and photography also interested him.

His older sister Marna recalled:

As a person, John was sensitive, kind, intelligent and thoughtful. He loved his home and family, but also his independence and was able to divide himself between the two without conflict. He was ambitious to do well in whatever he took up, working hard to get to the top. His sense of humour was such that he was involved in many youthful pranks, but he was sufficiently aware of the law to know when to stop! He would never do anything to hurt anything. I remember how distressed he was when he shot a green woodpecker in mistake for a pigeon, so much so that he had it stuffed and enshrined in a glass case in his room. He never went shooting after that day. One of the reasons that he went into Bomber Command was that he did not wish to see the immediate results of human suffering from the weapons of war. He felt that to be in the clouds would separate him from the awful act of killing. I know this worried him a great deal; he did not want to kill his fellow human beings. John was due to go to Corpus Christi College, Cambridge in 1939, but as war broke out in the autumn, he decided it was not worthwhile starting at university. Until he joined up he spent a few months articled as a Solicitor's Clerk to a friend of his father's in the City. He joined the RAF in 1940. John was 21 when he died; he had always given of his best to serve his country. He had known his chance of survival to the end of the war was remote.

His younger sister Betty says John was prone to tears and not a daredevil as a child; he was close and competitive with Marna, who was only fourteen months older. In contrast, Betty loved to climb trees, right to the very top, which she felt Marna and John were too scared to do, and she resented John for trying to shoot her beloved birds and squirrels. Betty enjoyed the company of her little cat, Susan, and felt she was just the silly younger sister. She remembers that, when young, John enjoyed drawing aeroplanes, and, as he matured, would often be found lying on the sitting room floor reading *The Times* newspaper. He was, however, always caring towards other people, sociable and sporty.

John aged 7 years at
Lanesborough Prep School

John's first school report, aged 5 years, from Lanesborough Preparatory School Kindergarten, near Surrey, said that his 'diligence and application' were 'very good' and he worked with 'perseverance'; even at this young age he was good at handwork and writing, and showing aptitude for sport and music. This was to be John's hallmark in the future when Guy Gibson recommended him for an award reporting that 'he pressed home his attacks with great determination'.

At the age of 10 years, a weekly boarder, he was already fiercely competitive, and very much enjoyed a challenge, as shown in the extracts from next the letter:

Mother and John, November 1921

John, aged 2 years,
with sister Marna

The five Hopgood children, 1926
(l-r Oliver, Joan, Marna, John, Betty)

John aged 6 years

Lanesborough School,
Cranley Rd.,
Guildford,
Surrey
May 1932

My darling Mummy,

I am sorry to disappoint you but I am not moved up but I may be moved up at half-term. If I am first and many marks above the rest I may be moved up at half-term, but do not worry I am moved up into a higher form in Maths and I shall be doing Algebra & Geometry in it and so far I am 2nd already and my same old rival is first who is Dean; he was first in Maths last term and I cannot beat him but I am going to try. I have played two games of cricket and on Saturday I made four runs.

... Last Thursday I went to the baths and I swam my length again, next time I went to swim 2 lengths. Last time I jumped off the side in the deep end, next time I am going to jump off the spring-board and off those steps, will you please tell Marna that and when I see her that I have done these things ...

... I am very happy.

Love to everyone from John Hopgood.

John clearly wanted to impress not only his mother but his older sister Marna as well.

He had always been keen on sport; the picture shows him sitting second from left on the bench in the first XI football team in his final year at Lanesborough Preparatory School.

Betty remembers John, aged about 11 years, talking earnestly to their mother as to how he could possibly ever fight in a war and kill people; he would have to be a conscientious objector. Grace replied that, as he grew older, he was bound to change his ideas and perhaps be more able to cope with the things he feared now.

In 1935 John, aged 13 years old, reluctantly went on a French exchange to the Hoepffner family, who lived in the Vosges. His mother had insisted he go and it proved to be a great success. Grace wanted him to be fluent in French and felt it would be good for him. So probably in order to ensure that he went, she arranged for John's father, Harold (born in 1865 and so too old to be conscripted in the First World War), to take him and show him the Menin Gate memorial and the First World War sites on the way. Grace's two brothers, Elliot and Harold, had both been in the trenches in the First World War. This certainly had a big impact on John, as he built up his knowledge of, and attitudes towards, war – and how the other half live.

Lanesborough Prep football team (John second from left on bench)

Letter from
Lanesborough Prep

2.

but it was nothing much. Last thursday I went to the baths and I swum my length again, next time I want to swim two lengths. Last time I jumped off the side in the deep end, next time I am going to jump off the spring-board and off those steps, will you please tell Marna that and when I see her I shall be able to tell her that I have done these things. I expect Seaford will be crowded to-day and to-morrow, are you going to that fete on the recreation ground to-morrow. as we have got a new master his name is called Mr Fry (chocolate) he takes us in French. He is very nice. Yesterday it was the hotest day we have had this year. I am enjoying myself. I am getting on with my music I have got a lovely book out of the libry. In criket there was a boy who trying to catch a ball had a bit (at least 1/4) of his tooth broken. There have been two good catches this term. The captain of the school is Burke m

John's passport photo
1935

He wrote the following letter to his two sisters on Sunday, 28 July 1935:

Dear Marna and Elizabeth,

We arrived safely on Tuesday night at Ypres, Ieper or Yper (Flemish). On the Boat-train from Victoria to Dover we saw a lot of Hops and Kentish Orchards.

It was a smooth crossing yet a lady was sea sick just after we started. We had lunch on board. At Ostende we had tea and then caught a train to Ypres. We travelled 3rd class and when we got in a carriage there was an old Flemish peasant woman who, when we looked at her, took off her shoes, poof! Then she started to eat some bread, 1" thick, with some meat. When the train started she made a cross on her body and murmured a prayer. After a while she took off her stockings, pooh! Her feet were absolutely black; when she last washed I haven't any idea. At last, to our relief, the ticket collector came round and he swore at her and she kindly obliged by putting on her shoes.

In the train we saw some oats, corn, wheat, flax, tobacco plants, potatoes and cabbages, the whole way, in large quantities. After supper in the Hotel Regina, we went along to the Menin Gate and saw the names of dead soldiers on large stones inside. We also heard the Last Post at 9 o'clock (21 o'clock in European time). They play it every night there and also in the morning. (N! I found out afterwards that they only play it at night).

On Wednesday morning we went in a car which took us round the battle fields and cemeteries of the Great War. We saw Hill 62 and Hill 60. And on both, more so on Hill 62, we saw the Trenches and Dug outs, also the Helmets, Guns, pistols, and various shells which were used in the Great War. I don't know. In a book on Belgium it said that they (Trenches) were so full of water that the English and the Allies had to build parapets in water and also get under cover. Besides trenches we were able to see shell holes and broken trees and other G.W.R. (Great War Relics). I took some photos. Oh! I forgot on Hill 60 we went in an underground trench. It was wet on foot and very damp and it would have been very dark had it not been that there were electric lights there. It was made, or constructed, rather, of wood and occasionally steel girders to keep up the earth. Also when they first found it, they discovered a soldier's body lying on a bed, which they think was the hospital ward.

Your brother John.

What an extreme impact the realities and sordidness of trench life must have had on the impressionable John; no wonder he would decide to opt for the RAF and the air.

At home in Shere, in the early days of Hurstcote before money became short, the Hopgoods were very sociable, attending and hosting dinners and dances with others of their social class. They had servants in these early days who would have referred to the children as 'Miss Marna', 'Master John' and 'Miss Elizabeth'. However, the Hopgood family lost their wealth in the Great Depression of 1929 and soon only the gardener was left. Hurstcote was turned into flats, and a smaller house, Southridge, was built on the land. The children mucked in to cover the practical duties needed to keep the estate running. Their mother, Grace, started a poultry business and lodged in guest houses whilst building works were under way; their father, Harold, often stayed in London near his law firm.

John continued to practise the piano daily and often played Bridge with his mother. The family attended church regularly and were upright members of the community. John wrote in his diary, aged 16 years:

JAN 2 SUN 1938: As usual we went to church at Shere. … **The address was outstandingly good. The theme was that the greatest gift of God** to mankind was the inability to foresee the future, and that to face the future we need God and so we must push forth into the New Year with God.

JAN 9 SUN 1938: … In the evening we listened to the service from St Martins-in-the-Field. **The theme was that we must not live in the past, but forgive and so build up love. If only the Nations could have forgiven each other at Versailles there would be unthreatened Peace now.**

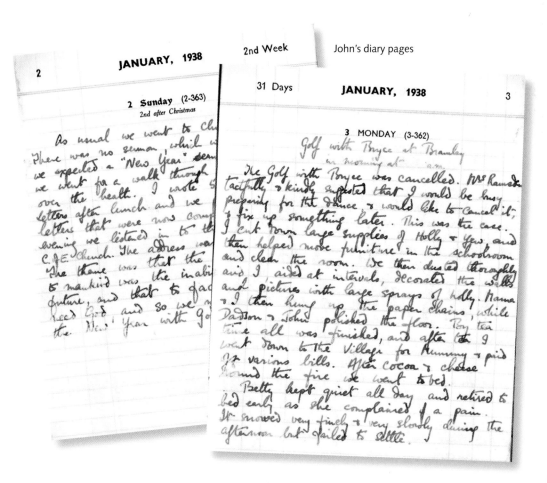

John seems to have taken the subjects of sermons very seriously, and this would have moulded his moral attitudes and given him a sense of duty to God and his country.

Enjoying a love of fresh air, wildlife and the countryside, John played golf and cycled miles. The Hopgoods took part in traditional country sports, including beagling and hare-coursing; the poor hare's head was often saved, stuffed and preserved, and they had some mounted on their walls at Hurstcote.

A hare trophy mounted
on the wall

Summer 1938 at Hurstcote (l-r cousin Laurence (later killed in a tank at just 18 years), Betty, John, Marna)

John, Betty and Marna making the most of the snow, Christmas 1938

2

M – Marlborough College

Despite money constraints, John spent his school life, from the age of 14 to 18, in Marlborough College, Wiltshire, following his mother's family tradition. John's name appears in the Book of Remembrance, along with his cousin Wilfred Fison's, and on the Roll of Honour in the chapel at Marlborough College.

Marlborough College always had a rough and rustic character among public schools, and the accepted amount of institutionalised bullying, which fits in with his mother's idea of bringing up her children to be tough. Marlborough College undertook to give bursaries to all sons of Old Marlburians who had been killed in the First World War, and so there would have been a strong ethos of respect for soldiers and officers.

Whilst John was at Marlborough he overlapped with David Maltby (Marlborough College from 1934–36) for a year. David Maltby was also to become a pilot and take part in Operation Chastise; in fact, it is the bomb from Maltby's plane AJ-J that puts the finishing touches to breaching the Möhne Dam. Interestingly also, it is David Maltby who signs the last page in John's Log Book (see end of chapter 9). David was to survive Operation Chastise only to be killed four months later piloting a Lancaster during an aborted operation to the Dortmund–Ems canal.

John started Marlborough College conscientious, competitive and desperate to make the most of his opportunities to please and impress his mother and family; he was also thoughtful and literate, coming top of the class in his first Michaelmas term. You will see in the summary below that John also came first and won the form prize in the summer term of 1938, when Jennings, whom he admired, was his tutor. However, by the time he left Marlborough College he had become a pretty rebellious pupil altogether, and he conspired to be bottom of the class when Wylie, whom he did not like, was his tutor (see John's diary entry for Monday, 19 December 1938).

(Historically Marlborough College had had many rebels. In 1851 the pupils had caused a riot and the headmaster had fled.)

John at Marlborough College, 1936

Detail from Marlborough College Book of Remembrance

John Vere HOPGOOD's record at Marlborough College:
Son of H.B. Hopgood   Born: 20 August 1921
At Marlborough College from Sept 1935 until July 1939

Term	Form	Form Master	Position in Form	House	Housemaster
Mich. 1935	U.4c	A.R.Pepin★	1st/63 won Form Prize	A House	W.I.Cheeseman
Lent 1936	Shell d	E.C.Marchant	46/98	A House	W.I.Cheeseman
Summer '36	Shell d	E.C.Marchant	6th/115	A House	W.I.Cheeseman
Mich. 1936	Hundred a	A.E. Spreckley	80/90	C1	L.F.R. Audemars
Lent 1937	Hundred a	A.E. Spreckley	46/98	C1	L.F.R. Audemars
Summer '37	Hundred a	A.E. Spreckley	6th/115	C1	L.F.R. Audemars
Mich. 1937	Modern 5b	R.A.U. Jennings	13/27	C1	L.F.R. Audemars
Lent 1938	Modern 5b	R.A.U. Jennings	12/26	C1	L.F.R. Audemars
Summer '38	Modern 5b	R.A.U. Jennings	1st/24 won Form Prize	C	L.F.R. Audemars
Mich. 1938	History U5a	H.Wylie	17/17	C1	L.F.R. Audemars
Lent 1939	History U5a	H.Wylie	14/15	C1	L.F.R. Audemars
Summer '39	History U5a	H.Wylie	11/14	C1	L.F.R. Audemars
Joined the O.T.C. Sept 1936 Passed Cert A. Part II on 7th March 1939					

★ His first form master, A.R. Pepin, was a very enthusiastic member of the Signals Section of the College OTC, and it was his pioneering work on radio between the wars which resulted in the development of the basic army walkie-talkie radio set used in the Second World War.

C1 House, Marlborough College

There are few letters surviving from his first years at Marlborough, but they were always respectful to his parents and well written. Here John was just 15 years old and on the main campus in C1 House:

C.1 House
The College
Marlborough
Wilts
18.10.36

My darling Mummy & Daddy,

Thank you so much for the letter …

So glad to hear you can all come on the Sunday. Confirmaga is A.M. at 11 o'clock (BE V. PUNCTUAL), come at 10.45.★

I played for house 3rd on Thursday but we lost; ahem! I'd rather not say the <u>cricket</u> total against us!! But as a result I was put on to top game yesterday, but it was too hard to play. House teams are:– Upper, Lower, 3rd, Remnants. I might play for Lower next time.

I did some more Vol. shooting and did a group of 4 in a halfpenny easily.★★

I am getting to know the Oboe better now and can play a <u>few</u> scales. I might be able to take my piano exam by about half term as I am practising very hard and know the stuff pretty well now.

… A boy has just returned with a rabbit which he saw being killed by a stoat. We don't know what to do with it, whether to 'paunch' it and sell it 'down' town, or to see if the cook will prepare it for him to eat, or What?

On Wednesday we were allowed to try and command our section. I volunteered and was quite efficient, except that I let them get out of hearing once and they rather fell to pieces. On Friday we were allowed rifles and have begun to learn rifle drill.

On Tuesday there was a school match against Bath which we lost I think. And yesterday the school played 'Harlequins A' and won 16–0.

This morning the preacher was of Blundell's School.

As an English book this term we are doing Hamlet. I think it's quite one of Shakespeare's best. We always have to do a 'set' book for the 'cert', and this is what the school has chosen.

I think that exhausts the news for the week.

Much love to all,

Your very loving Son.

★ It was very important, not only to John but to John's mother, Grace, that John was confirmed. That he had been confirmed was to be a source of extreme comfort to her in the future.

★★ 'Vol' shooting is rifle shooting.

Note in the next letter that John was beginning to take interest in the opposite sex.

C.1 HOUSE
THE COLLEGE
MARLBOROUGH
11.37

My dearest Mummy and Daddy,

You will doubtless be pleased to hear that I have passed my music exam with 120 out of 150. 120 is the prize mark, so I am lucky enough to get a prize! Lucky!

… Did you see that my friend Dart's father has been having a row with the Duke of Windsor over the Armistice Celebrations in Paris. Dart's father is the chief English Dean in Paris and he, as most clergy, is anti the Duke of Windsor.

Confirmation Sunday today. There was no-one whom you know being confirmed but I went to the service (and in order to get a decent pew in the balcony, sneaked in 35 minutes before the service was due to start and learnt my repetition prep! And also dodging the wary eye of the school porter who was attending to the benches; there were a few others also). I met Mrs Ramsden, & Mr & Jill, outside the Chapel, and she told me about the wives fellowship Dance or something next hols (meanwhile I was expecting to be asked out!), but I tactfully withdrew. I was later accosted by many boys to know who the pretty girl was, I was talking with!!! (and was it my sister!)

As we only read one chapter of Gibbon* a week we have not got much further than halfway (Vol. 1). We had to write an essay on the Constitution of Upper School in the style of Gibbon, and unfortunately the master in charge read mine, and I had written the most licentious and treasonable things about him** and how his inward fear and trepidation was severely veiled over by a mask of authority, etc etc!!! (My essay was appreciated by Mr Jennings).

Last Sunday we heard a most boring lecture on Alchemy and Alchemists. I learnt practically nix, and certainly could have spent my time more profitably.

I really must stop now and write to Marna.

With much love,

From your very loving Son.

---

* Edward Gibbon (27 April 1737–16 January 1794) was an eighteenth-century English historian and MP. His most important work, *The History of the Decline and Fall of the Roman Empire*, is known for the quality and irony of its prose, its use of primary sources and its open criticism of organised religion. (Amazingly enough, when, in 2013, the author visited the archives at Marlborough College and was shown around the school, these books were still in evidence in the Adderley Room, a gracious room used, then and now, for quiet study.)

**This could not have been the most tactful thing to write about your own master, who then read it, and shows John's increasing questioning of authority. It seems he would do anything for someone in authority he admired but didn't suffer fools gladly. (Note later in this book how John must have greatly admired and respected Guy Gibson.)

Thus it seems that Marlborough boys were not protected from controversial writings, so not encouraged to conform. John must have taken this on board and, as shown in his diary entries, had his own opinions!

The letter above also illustrates the calibre of his peers and their parents' attitudes to authority and those in high places. No wonder John came across as arrogant at times. Maybe it was this type of situation – along with his changing hormones – which began to mark a significant change in John's hereto compliant nature.

John kept a detailed diary from January 1938, in which, as well as noting his school curriculum, officer training and friendships, he refers to war rumblings in the country's politics and speakers who had impressed him, moulding many of his attitudes:

FEB 2 WED:
Long Parade – I changed quickly and obtained a shine to the brass of my belt. On Parade we did the usual boring arms drill, and a few field signals.

MAR 2 WED:
I am now determined to try and strengthen my personality and not always do what everybody else does – I want to be a captain one day. Chapel was at 11.15, and 3rd period was excused. As I really can't see any reason to give up something in Lent, and as it would do me no good, for, at the moment, my Christian principles are not strong, I shall not give up anything for Lent. … After lunch we paraded in flannels. Knight is far too beyond himself and is far too bloody officious. We just did the ordinary arms drill, and section leading.

MAR 3 THURS:
In Jenning's double period we had a long discussion on Socialism and the state, and the probabilities of another war. According to Jennings the state which had the most necessary food stuffs would win in the end, but he heartily advised us not to think of war, and not be too keen to sample it, as each generation always has done.

MAR 7 MONDAY:
In Mole's period I drew faces, as it was so dull. Double Jennings was more interesting. He gave us back some papers and we discussed the History Chapter and the troubles in the Balkans, which led up to the Great War. … I had a long fight (friendly) with Hope, in which he was victorious.★

★ John's friend Richard Hope will be referred to many more times.

MAR 9 WED:

In Economics, Jennings preached an interesting lecture on atrocity stories. We all recalled various *Daily Mirror* extracts, such as child slaughter in the ensuing Chino-Japanese War, and also Spanish Civil War. **It seems extraordinary – all these wars and rumours of wars. Austria is to have a public vote for Pacifism or not, whilst we are arming to our teeth and Mr Eden has just resigned, with semi welcome and opposition. Who knows but there may be a World War soon and we shall be drawn into it on account of our trade and colonies, although we English people don't really want to fight!!** ... After lunch we paraded as House Platoon and were completely lousy and inefficient, chiefly owing to the inefficiency of Phillbrick – Platoon Commander. After Parade until work I practised the Piano.

MAR 12 SAT:

O.M. Club Day – and what a lot of O.M.s! All chattering about 'When I was here', and 'So you remember', etc etc. I saw the Coxons and Hugh Pothecary, also Robert and Wilfred Fison.★ It was quite a nice sort of day. With Jennings we first of all discussed the History, **then he told us and explained the present day situation in Austria (Hitler invaded Austria and is in Vienna),** and then we read on in our History Books, and made notes. I greened my belt at night [for camouflage].

★ John's cousin Wilfred Fison went on to join the RAF in October 1941 and was killed in January 1943 night flying with Robert Hope Hillary, by then a well-known author.

MAR 16 WED:

After lunch I stayed in Classroom and read the papers – **it is interesting now that Hitler has invaded Austria and practically annexed it. Poor France hates it all, but I think it's a damn good show; but of course, one never knows where Hitler may go next. I think it will be Romania, as she must have oil and petrol for her army. We had a long discussion in classroom about it.**

MAR 17 THURS:

We read on in our History books, and finished it. **It was rather interesting, as it dealt with the present day situations up to 1932. Of course it was not accurate – Austria is German now!**

MAR 18 FRI:

After lunch I filled my pockets with chocolate, etc for the <u>Field Day</u> and then slowly donned my uniform. Of all the bloody Field Days this was

about the bloodiest. Without any exaggeration, lies or misstatements, I did not even see the enemy until 3 mins before the bugle blew for time! We were reserves, and just followed on miles behind everybody. We went over the golf course and down into the Ogg Valley, and finished up about 250 yards from the enemy, behind a ridge on the other side of the valley. The march back was also rotten, as we were right at the very back, could not hear the band, and found it very hard to keep step! Tired and weary with doing nothing, I had a foul lot of Prometheus to do … write a précis as well.

The photograph below shows Marlborough College OTC marching back after a Field Day. Marlborough College continues to train pupils for the military, but it is now a Combined Cadet Force, and the updated sign adorns the building where they currently train.

MAR 23 WED:
Field Day: We advanced for 2½ miles over the Downs (with no shade) and then had lunch.

John described in his diary: 'An aeroplane gave a demonstration, 150 yards in front of us, in picking up a message 9ft off the ground at high speed; each time it only just cleared the 35ft trees above us – a menace.' But John explained this in different terms in a letter to his parents, written that very same day:

Marlborough College OTC marching back from Field Day

While we were having our lunch (bare-chested), one of the aeroplanes gave a demonstration in picking up a message off the ground at high speed, without landing. They put up two posts with a line, and message tied on across the middle. This was about 150 yds (no exaggeration) from where we were under some trees, about 20–30ft high. The aeroplane then swooped down, and by sticking out a short stick from its undercarriage managed to pick up the message, with its wheels about 9 ft off the ground! And in 150 yds it managed to just scrape the trees each time! It was really thrilling.

So, if John thought this was thrilling, it is poignant that his last mission in *M-Mother* should also have involved very low flying and coming back to Scampton with bits of tree caught under their Lancaster.

John had become a pretty normal teenager, with a typically teenage sense of humour:

MAY 2 MON:
God! How damnable – work. The only amusing incident this morning was when someone was asked the p.p. [past participle] of scrire – answer: 'scru'. Ha, ha! After lunch I went down town and then had a music lesson; there is a new man taking Ferry's place, who is ill with scarlet fever – he is no good and I hope Ferry comes back soon. I am going to learn Beethoven's 1st Sonata.

A letter home, dated 12 June 1938, came when John, aged nearly 17, was at an academic peak, having won the form prize by coming top; it also showed a serious bent towards deep, logical and practical thinking:

My dearest Mummy and Daddy,
   Thank you for your long letter. I hope you have good weather, and enjoy yourselves. About Prize Day: will you please tell me exactly how many you will be for Prize Day, as soon as possible (because of getting tickets). I hope Jane [Marna's friend whom he likes] will be able to come; and she wants to know, sort of thing, because she is holding another invitation open. Is Joan [John's half-sister] coming etc etc. We can squeeze 5 in for the concert (it's easy to gate-crash, if I haven't got enough tickets, and they can't refuse to let you in, but I can get 4 tickets for certain, and probably 4 for Prize Giving).
   I haven't played any cricket this week, except one net. Otherwise I have watched cricket or bicycled.
   On Thursday, Mr Dalton, the ex-under-secretary for Foreign Affairs (in the last Labour Government) spoke to us and said:– that to prevent London, or other such large towns, spreading, and spending millions on improving roads etc to accommodate for the great population, it would be better to make new towns! His idea was to take a factory from London with its dependent population (or workers), and plant it and them down

in some village or town in the country, so that all the people who came into London to get work, would have to go into these new towns! (He seems to forget that this is free England, not communistic Russia!) I asked thousands of questions & really pestered him. I could not see why to make say 6 new towns, with new roads and better railways to them, should be less expensive than improving the roads round London. I also asked him if he realised what was going to become of the country, with all these new roads and increased traffic on them from new town to new town etc. I also suggested an agricultural slump 75 years ahead* since farm labourers would desert the land, to work in the nearby factories where they would get a better wage, better securities for living, and an easier job. He said that mechanism would rectify that, to which I replied that since a mechanical machine quickened the process of harvest (for example) it was therefore able to farm greater extents of land, and to make this mechanism worthwhile, larger areas were required, but since his factories and new towns and roads could spread all over the country, it did not look as though mechanism would really be much help, since the farms would remain small, and become smaller and so many labourers would still be required for each farm. He was quite pleased with my questions, and said there was no satisfactory answer at present to the agricultural problems. He confessed ignorance of agriculture – I wish he would just consider the farmer's point of view before he puts his artificial towns down! I enjoyed it very much and we kept him talking, getting keener and keener until we were stopped at nearly ½ past 10 …

Looking forward to seeing as many of you as possible on Prize Day (also hoping to hear soon how many).

Much love to all,

From your loving Son.

---

* That would be 2013 and he wasn't far off the truth! If John hadn't been a Dambuster, perhaps he would have been a politician, or even prime minister – Conservative of course!

What an active mind and sensible ideas he had, and how he liked a good debate! John was certainly a strong and resolute character, and, although we do not know how fate would have served him if there had not been a Second World War, the RAF seemed to provide just the challenge he needed. Yet what a waste the war proved to be when young men such as John were killed in their thousands.

JUNE 18 SAT:
Marna's birthday (18) <u>send large present.</u>

Note in the entry above just how John dotes on his closest sister.

John was still very much involved with the OTC and military training, and he wrote this letter from the school's OTC military Camp on 31 July 1938:

My dearest Mummy and Daddy,

Here I am, sitting in glorious sunshine, with only shorts on. As far as I can gather we never do get bad weather at Camp! Thanks very much for all your letters. I can't let you know exactly what time I can get home, for I have to go by train the army tells me and they won't tell me yet! As I live near I shall have to help clear up so I probably shan't get off until about 11, getting home in time for lunch. In which case you won't be able to meet me, so I will get home independently.

I am enjoying Camp immensely. From 3.30 until 10.15 we can do anything we like – the gritty part of the day is in the morning. Up punctually at 6.30, clean uniform & equipment; make piles, clean out tent; breakfast and then parade. Army prayers are very funny, and most of Marlborough accompany the padre in a special military prayer, and also his speech on where the H.C. [Holy Communion] tent is. After prayers and a spot of drilling by a major Catt ('pussy') with lovely whiskers who talks too much; and then we go for a march to a place about 2–3 miles away, watch a demonstration by the Grenadier or Scots Guards, and do about an hour's 'field day' and then go back for a 1.30 or 2 o'clock lunch. We get on our paillasses at about 10.15 pm.

Last night we went on night operations, which were awfully good fun. But it was a bit of a strive having to get up at 7 this morning, and getting everything done extra well and half an hour earlier for church parade, after being up until 2 last night.

By the way, Wilkie Rowe has invited me for a week on the Broads, Sept 7th – 12th or 13th, and I am wriring to accept. I hope that is OK I shall probably have to come back on the 12th as Lanesborough Old Boys match is then.

Please convey my heartiest congratulations to Marna on the Driving Test. Am also very sorry to hear about breaking up of Birtley House [Betty's Private School that she loved so much]. Will tell you all about Camp when I see you,

With much love,

Your loving Son.

John certainly learnt to understand military discipline from these camps, which would serve him well in the future.

Although we have nothing in John's diary for the rest of September and the whole of October, we do have some letters. One to his parents is dated 25 September 1938 and describes a glimpse of Queen Mary, but more importantly, it indicates that there are now even more serious concerns that war might be imminent; it is written from C1 Marlborough:

On Friday Queen Mary drove through Marlborough. Being a 6th form I lined the road. She came through ½ an hour late – so we missed the whole period. I had a good view from some railings.

… I should get as much holiday as you can!! No one here is very optimistic – I for one am not, and I think it will be a good thing if the English army hurries up and mobilises, and not be left in the lurch by other nations.

At this same time, his sister Betty was beginning to worry about war. She says, 'The possibility of imminent war was played down by the authorities. Nevertheless we picked up frightening vibes and I had nightmares at night!' Grace, her mother, must have been alerted to her worries by her letters and tried to reassure her in a reply:

Don't be alarmed at all this <u>War</u> Talk – Thank Goodness the authorities <u>are</u> bustling about & taking all precautions – But jut keep calm & pray that the forces of Charity and reason will prevail – Hitler has invited Mussolini, Chamberlain, the French and Czech prime ministers – to have a talk with him – and it looks as if Hitler <u>does</u> realise that the whole world would be shocked unless he <u>does</u> have the matter arranged by <u>talk</u> instead of by <u>fighting</u>. Unfortunately the German <u>people</u> as a whole have not been allowed to hear what America, England etc are trying to do for Peace.★

★ In fact, Foreign Secretary Anthony Eden, who had always tried to find peaceful solutions to political problems, resigned suddenly, having made some bad decisions around the Suez Crisis. There followed the Munich Agreement on 30 September 1938. This was an informal pact between Neville Chamberlain, our prime minister, and Adolph Hitler, which was meant to guarantee 'Peace in Our Time', but as we know, the deal was not to be respected.

John's letter of 2 October perhaps provided his parents with a brief respite from the worries of war:

My dear Mummy and Daddy,
    Well, I think we may safely breathe again.
    On Thursday, the College at last threw a panic and Pont★ gave us a long lecture on A.R.P (Air Raid Precautions) etc etc. and we tried on gas masks. On Friday 'Pont' shewed [showed] us where we had to go if there was an A.R. [Air Raid]. It was half way up a very steep bank. When he shewed us it was raining hard and the bank was frightfully slippery so we all slid down on top of one another, and poor old 'Pont' didn't know what to do. On Sat night we were going to have a practice at 10 o'clock, but that was cancelled, thank goodness! Today, Sunday, the Master gave the Upper School a long talk, instead of Scripture, on the present crisis from his own point of view. It was really a lecture on what a bad thing war is, with examples of last war and what would have happened if there was a war now. Still it was quite interesting.
    Today I went out to tea with Owen and his parents and two sisters (one is very pretty). It was very pleasant and there was plenty to talk about.
    From Friday until now we have scarcely seen blue sky, for it has rained very heavily indeed, and everything is very soggy. I am in the middle of a cold, but so is everybody else.
    I have joined the Musical Society. We are singing Bach's B Minor Mass – so of course I joined. I am trying to sing Bass, and enjoy it very much. I am going to take Grade 6 this term on the Piano, as there are some very nice pieces in it, and it is worth doing.

Rugger is going OK this term. It is being organized on a different system. It is arranged for the whole school, and not by houses. I am on the 2nd Block of Games. The 1st of course, is where all the tough people play. I am also one of the 40 select people allowed to use the new squash court.

By the way, have you put me down for a college [at Cambridge University] yet, and what did Wilkie say?

I have written to Betty, and I hope I have cheered her up. ★★

Please give my love to M & thank her for her letter – will write when I have time. With love from your loving Son.

★ 'Pont' was L.F.R. Audemars, who was John's housemaster in C1 boarding house.
★★ Grace must have pleaded to the whole family to write to Betty, who, following the closure of Birtley House, which she loved, was now hating her new school, a PNEU school at Burgess Hill.

In his letter to Betty below we can see that John had learnt to put up with what he didn't like and make the best of things and was advising her to do the same:

C.1 House
The College
Marlborough
2.10.38

My dear 'Betty'

Now that I have not got to go and fight Germany, and put on a gas mask etc, I have time to write to you. I hope you have got into things by now & that the strangeness has worn off. You can't expect it to be like Birtley, so if I were you, I should forget all about Birtley, and make the best of what you do get. When I was in Upper School I used to have to do my prep in a large room, containing 200 boys, all fighting, dashing about, yelling, singing & whistling, while there was a wireless and gramophone going on as loud as possible!

Have you been trying on gas masks and digging trenches, etc and having A.R.P. practices? The College decided to wake up the other day, and 'Pont' gave us a long lecture on Air Raid Precautions, and we were all fitted with gas masks and shown where we had to go if there was a raid. Of course all that is unnecessary now, and in a way I am rather disappointed, because I had made up my mind that there was going to be a war, and that I shouldn't have to do any more work!★

… You will be pleased to hear that I have got Lucien McGrath stuck up in my study and everybody agrees that she is damned beautiful!★★

In my new form I have a beastly lot of work to do. I have 18 History periods out of 30 a week! I only have 12 periods a week in which I do something else. 1 period lasts for 40 minutes.

Mind you don't get Measles or anything like that. And I hope you will enjoy yourself (and I'm sure you will if you don't make yourself objectionable by saying, 'I don't like this', etc.)
 Best of luck,
 With love from John.

★ John was clearly trying to impress his sister Betty with a casual attitude to the relaxing war threat.
★★ Presumably Lucien McGrath was a pin-up.

Betty says she was blissfully unaware of approaching war in the main, but one thing she does remember is her gas mask training:

An interesting event when I was at Burgess Hill School, was the introduction of GAS MASKS. A team of people arrived with these items each concealed in a square cardboard box. Each girl was personally fitted with one. We placed our faces inside a rubber mask which was attached with straps over the head. We were instructed how to put it on and to breathe. Then we had to carry them everywhere we went, onto the sports field, to church and even to the loo.

Even their father Harold had been moved to write to Betty; his letter below shows that once again the threat of war was being taken very seriously indeed:

11, New Square,
Lincoln's Inn
LONDON W.C.2
20th Oct 1938

Dearest Betty,
 You want a letter from your Daddy so here you are –
 I saw nothing very exciting about this war crisis. I was surprised (and annoyed with Hitler) one morning, when walking from Holborn Station to my office in Lincoln's Inn through Lincoln's Inn Fields, to find gangs of men making an awful mess digging trenches round the roots of the magnificent beech trees there (the best in London) and spoiling the green turf on which children used to play, and anaemic clerks play at putting in their luncheon hours. ★ At Guildford they piled up hundreds of sand bags blocking up the door through which I usually went when leaving the station.
 … I was going to stay in town to be bombed and to look after the office whilst Oliver was prepared to join up wherever he was most wanted. In the big war (WWI) when there were only 1 or 2 airplanes to the 1,000's that now exist we were bombed twice here so what it would have been if we had had a war now, heaven only knows …
 Much love,
 From your Daddy.

★ The next day Harold sent a postcard to Betty saying, 'In my letter of yesterday, there is a "Lapsus Calami" – for "Beeches" please read "Plane trees".' Doesn't this show the exactitude of character and upbringing to which they all, including John, must have been subjected? This may well have been contributory to John's excellence as a pilot.

John's diary picked up again on 6 November; he was now seemingly ignoring the threat of war and indulging in his own teenage high life. 'Live for Today' had suddenly become his motto, and in the light of hindsight, why not?

NOV 6 SUN:
Had a hell of a hearty party with Fraser, Scott, 'Bimbo', Dart, Faith, Whitney, in Fraser's study. It was a crush, but it was hellish good fun, & there was plenty to eat. Dart took off his shoe to get his feet cool – so Hicks threw his shoe out of the window. We all then promptly threw Hicks out of it (hanging on to his feet). He was promptly sick (gluttonly), so we hauled him back. Hicks then poured some milk over Dart – a general fight ensued. We then had a competition to see who could eat the most in a mouthful! After a lot more heartiness we all lay back and laughed (in our shirt sleeves). Then with cushions, chairs and tables all over the place, we began to clear up and wash up. While we were doing this the Master walked along, and asked if he could show an O.M. friend a specimen study!!! He did & asked us if we all lived there! He couldn't have chosen a more inopportune moment to come for we were all dishevelled, & the room in chaos. It was good fun.

John had at one time written in his diary about wanting to be a captain, but now he was not so sure as he didn't want to compromise his own moral high ground.

DEC 14 WED:
This afternoon I went for a walk with 'Faith' [Richard Hope]. We both decided that Bower's oilings ['buttering up'] to be a captain were a hell of a poor show. He quite agrees with me in not being too keen – yet jolly – the two are not compatible. I am resolved not to 'oil' to be a captain, he can – & I shall definitely continue my reform, yet I intend to enjoy life. Pont has told me that he wants me to assert myself by being keener – so that he can make me a captain. But I think it is quite possible to assert oneself without being keen. To be keen, it means being hypocritical, and I can't be that unless it is to be polite.

DEC 19 MON:
Lists – I came bottom! That swine 'Faith' who had said he was going to keep me company at the bottom of his form came 2nd to last!

Contriving to come bottom of the class shows that John is taking rebelliousness a step too far.

There is one surviving letter from the beginning of 1939, and it is from John to Betty, still at the school she hates. It shows that John was becoming more of a daredevil and was still frightfully competitive:

C.1 House
The College
Marlborough
30.1.39

My dear Betty,

I wonder if you have had much snow? Here we have had it at least 2" thicker than at home last hols. It snowed continuously for two days. But it was a very wet sort of snow, & the temperature was only just at freezing point. Nearly all the roads have been completely blocked near here by large drifts of snow well over 6 ft deep. I saw one myself, and helped cut through it. A village near here was completely isolated for 2 days! Now it has thawed quite a lot and although the views are still white, the roads are quite clear. In fact we were quite snowed up! Needless to say I had great fun tobogganing and assisting in snow-ball fights. We made a grand toboggan run down the side of a very steep escarpment near here. It had a jump in the middle of it, and we flew into the air for at least 3 or 4 yards:— the record jump was about 10 yds. The only trouble with the run was that there was a river (the river Kennet) and hedge at the bottom so that one had to either throw oneself off at the critical moment or do a spectacular broadside, to save oneself from taking a swim in the Kennet.

As a matter of fact the jump was forbidden after a time, as a master who was testing it came to a hell of a crash himself. It was much steeper in parts to that run at Netley, but was not quite so long.

When the jump was forbidden we resorted to other runs, and had races. This was even more fun as about 12 of us all started together in a line and raced to the bottom. I was only beaten once!

I am writing this in the evening by the sight of one eye! You see we had nothing else to do this afternoon but snowball, as there was not enough snow near M'borough for tobogganing purposes. While I was bunging one at someone, someone else bunged one at me and got me plumb in the eye. The result is that I have to report the death of one eye (for this evening).

On the first night of term I saw a jolly exciting film, called 'Test Pilot'. It was all about aeroplanes and was most thrilling. I expect you would have been horribly bored.

We have bought two marvellous pots of flowers for the study. One is a cyclamen, and the other a begonia.

Hoping you are working hard and liking school this term,

Ever your loving Brother.

Betty admits to always being an out and out tomboy, even into her late teens. It seems that John had not been able to compete with her tree climbing, despite being older than her. However, note that in the letter above John was proudly relating his exploits, trying to convince his sister of his bravery.

John's next correspondence shows that he was pleased to have some reduction in the rigidity of life with a relaxation of Sunday rules:

> C.1 House,
> Marlborough
> Summer Term 1939

Dearest Mummy and Daddy,

At last the reforms have come, and there are no longer any more Victorian Sundays. We are now allowed to play Tennis, Squash & Fives, go for bicycle rides, and wear soft collars on Sundays! In the words of an old master, in a letter to a boy here, 'George Turner was more of a schoolmistress than a schoolmaster'— but I think, that even if he was a school mistress, he was a very good one. ★

★ It appears that a Sir George Turner, who was Premier of Victoria in the early 1900s, coincidentally bearing the same name as the Marlborough College master, started a Royal Commission on Religious Instruction in Schools, and instigated a reforming Act, relaxing the formalities of Sundays.

John had gone to Corpus Christi College, Cambridge, for his entrance exam on 16 March but, being aware of the difficult financial situation at home and their struggles to make their estate viable, was willing to forego this as a next step; musing on his future, he continued:

Look here, I am not going to have you and daddy crocking up just because you want to send me to Cambridge. I hear from Marna that Daddy got about £80 on the Derby – well that certainly ought never to be spent on settling up bills etc – you know that it ought to be used in paying for a long holiday for you both – in Italy perhaps, where I know you both long to go again. I have been thinking it over a lot lately, and I have come to the conclusion that what little I can get in the holidays – say £5 at the most – is not going to relieve the strain on the Hopgood finances. I know that you said all along that you are going to send me to Cambridge, but, I think, that to continue in that frame of mind now is rather obstinate. Much as I want to go to Cambridge, I do not want to see you both crock up trying to keep on and pay for my 'varsity' Education. I honestly think that the sacrifice, which you are nobly willing to undergo to send me to Cambridge, is not really going to be worthwhile. ★

Hurstcote must be dealt with, for obviously, you, Mummy, cannot keep on at it much longer; Daddy ought to retire now; and so on. And it isn't as though a 'Varsity

Education' was essential – since I am not going into the church or going to study Science, etc. I am quite prepared to think about some other profession or job. Why shouldn't I go into business or something like that? At any rate, do you really think it is worth-while sending me to Cambridge? I feel that there are many other things which are doubly as important. I know that you will say that I am young and have a whole life before me [little did he know that in less than four years from writing this letter, he would be dead] but really I don't think that argument still carries. There are plenty of other jobs and ways of earning a living – and it doesn't need a Varsity Education to get started at them ...

... I think the time has come to face the fact, ugly as it may be, that I cannot go to Cambridge, and that I must look around for something else to do (not school mastering).★★

With much love John.

★ His conscience must also have been pricking him, seeing that he was aiming to, and did, come bottom of the class!
★★ This last bracketed admission is perhaps indicative that John wanted something more exciting in life than being stuck in a school situation forever and may also explain some of his rebelliousness.

John was certainly trying to dismiss Cambridge from the equation in the previous letter; however, he must have had very positive replies from his mother and father, counteracting these doubts about Cambridge, to which he replied with the following:

C.1 House
Marlborough
18.6.39

Dearest Mummy and Daddy,

I was glad to get your letters allaying my doubts & fears. I am very glad that you are really determined to send me to Cambridge, &, of course I am <u>very</u> thankful.

I am very busy just now for we have got a 'prize' on Tuesday next. It's an English prize, with its subject as 'Classicism to Romanticism'. So badly have we been taught, that the whole form has just realised that they don't know much about it – and we are expected to show up pretty good papers, because we have been reading it, on and off for a year.

On Wednesday, I saw 'Macbeth' acted here by a group of so-called Classical Players. It was not first class, but good enough to prevent it passing over to the absurd side. Of course, a college audience must be a very difficult audience to act to, for we invariably laugh at the wrong moments, and there is usually a hum of conversation whenever they come to a well-known bit!

On Thursday, Tony Whitney & I won a doubles match in the School Competition,
which I got a 'walk over' in the first round of the singles. But on Thursday, also Tony and I,
as 1st pair, for House, lost our 1st House Match against C.2 rather badly.
      Sorry I haven't got time to write any more,
      Love John.

John continued his love of sport and action throughout his time at Marlborough
College. The photograph below shows L.F.R. Audemars Esq (nicknamed Pont by
the boys), who was housemaster of C1.

The next letter shows that, as a soon-to-be school leaver, not only are the
pressures of earning money and finding a career dawning upon John, but also the
discovery that people in high places, including the Bishop of London, are often
as fallible as any other. What a troubling time this brink of adulthood is! And on
top of it all, John's mother was now ill. John wrote from C House, Marlborough,
on 16 July 1939:

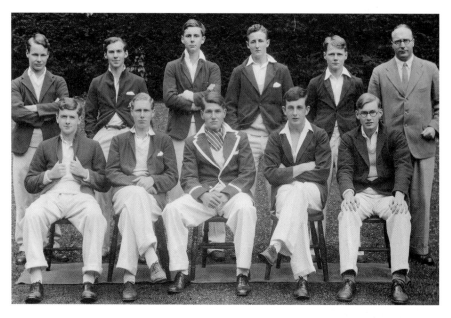

June 1939, C1 Cricket Team: John front row, second from left; Richard Hope back row, third from
left; Mr Audemars back row, far right

Dearest Mummy and Daddy,

I am very sorry to hear you are crocked up, Mummy. I hope the visit to France will do you a lot of good.

About this job, I have not heard of any other yet, but it will be an awful pest if it is daily. I should never dream of inflicting myself on Batings or Ramsdens – because if they aren't away, it will mean that John or Bryce will be frightfully tied down by me, unable (or not wishing) to take the whole day off, and always having to drag me around to his friends etc etc. That idea is quite impracticable. But it would be wise to fix it up for September, so that, if I can get another I could try to get it for August, or if for September, then I would cancel the other. If I took Walker's job in September, I could easily pig it out somewhere for a fortnight or so.

About the car. Even if I did buy it, I should not be able to have it until middle of September! I shall not get it chiefly because I have now bust my tennis racket & must get a new one. Daddy is quite right – it would cost a hell of a lot to run it – and I am not going to waste out my capital on petrol. It would have to be run on pocket money, & obviously Daddy can't afford that. So that's that.

The Bishop of London gave his last sermon here today. Never have I heard such sentimental nonsense spoken – such stuff may go down with the very young or old – but certainly not with Public School Boys. I think it is shocking that such a dear, sentimental, old man should have had spiritual power over so many people for so long. He may be a dear old man but he is certainly not the man to be entrusted with such a responsible position as Bishop of London.

Yesterday I played cricket and tennis. Cricket versus the Swindon boys' club. We drew, and I made top score of 33. And in the evening I played off my 4th round of the Tennis Competition, and was beaten in 3 sets: 3–6, 6–4, 3–6. The other chap was a school player, and had had much more practise. Still it was a jolly good game. Hope you get on well at Wimbledon, Marna!

We have just been arranging about our end of term party – bottles and otherwise. I have just been talking to the old chef, who is a jolly good fellow, & treats me to anything I want every time I go and see him (he gave me 2 lbs of sausages last week!) and he is going to cook us a damned good feast – we leave it to him to choose what. (It'll be jolly cheap, because he will insist on only charging for half!). as for drinks, we got the postman to pack up the bottles in paper parcels, & address them to us, & we then collect them! – Subtle.

Hoping you soon get better,

John.

So John was full of initiative and still very competitive; he had a growing sense of justice and injustice, a more and more questioning attitude towards religion and his opinions were still seasoned with a touch of arrogance.

JULY 1939

Only a few pages of a 1939 diary exist, and show John continuing to be more and more rebellious by the day. John was certainly critical of many things at Marlborough College and was courageous enough to be open and honest about these when he had his 'leaving session' with his house master, Pont.

> JUL 22 SAT:
> Was quietly smoking in study with Tony D., Tony & Edward, when I was told Pont wanted to see me.
>
>   Pont wanted to give me my leaving session. I was very prepared and had longed to be frank with him. I told him his system was all wrong – at a public school, discouraging any natural growing boy, and tended to wreck many careers in his house such as mine. He was also frank, but could not reply about the system. He is a fool, but an old man, whose system does not take into account the average public school boy and merely favours the goodies and gutless! I then drew his attention to his captains – weak and stupid suckers, and explained why we were called the Nursery – I then explained that our gang had done much to get rid of that name. He said that he didn't mind that name as he and his House (ahem) were fighting a good cause – high morality – he and his bloody system!

John the rebel, smoking a pipe and in shorts, July 1939. Look at his arm muscles – he is no wimp!

JUL 23 SUN:

Ariston's Day

Smoked cigarettes before and after Chapel. Played and won a House Competition of tennis after lunch, having signed off from Marlborough and joined O.M Club [Old Marlburians' Club].

Then walked for half an hour. Then went out to tea and dinner with Micky Gibson. We smoked and then went for a walk after tea. I shot and bust a street lamp bulb with his airgun pistol. We then shot at birds, females etc. Then dinner when we got very hearty and slightly drunk. Of course none of us had got a leave (and we met old Wilcox)! Then we staggered back, very happy, to college and smoked. I then worked.

JUL 30 SUN:

I spent most of today packing. Rather grim thought. I am sorry to leave Old M.C. I have had a damn good time and plenty of friends. Tony Whitney & I had a pretty good record – we have smoked every day at least 3 or 4 cigarettes for the last 2 months, and about every 3 days at the beginning of term. And I have had at least a pint & usually 2 pints daily (at Bernard's & pubs, etc) for the last 3 weeks. I have also been every now and then to the cinema.

I have learned lots of things – had to love and serve others – my friends. Hate and thoughtlessness & unappreciating others. But the remembrance of Marlborough will be a strength & power & inspiration for the future.

M.C. has meant much more to me than to Richard Hope. I am not happy at home, but have found all that I looked for at M.C. I have looked forward to the beginnings of term more than to the ends – the opposite view to Richard's. How I long for the old days at M.C. all over again.

The learning at Marlborough College that John particularly emphasised here, 'to love and serve others – my friends', is very poignant: in his final minutes, as he knew his life was at an end, John, selflessly, and with all the skills he had as an exceptional pilot, kept the flaming Lancaster *M-Mother* flying long enough for the remaining live crew, who were indeed also his friends, to jump free. That is the ultimate in heroism.

Betty says the line 'I am not happy at home' may well relate to his relationship with his parents at this time and probably in particular to his mother, who was highly principled and therefore 'terribly critical' of her son with his mushrooming rebelliousness. Grace should, however, have been more prepared for this in John, having been a rebel herself at the same sort of age; she had been so strong-willed and opinionated with her extreme feminist ideals that she had left home at a comparatively young age, leaving her father and brothers to her mother, whose subservience she had come to despise. There must therefore have been something of a shared mindset between John and his mother of which she was fiercely proud. But there was the added stress of her now elderly and frail husband, John's father, and the considerable financial strain they were under, converting Hurstcote into flats, moving out, and still somehow finding the money to keep John at Marlborough College. The tensions were certainly contributing to Grace's heart trouble and general ill health, and John was not insensitive to these issues, as seen in the earlier letter. Perhaps, with his increasingly adventurous nature, John was just fed up with the stressful and critical home atmosphere and his cooped-up existence at school.

But was this perhaps the very explosive mixture that the RAF and the Second World War kindled and which went on to make John the daredevil Dambuster he was later to become? It is interesting to note that two commanding officers of John's 617 Squadron, who were both awarded the Victoria Cross (VC), were also rebels at school. Guy Gibson was certainly no angel at St Edward's School, Oxford; indeed it is rumoured he was expelled from this school. Leonard Cheshire (who became CO of 617 Squadron after Operation Chastise) was a 'challenging' pupil at Stowe School but carried out 102 missions with 'sustained courage and outstanding effort' and, after the war, was responsible for starting The Cheshire Homes charity, now called Leonard Cheshire Disability. Interestingly, both Gibson and Cheshire were outspokenly critical of Bomber Command's indiscriminate bombing in the last half of the war, and I am sure John, with his deep-seated principles, would have been equally unhappy.

In the meantime, though, John was still trying to shock. And he was enjoying his drink, which would certainly help him relax in the officers' mess and Lincolnshire pubs in the future. As Guy Gibson was to say of John, 'He used to go out with us a lot, get drunk … he was a good squadron type', and I imagine he would have been a big social asset with his piano playing for rowdy squadron sing-songs – 'Roll Out the Barrel' etc. However, Betty remembers her brother as being very self-conscious about playing in public and generally only playing classical pieces.

And John was not cowed by authority, which may have been one of the reasons he became a close friend to Guy Gibson, renowned for his authoritarian leadership.

As Marlborough College was to have had a great deal of influence on John's short, but action-packed, life, it seems appropriate to quote a verse from a Marlborough College song that John sang in his leaving concert on Monday, 31 July 1939; how pertinent some of the lines were to be to his future, what 'grander glory' could he have achieved?

Onward go, without check or turning,
School of manhood and king's highway;
Speed the commerce and spread the learning,
That Britain trusts to your charge today.
Greater ever and grander glory
Still than aught that the past bestowed
Shall be your share in your country's story,
Marlborough School and the old Bath Road.

John did come away from Marlborough College with two certificates, which, although not specific about his academic achievements, showed that not only had he experienced a good education but also the basis of a military and officer training.

It was very soon after John's return to Shere that family life was to change dramatically – and not only for the Hopgoods.

3

Family Life Changes as War is Declared

Having left Marlborough College in August 1939 John went with his mother and two sisters for a summer holiday to St Briac in Northern France; it was there that they heard the following announcement on 3 September from Britain's prime minister, Neville Chamberlain:

> We are at war with Germany.

Britain and France had agreed to support Poland in the event of a German invasion, but their agreement did little to deter Hitler, who had attacked Poland on 1 September 1939. The deadline set for withdrawal had overrun.

Marna had joined the ATS within its first year of existence, having done two terms at Queens Secretarial College. She had to get back to 'join up', and John returned home with her as her support.

John's mother, Grace, and his sister Betty were left together in France, wondering what they should do. Everything was very normal in Brittany, and they were sure 'La Ligne Maginot' would protect this part of France from the advancing enemy. Betty had loathed her English school, so it was seen as a fresh experience for her, an opportunity to attend a French school and learn the language. Always very resourceful with ideas, Grace worked out a solution: she would stay on throughout the autumn and keep Betty with her. They stayed in a very nice guesthouse, homely and with delicious French cuisine.

The outbreak of war led to large-scale evacuation of women and children from London and other large cities in Britain. However, for the next few months there were no air raids and many evacuees returned home. This period is now known as the Phoney War.

John, who had just turned 18 years old, was at home in Shere with his ageing father, and was shouldering a great deal of responsibility. Not only was John looking after the family, their possessions and their estate but he also had to make decisions about his own future (deciding between the Univeristy of Cambridge or studying law in the City) in very uncertain times. Given that John, despite their recent clashes, was devoted to his mother, he was trying to organise this assault on Hurstcote to provoke minimal upset to her when she returned; he thought his mother would not want refugees using her kitchen. John's half-brother Oliver, wife Celia and baby Susan would also be moving in.

What a sudden turn of events from the irresponsibility and rebelliousness in his last year at Marlborough College. John was now a very worried young man, struggling to keep everyone else from worrying, with no time even to play golf, and in this vein he wrote to his mother and sister in France:

Hurstcote

Shere

September 1939

My dearest Mother and Betty,

At last we have got your letter written last Saturday. Daddy, M and I had been getting very anxious, and are very glad to hear that you are both well.

It worries me to feel that you are worrying so much. I know what it must be like to feel that your belongings are not under your own eye, and, of course, Marna and I will do all we can to see that they are put under lock and key. Next week-end Marna and I are going to collect all yours and E's things and <u>lock</u> them up in your bedroom and boudoir, where they will be perfectly safe. I will lock the silver in the Bank if you think it safest. You will then have nothing to worry about.

I hope I can make this clear that in England in the Reception Areas at the moment every house is liable by law to have 1 person per every room in the house. This means that we have a good many rooms liable to be commandeered. We have been obliged to have a married couple to sleep in our part of the house. They will feed with the Noves and will bring their own sheets and blankets. ★ We shall put them into Betty's room – and I will see that all valuables are cleared out first. I am sorry but I could not help it – nor Daddy either (and we had already managed to prevent a mother and child being billeted to us). But, first it is infinitely more preferable to have the Nove's friends using a room because they will not want to use the kitchen nor the ping pong room and (chiefly) nor will they be infected with bugs in their hair and break out with some horrid disease like Dyptheria (both of the cases I know about). As we are at war I am afraid we must do our bit and help.

So what we are doing at the moment is we are calling your bedroom and boudoir store-rooms one room, that leaves us with 7 people to 9 rooms (counting you and Elizabeth and Oliver and Celia). That means we are liable to have two evacuees planted on us. Daddy and I have already argued [the billeting officer] off once. Our excuses are that there is no female member of the house permanently about to supervise, and daddy goes up to town several times a week. We can also use the excuse that an invalid mother is likely to come back at any moment, and use your doctor's orders about evacuees. But supposing London and other towns are seriously bombed, then it may not be possible to avoid having evacuees. You may be sure that we will do all we can to avoid anything so unpleasant happening, but war is war …

About your idea of making another home for us … At the moment I think it is quite impracticable. I shall be in town all this week and Marna will be working, only getting the Sundays off. So Hurstcote, in spite of Daddy's regime and other inconveniences would be all we could desire. We should all be together at the week-ends, and I should hate the feeling that we were separated from Daddy and Oliver and Celia [Oliver's wife]. Oliver and I are now brothers not mere acquaintances as we used to be, and we have good fun at the week-ends. On the other hand I <u>do</u> want to see you. I do wish we could all be together and happy again – something so nice when war clouds are blowing and things outside are so gloomy. I do wish you had not misjudged Daddy so hastily and bitterly. Of course we were going to look after your things – hang it, we are sane and gentlemen. ★★

Things in England are quite changed. On the roads, there are army lorries & aeroplanes all over the place and soldiers everywhere. Buses only run 3 times a day, but trains are normal, though more expensive. Not a sign of any light must show from any window, while driving at night with a very restricted headlight is a real nightmare. The reflector has to be blackened (I have done it with cardboard), whilst there must only be a thin slot 7/8 inch for the light to shine through – and then one must have a hood to throw what little light there is on to the road and prevent it being reflected upwards. Road signs are mainly painted over with white paint whereas others have been swapped over to foil the enemy, should there be an invasion; all it really serves to do is to confuse some of the villagers!

About 'Guy' Marna and I are going to lock him up as we are only allowed 6 gallons a month and taxes are going up. ★★★ *It will be too expensive to make it worthwhile. .And I have placed the car and myself at Stumber's hands for A.R.P. work if a bomb should fall in this locality – but I doubt very much if such a thing would happen. To-morrow I am going to mess around with sandbags at the Guildford County Hospital.*

Well I am now articled to Noel Dowson and am starting work on Monday (25th)! ★★★★ *I shall have a bed at Philis's and come down with Oliver at the week-ends. I shall work from 10 – 5, and get Saturdays off! I'm terribly anxious to start. I went up last Wednesday and had lunch with Daddy and Dowson at Daddy's club, which is all very new now. Dowson seemed very nice and easy to get on with. He was jolly nice and let Daddy off a premium of £300.*

Although I have registered, we chucked Cambridge. It isn't worth it – only 3 colleges open. No life, only people swatting away very hard. So it is better to get on with my necessary education, which I can, as it may be delayed Heaven alone knows by the war.

Thanks for getting golf clubs – of course I have not a minute to worry about playing games or amusement now, so I do not miss them at all.

... I am very sorry for you, knowing how lonely you must feel. Get better quickly and please don't worry!

Much love,

Ever your loving Son.

★ The Noves were a Jewish family which Grace was not keen on, having previously fallen out with them over rules of flat tenancy in the Hurstcote downstairs flat.

★★ John includes himself in the term 'gentlemen'. Aged just 18 years old, he is already feeling very grown up (the age of majority then was actually 21 years old).

★★★ Guy was a car, an Armstrong Siddeley.

★★★★ Messrs Fisher & Dowson (the London Solicitor's Firm, to which John was articled).

Notice that in the letter above John expresses the Hopgood assumption that refugees must be contaminated, i.e. 'infected with bugs … and disease', and be dirty in some way. Things were not altogether happy between his mother and father and, being a sensitive young man, and loving both his parents, John was trying to do his best to rebuild bridges. He was also getting on very well with his half-brother Oliver, whom he knew his mother thought a bad influence. It also shows John was a peacemaker, not a warmonger, by nature.

7, St James Place,
London S W 1
11th October 1939

Dearest Mummy and Betty,

I have received a good many letters from you of late, of which one dated Oct 6th was the last. Thank you very much. I am very glad to hear you are both well and enjoying your existence. About the trunk we sent you – if it hasn't arrived you had better stick a pin or two into the nearmost parts of the St Malo S.R. officials. I am also glad to hear that there are plenty of English out there for company.

Well about myself – if you really are so eager to get answers to such detailed questions. My work at the moment is decidedly dull – I read and read from 10.00 to 5.00 with a 3/4 of an hour break off for lunch. It is much harder work than reading at school because there is no-one always able to help me. However I have asked, with Daddy's support, for some practical work, and I got some today. Also we are making inquiries about a crammer and correspondence courses, so that my studies may be assisted with professional guidance. As I hope to take my Intermediate next summer I have got to work twice as hard as an ordinary articled clerk, who usually has about 3 years before the Intermediate. In my case the idea is to get the b....y exam over before I am called up and join up. Hence all the haste and hard work! Everybody says it is very dull and stiff to start off with, but once one gets knowledge of law it becomes vastly more interesting.

I am on an allowance of £100 a year – not much when it has to pay for everything except Doctor, Dentist and Holidays. I am sleeping with Oliver in Aunty Vi's flat free of charge, because this aunt has been evacuated. We feed with Phyllis – 1s 3d for breakfast and 2 shillings for dinner, and she gives us good food. I have my lunch anywhere and everywhere, but mostly in Lyons's – because they are the cheapest. I never spend more than 1/- on lunch, and usually it is only 8d. I get off Sat and Sun and go down to Hurstcote on Friday night returning on Monday morning. In the evenings in London we play Bridge (1d. per 100) [Guy Huntly who boards with Phyllis makes the fourth], Bagatelle, read and listen to the wireless or go to the flics. We go to the flics once a week, and pub-crawl back. I like it very much.

Noel [Dowson, the lawyer] is a very Easy-to-Get-on-With person. He is kind and ready to help, but being very busy has not much time to waste on me. However I have made friends with a clerk here, who tries to be a gentleman, and he is only too willing to assist me and explain things and give me some practical stuff to do.★ So you can see I am getting on all right.

At the week-ends we have been doing some exciting forestry in the wilds of Hurstcote garden, and I take exercise by walking or bicycling to Guildford. Discontent against the rector is growing more manifest everywhere – his sermon on Oct 1st was no better than a 'leader' in the Daily Mail – he even condescended to tell us where the Siegfried Line was! – Daddy and all our friends were furious, & we go no more to church at 11.00 when the rector is preaching. Instead we go to Peaslake, or early Holy Communion. I hope to get some golf and squash soon.

Have I satisfied your curiosity?!

Since I am getting bored doing nothing while the war totters on, I am seriously debating whether I shan't join the R.A.F. next summer as that seems to be the only thing which actually does anything, and which takes boys of 18. However there is a long time until next summer, and you may rest assured I shall do nothing in a hurry.

We have all been given our Identity Cards, and rationing will start soon. O& I are going to experience some difficulty in getting meals, as we cannot register just with one butcher. However I don't suppose we shall starve.

Much love to you both,

Your loving Son and Brother.

PS All your belongings are safe at Hurstcote and there are no aliens in the house.

★ John was assuring his mother that, although this clerk is somewhat below their status, he is trying to better himself.

Hurstcote
Shere
December 1939

My dearest Mother,

This was meant (and is meant) to arrive on Christmas Day, but I am afraid I may have left it a bit too late. However, here's wishing you a very happy Christmas. I do hope you manage to have a happy one; anyway you may be sure we shall all be thinking of you both. I hope you get the wireless in time, and also that it works! By the way I am sending out a box of toffees to Betty, and hope it will arrive in time for her birthday.

We ought to have a pretty merry Christmas here if all goes well. Marna & Celia have just compiled the menu, and have tried to get things shipshape. I hope Marna will not go down with German Measles. She appeared to be in more or less daily contact with it in the barracks – quite a lot of her A.T.S company have gone down with it, and she will be lucky if she escapes. Let's hope she won't, and be optimistic.

This weekend was pretty dull. Marna only came over for the day (Sunday) as she could not get leave for the week-end, because of her quarantine. This morning Oliver & I did some more axing – we trimmed off a few old dead stumps, and also shot a squirrel. We also saw a hen pheasant pecking around in the Victoria's garden, but it got mixed up in the bracken before we had time to fire. Yesterday we played golf and although it was (and is) intensely cold with a bitter north wind and almost snowing, we got a good game and both played pretty well.

Last week I had dinner with a half-brother of Richard Hope's, John Hope, and then we went on to The Cumberland to drink. ★ Gibson and Weldon seem quite satisfied with me. I got 75% on my last paper. The work gets more dull and boring and I hate it, – but I suppose any job must be boring and loathsome to start with – at least everybody seems to find it so.

It looks now as if the war is going on for some time now, what with this Russo-Finnish complication. Daddy had a bet on that it would be over before Christmas – well, he's lost that all right. From very selfish reasons I should like it to go on for a bit, so that I can have a good time in the RAF before I have to settle down to the monotonous drudgery of life in town and at law. ★★ Everybody wants to have a good time at my age before they have to settle down. However it's all very selfish but natural.

I have found a very good new flic place in town, where they revive old films. It's a 2 hour show and only costs 6d. – quite surprising really. I go there occasionally after work before dinner.

Wishing you a very happy Christmas once again,

From your very loving Son.

★ Richard Hope was the very same good friend John wrote about in his diary from Marlborough College, whom he nicknamed 'Faith'.
★★ This is very significant and shows how open and honest John was. It also gives us a huge insight into what attracted young men to the war.

Betty remembers her mum discussing the possibility of her father coming out to France for Christmas, and a dinner party being organised for him, with a menu, and all her friends and associates from working parties (for knitting socks and making things for the troops) to meet him. Grace was about to meet him off the boat, with a bag containing brandy to revive him after his long trip, only to get a wire at the last minute saying he couldn't come; it seems that new war-time red tape was insurmountable even for the landed gentry. John's father, Harold, was devastated.

Hurstcote
Shere
6th Jan 1940

My dearest Mother,

We had a very good Christmas, though of course we missed you both very much. On the Friday night I met John Coulson at Waterloo which was pretty lucky in the black-out and amongst a solid mass of soldiers, sailors and airmen, and we came down together. On Saturday we went shopping in Guildford in the morning. Going into G'ford we had an exciting skid down Newlands Corner, just narrowly missing a bus and a car. The roads were iced over the whole time, and there was a thick fog as well.

We had our Christmas lunch, helped down with Sherry, Champagne and Crème de Menthe. We then digested it and heard the King's speech.★ After that we decided to shake the meal down, and O, Joan, M and I played squash down at the Warren's. We played a foursome and had great fun.

On Boxing Day, Joan and Oliver having arranged to do other things, M and I went over to Cranleigh to beagle. It was a very good meet, and I have never seen such a large field event on Boxing Day. Although we did not kill there were plenty of hares and we were on the run for nearly 3 hours. On one occasion we nearly caught the hare ourselves. It got in a small spinney, and we formed a cordon round it to prevent it escaping, so that the stupid hounds might have a chance of killing. However after a lot of yelling the confounded thing dived through somebody's legs and got away having been hit across the back by a small boy and nearly sat upon. We all got very muddy, hot and thirsty and as it got foggy and cold again we left just before the end, and M and I were very lucky getting busses back home.

On Thursday and Friday I went back to work. It got very much colder and snowed on Thursday, and froze hard all day Friday and Saturday. So on the week-end there was snow and ice to choice. We chose the snow – though the snow and ice on the roads was unavoidable, as you will hear …

Oliver brought a friend down with him for the week-end and we went over to Box Hill all day Saturday and Sunday; the slopes there were beyond comparison. There was one long and very fast slope a quarter of a mile long, and two precipitous ones sloping away from it on either side. We tried the more precipitous ones, but as a chap killed himself on one of them, and as it had no run-out before the road, we gave them up, and got more fun on the big one. … We all got very bruised, and smashed the toboggan rather badly when we had a crash at the bottom in order to prevent ourselves from going into a tree and/or pit. On Sunday Marna came and did some skiing. It was rather too hard and fast for it, although there were many others. I also tried and got on very well, and managed to 'stem' the whole way down without falling.

On Saturday as we were driving home we crashed into a ditch. I was driving, as Oliver had bust his spectacles tobogganing, and I was doing a steady 40 just between Abinger Hammer and Gomshall. I got behind a cyclist and was accelerating to overtake before the next corner. However a b….y little car crept round the corner in the opposite direction, rather upsetting my calculations. So I jammed on all brakes, which was rather fatal on a road that was completely snowed and iced over, and hey presto! We landed wrong side up in a deep ditch on the left-hand side. It was either that or the bicyclist or the car or a 10 to 1 chance of getting between both. The nose of the car stuck down in the ditch while the whole car was canted on one side, with the back in the air. However nobody was hurt, though we all got bruised, and after 2 hours digging … we extracted the car. By a miracle it was hardly damaged – only rather bent about in the front. It started up beautifully and only a few minor repairs have had to be done to it.

★ The king's speech John referred to was given by King George VI, from his study at Sandringham House, to the British Empire on Christmas Day:

And to all who are preparing themselves to serve the country, on sea or land or in the air, I send my greeting at this time. The men and women of our far-flung Empire working in their several vocations, with the one same purpose, all are members of the great family of nations which is prepared to sacrifice everything that freedom of spirit may be saved to the world.

Such is the spirit of the empire; of the great Dominions, of India, of every Colony large or small. From all alike have come offers of help, for which the Mother Country can never be sufficiently grateful. Such unity in aim and in effort has never been seen in the world before.

Let us remember this through the dark times ahead of us and when we are making the peace for which all men pray.

A New Year is at hand. We cannot tell what it may bring. If it brings peace, how thankful we shall all be. If it brings us continued struggle we shall remain undaunted …

Vol Hopgood W/13342
10th Surrey ATS
Metrapole Hotel
Folkestone
Kent
26.1.40

My darling Mummy,

Monday Jan 8th
… I heard from my friend Richard Hope the other day. He says he failed his Marine Exam, and is going as a deck hand on a small ship, which is sailing round France, Spain and Africa I think. He then hopes to try the exam again next summer, if he is not mined or torpedoed.

Many, many, thanks for your last letter, which I got last week. If you are really well by next spring it would be really marvellous if you could clear out of Hurstcote, and set up a new home. I should be all for it, because I miss a real home very much. At any rate Hurstcote is an impossible place, and still worse when there is no-one to look after it and keep it nice. … I hope to get into the RAF next summer when the exam is over, and I shan't expect to get more than half-a-dozen or so leaves per year.

You suggest that O & C might like to rent the ground floor of Hurstcote, well as far as I know they both loathe Hurstcote as much as we do. …

Daddy is whining a lot just now about money, and I had a hard job to persuade him that £25 was not at all sufficient to meet my expenses per quarter, and to get £30 out of him. He expected me to give up golf, merely because he is giving it up! So I expect there will be great difficulty about getting him to pay for a new home. It's a nuisance but it can't be helped.

Well I think I have said all I've got to say,
Much love from your loving Son.
PS A Happy New Year

On 26 January, Marna (aged 19½) wrote from 10th Surrey ATS in Folkestone:

On Wednesday the King stopped at the Barracks to inspect the Canadians; they all lined up along the road and then he walked past them. We unfortunately were not inspected, but were allowed to see him as best we could. I rushed to the beginning of the line and when he passed, rushed to the middle to see him again and then rushed to the end to see him get into his car. He looked very grave and serious all the time but smiled as he talked to some of the men. I wish he had talked to some of us! Before he came we were told we could not see him as there was too much work to be done; this made my blood boil, so I snatched my hat and flew with the risk of a punishment afterwards, because as a member of the King's Army I thought it right to see the king, and there was certainly not enough work to be done as half of us had not done a thing all day. I got there to see all the men being marched along and put in position; there were about 1,500 altogether. Later the rest of the company were allowed to go and no one knew that I had gone before the order came through so I was not caught.

In the meantime, John was bowed over with the weight of troubles at home. His father was unwell and very stubborn, refusing to let John rescue their finances by selling Hurstcote. John was staying at Earls Court in the week and working hard at his law course, which occupied him 'up to 11 to 11.30 at night'.

He wrote to his mother in France at the beginning of February:

Hurstcote,
Shere

My dearest Mother,

I meet a nice lot of chaps at the Law School – though almost 75% are the Grammar (or worse) school type.★ I went to a revue – 'Lord Haw Haw' – with one chap, and have been asked out to dinner with another. Last night I met John Hope, brother of Richard, and did a dinner and revue. He is an engineer in the Merchant fleet, and was just back, from a sail to Ireland and back, for an exam. He took Richard on his ship, who has now gone on to France and Spain in it.

Well we really have had a bit of winter weather. There has been skating daily from Xmas day to the beginning of this week – about 6 weeks or more!

We are going to be rationed to only 1/10d worth of meat per week – I shall positively starve!

Much love to you and Betty,

Your loving Son.

★ This illustrates how different life was before the war and how families who were able to educate their children in public schools felt superior to the other classes. Even in Shere, the landed gentry sat on one side at church (with named, printed visiting cards slipped into a little frame on the side of the pew, reserving their seats), whilst the workers sat on the other side. As a verse from the hymn 'All Things Bright and Beautiful' goes:

The rich man in his castle
The poor man at his gate
God made them high or lonely
And ordered their estate.

Betty says that the war saw the destruction, to a great extent, of these class divisions and was a great leveller.

In this next letter John was wrestling with the many demands of his home and a very sick father; he was also trying to study for his law exams; Grace must have written to John saying that she would return home. This letter also shows that John was now determined to join the RAF:

18 Longridge Rd.,
Earls Court
LONDON SW5
1st March 1940

My dearest Mother,

Many thanks for your last 2 letters – sorry I haven't written before – but Daddy's illness and my work have not given me much time. I have also had the flu with a very sore throat – but am quite OK now.

I am certainly looking forward to very much to seeing you – it will be grand after so long – since September, and will arrange to spend Easter at Folkestone or wherever you will be.

Daddy is much about the same – that is his temperature is erratic and won't remain normal. He is eating very little and feeling bored and fed up with life and his present condition. He has a nasty cough, but no pain anywhere, but is, of course, rather weak and worried because he doesn't get better … he is now refusing to take his pills or eat breakfast.

… I'm afraid Daddy's illness has put a complex on the Hurstcote question – he is quite unable to tackle any business and cannot concentrate, and there will be a heavy bill at the end of it all, which will be a drain on the money needed to move into another house. I quite agree the only way to move him over would be to present him with an attractive house – but will a house large enough to suit us and cheap enough for us be possible to find. It will certainly be a miracle if we find one, however we can but try.

… I am working pretty hard now. I have got the terminal examinations coming on next week at the Law School, which means a solid spot of revision. I got 85% the other week in a paper for Gibson and Weldon, and they were quite pleased.

… I see that it is very difficult to get into the RAF now. They have a long waiting list already. However I met a chap – Hicks – who was at Lanesborough – in the tube the other day, and he knows of a chap through his uncle – Sir Seymour Hicks – who gets people through the back door into the Air Force with a commission. I hope to see him soon and find out further details. ⋆

I like your idea of flying – it's probably the safer way to cross the channel these days – I hope you like it, and are not air-sick. I'm afraid you'll find it very noisy – however plenty of cotton wool should help. Let me know where you land and I will meet you.

Looking forward to seeing you, Love to Betty,

Your loving Son.

★ 'Lanesborough' refers to John's preparatory school in Guildford. In those days it was, even more than now, a case of 'not what you know but who you know'.

Grace was obviously planning to return to England by air, but circumstances developed rather quickly and this was not to be. On 15 March, although Grace had still not managed to receive the correct papers to enable her return to England, she and Betty despatched her large trunk from St Malo, travelling together by taxi. Then on Saturday, 16 March 1940 they received a telegram to say that Harold had passed away that morning.

Betty says:

Mummy was held up for several days awaiting her passport; she travelled back by boat, arriving just too late even for the funeral. It must have been so upsetting for her … And it shifted a huge weight of responsibility onto John (and Marna) to make the necessary decisions, and arrange both a cremation and service, as well as managing the estate and staff. All this must have helped mould John's character and confidence in stressful situations, of which he was to experience much more in his short future!

Mummy then pulled things together, sorted out the three flats, made a comfortable home on one side of the house, at the same time being landlady for the 3 tenants of the flats. She made a flat in the kitchen quarters of the house for an undertaker's refugee family from London with 6 children; he travelled to and fro to London, as business was good due to war! Attached to the house was a gardener's cottage in which lived a gardener and his wife, and with their help, mummy ran the whole place and kept it ticking; there were 6 families now living at Hurstcote.

John wrote to Betty on 20 March, with great empathy, realising that she was away from home at a significant time:

My dearest Sister,

I am sorry I have not written to you before, but there has been a lot to do lately, and I was waiting until the Funeral was over so that I could tell you everything. I am very sorry for your being out in France all alone at such a time – but cheer up! For a death is not such a sad thing if you look at it in the right way. Of course it is very sad, and a great blow to us all, that Daddy has gone from this world, but then it is very consoling to think that he has gone from such a war-minded and troubled world, and also that he has been spared what would have been a very boring and troubled convalescence and also retirement, when he would have been very weak, and unable to garden and play golf – which as you know, are his two hobbies so to speak.

We have had lots and lots of letters and telegrams in sympathy, and they all stress the fact that he was so good, upright, kind, willing to help others, a gentleman and friendly. – But we will send you out a selection when Mummy has seen them; and we are expecting her today or tomorrow … Once we had told him he was going to die, he was very happy and prepared himself for death … he was never in pain … he remained very intelligent, and spoke of theoretical matters mostly. He was blissfully happy when we were all there and spoke of you, whom he missed a great deal … After he passed away, we picked spring flowers and put them on his bed….

… Mummy was telling us all about you … I hear you have cut your foul pig-tails off, and put up your hair, and spend half the day in front of the mirror – marvellous. I expect you are now wearing lipstick now Mummy has gone?★

Much love John.

★ Note that near the end of this letter, John could not resist a brotherly tease. This would have been particularly galling to Betty as she had always been a tomboy and would have wanted to impress John that she still was. But at least it would have distracted her from her grief and return some normal emotions – i.e. annoyance!

Whilst the Hopgoods were dealing with their grief, there were important developments happening on the world stage, with Germany attacking Norway in April 1940. Until now the RAF had only performed intermittent raids on shipping and dropping leaflets over Germany. Although there was never any evidence that these propaganda leaflets had had any effect on making Germany less warlike, it had given pilots and their crew a means of becoming expert at flying, particularly night flying over enemy territory. Bomber Command had also used the time to become better equipped with planes.

Grace wrote to Betty in France from Hurstcote on 4 May 1940, in the thick of transforming their erstwhile elegant home into practical flats for tenants. Their financial situation was becoming increasingly problematical now that the family's primary wage earner had died.

My darling Bets,

We've had the workmen in for 10 days & Celia only left 4 days ago, so I haven't had any time for writing letters … John has moved down to what used to be my little room, but there are still his pictures & books to move. I don't <u>think</u> I can get his old room redecorated before you come home, but if I can, have you any choice of colour? … <u>Your</u> beech tree is just out – But <u>not</u> the Spanish Chestnuts nor acacias, nor poplars. John has a mania for climbing the Beech Tree now and does so every weekend!★

John is taking your box of summer clothes up to town on Tuesday 7th all being well – My darling, I <u>am</u> so sorry it has not gone before, but truth to tell when we got the news of Germany invading Norway [9 April 1940], I felt it <u>might</u> be necessary to get you back at once (somehow) & so put off sending it. I had it all ready weeks ago! I wonder what the French are saying about the evacuation of Norway?

… Of course if the War allows, & if Marna's and John's arrangements allow, <u>I</u> shd <u>love</u> to come to St Briac for the month of July & bring you back with me!! But we must see – I'm hoping to have Marna here next weekend – she wd <u>love</u> to come to St Briac but thinks she will not be allowed to leave the Country.

With very much love from Yr Loving Mummy

PS I am going to a 'knitting' party on Mondays, beginning tomorrow, at Mrs Palmer's – her husband is Colonel of the 5th Queen's Surrey Regiment & we are going to begin working for its next winter comforts. ★★

★ Betty always had protected this towering tree as her property, to the extent of putting up a notice reading, 'Betty's tree keep out!' But now John, it seems, is trying to prove that he is every bit as dare-devilish as his younger sister.
★★ There were lots of women on the Home Front doing their bit for the poor soldiers, sailors and airmen; Grace was no exception and she threw herself into the work with any surplus energy she had.

On 10 May British Prime Minister Neville Chamberlain resigned and was replaced by Winston Churchill. The Phoney War was over. Britain appeared to the world, and America in particular, to be heading for certain defeat. Churchill understood that morale was as important as military force and he was determined to place this at the heart of his policy making and to boost the confidence of the British people – Operation Chastise became one of the ways Churchill was to do just that – and he hoped he wasn't too late.

On 15 May Holland surrendered to Germany and German troops continued advancing towards the extremity of the Maginot Line. By this time the war was really hotting up, and there were difficult decisions to be made for the Hopgood family, particularly concerning Betty, still out in France. Her mother wrote the following about the plan to try to get Betty back to England and home in this very unpredictable situation:

Hurstcote
Shere
Surrey
17th May 1940

My darling Bets,

Are you frightened? I'm sure you are not — we are not — Damn Hitler! But our poor soldiers have got a horrible time to try & keep us safe. I'm writing in the train & I've taken my gas mask just so as not to worry the ARP people. Marna is not allowed home & has been provided with what she calls a 'new summer hat' ie a Tin Helmet! Her poor little head.

Uncle Elliot has gone to Morocco on business and hopes to return about the first week of June — He may go to St Briac to fetch you.

… Poor John, there has been some carelessness (not his) for registering his Exam [a law exam], & so after all his hard work, he probably won't be allowed to take it in June. He is therefore going to have a week's holiday in Cornwall with Richard Hope, come home & finish his work for exam, & then 'wait & see'. He is much improved in every way after being quietly at home, but it is awful for all these lads having their prospects all messed up. ★

… Lots of love, my precious daughter from,
Yr loving Mummy.

★ 'Much improved' refers to John's poor behaviour at the end of Marlborough College, which mentions his drinking, smoking, swearing and general rebelliousness (see diary entry 23 July 1939).

By 26 May 1940 the Maginot line had been breached, and on 27 May Belgium surrendered to Germany. The advancing German Army trapped 330,000 British and French soldiers on the beaches around Dunkirk. Lord John Gort led trained men from the British Expeditionary Force to evacuate as many men as possible. Seven hundred private boats sailed from Ramsgate in England to bring men home. The British RAF fighter planes, including the new Spitfires, battled courageously and on the first day claimed over fifty German aircraft for the loss of only twelve of their own. This was a great victory for Britain, and according to Winston Churchill, had we been defeated, it could have cost us the war.

And Betty was still in France. She wrote:

Le 31 Mai

Dearest Mummy

Just received 3 postcards and 1 letter of yours which arrived all together. No I'm not worrying, and although I am so happy here, I am rather hoping Uncle Elliot will come to take me home, as I hate thinking of you worrying about me, am looking forward to doing my share of 'Digging for Victory' or in any other means. If we leave it too late I may not be able to get back at all as the news is decidedly serious now, but don't go risking coming over to fetch me – I'm not in the least bit nervous or frightened and would enjoy going back by myself if you'd only let me? Thanks for cheque all your friends here are ok plus sons.

God bless you,
Love Eliza.

Betty describes how she did indeed return home with her uncle:

Uncle Elliot [her Mother Grace's brother] did pick me up from France on his return home from a works trip to Africa. We waited for 3 days, enjoying French 'gastronomie' and doing long walks along the coast, waiting for news of a boat. Eventually I came back to England on the last boat from St Malo to Southampton, although noone had been told where we would land. It was a zig-zag crossing because the sea had been mined and the captain was taking evasive action. We heard that from then on, any English still living in France were pursued by the Nazis. They left their houses in France, and drove towards Marseilles, where they were stuck in long queues. They had mattresses on their roofs to protect themselves from gunfire and camped on the cliffs waiting for boats back to England; many of them were machine-gunned and killed. So we had a lucky escape from France!

Suddenly all priorities had changed and John, with his mother now at home, had taken the opportunity to escape from duties at Hurstcote, first holidaying in Cornwall. On 27 May 1940 he sent the following letter:

Penwarthe
Mawnan Smith
Falmouth
27th May 1940

Dearest Mummy,

I am coming back on Wednesday May 29th. … I do hope you haven't been doing too much. I am longing to help you. Glad to hear Betty is returning. I hope Marna will be safe.

My plans now are, a week or so on the Broads, starting next week, … then see if I can get into the RAF immediately – if not I shall join up in this new Home Defence Unit for chaps of my age. My exam will have to go by the board.

I am having a lovely time down here. We have been sailing every day and had a great time yesterday in a very strong wind. Today it is altogether too windy so we are going into the flics.

Looking forward to seeing you,
Your Loving Son.

Marna wrote from Folkestone on 28 May:

My darling Mummy,

We had an air-raid this morning, it only lasted about half an hour unfortunately. You see our section has to go into the sgt's mess which is full of arm chairs and all sorts of games – I played darts and then started a game of billiards on a full size table. I shan't mind if we have a few more air raids like this.

We are definitely going on Sunday to London, as far as we know round Kensington somewhere. We are supposed to be going into private billets, so I hope there will be plenty of chances for getting decent digs.

And then on 2 June from No. 57 Lexham Garden, London:

My darling Mummy,

Have arrived at last after a very interesting journey with some of the B.E.F. officers!★ Am very near Aunt Vi's flat, just at the back of Earl's Court Rd., we are in a Y.W.C.A. not too good and have a half hrs march to work every day!

★ The BEF (British Expeditionary Force) would have included the very officers who had masterminded the Dunkirk evacuation, which continued until 3 June when German troops were within 2 miles of the beach.

Betty was now back in England, looking after and helping her mother so as to free John and Marna. Betty writes the following of this time:

All was very bleak at Hurstcote: dear daddy was gone, my mother was very unwell, Marna was away in the A.T.S. and John still working in the family lawyer's office with Oliver in Lincoln Inn's Field, was champing at the bit to enter the RAF.'

The tenants in the 3 flats that had been made on the three floors at Hurstcote were a worry with complaints of 'no hot water' and 'no-one cleaning the entrance stairs' etc.

Because of the war the delivery of anthracite had been curtailed and so the central heating furnace for the house often ran low. The cess-pit for the sewage overflowed because the Council wouldn't come often enough to empty it (we had to pump it by hand).

A billeting officer came and inspected the house and told my mother she had enough room to receive a bombed out family from London. So we had to fit them in: an undertaker and his wife and five children. So including the gardener and his wife in the gardener's cottage, the cesspit had to serve 6 families!

We dug the kitchen garden and grew vegetables and Mummy ran a small chicken farm to supply eggs. So I was needed! And I convinced Mummy that I would study on my own every morning; I read History, Geography and English books and tried to make up what I had missed. I also cooked bacon and eggs for the troops at their canteen in Gomshall whilst they were on manoeuvres to the Front. There was blackout and barbed wire everywhere.

On 4 June 1940 Winston Churchill made his famous, rousing 'we shall never surrender' speech.

It was high on Churchill's agenda to boost the RAF in the eyes of the public – 'these young men, going forth every morn to guard their native land and all that we stand for, holding in their hands these instruments of colossal and shattering power' – and to encourage the idea that although the Luftwaffe had dominated the air until now, the RAF, with proper support, could become the dominant air power. He even articulated the following:

There never has been, I suppose, in all the world, in all the history of war, such an opportunity for youth. The Knights of the Round Table, the Crusaders, all fall back into the past … We shall prove ourselves once again able to defend our Island home … and to outlive the menace of tyranny … We shall fight with growing confidence and growing strength in the air.

Can you imagine the impact this must have had on John? Remember he was fiercely competitive. He had shouldered the responsibilities and duties surrounding his father's death. Now, sick of being bogged down by the practical duties at home, unsure about committing to a lifetime as a lawyer, not yet enrolled at Cambridge, he was ready for action. As an idealist, John had always been impressed by fine oration, and this speech appealed to his sense of justice, patriotism, challenge and adventure. He wanted to serve his country; in fact, he was champing at the bit to get out there. Plus a growing sense of responsibility and maturity was fast replacing John's rebelliousness of youth. He wanted to make his mark in history.

Over the next month, much was to happen on the world stage, with an escalation of the Second World War. On 10 June, under Mussolini, Italy declared war on Britain and France, potentially committing two of the most powerful naval forces to become part of Hitler's war machine. The threat of invasion became a real possibility, and the ringing of church bells was banned, except to warn of invasion. On 14 June the German Army entered Paris and a week later, Germany and France signed an Armistice much to Churchill's dismay. Soon after, Germany began occupation of the Channel Islands, and on 3 July Churchill ordered the destruction of the French Fleet to prevent German possession.

Now the war was in full spate. John was for action; he could no longer be just a bystander.

4

The Sky's the Limit

On 10 July 1940 the first great air attack on England in the Battle of Britain took place. It was immediately clear that Britain needed more trained pilots.

I wonder if John, being a deep-thinking, impressionable and principled young man, had any doubts of conscience in these formative days, weeks and months. Did he ask himself whether indeed he wanted any part in a war? As well as listening to Churchill's speeches, had John listened to the regular BBC broadcasts on Sunday evenings? Amongst the regular BBC broadcasts John might have heard would have been those by J.B. Priestly, who had fought in the First World War,

John when he joined the RAF, 1940

was a Cambridge graduate and quite left wing, being against accepted class and social order.

John probably realised that conscription of his age group was likely in the near future. Having been educated at Marlborough College, he was ready for tough action. He had always enjoyed sport and competition; he liked excitement and action. Would the option of becoming a conscientious objector have entered John's head? It had, apparently, at the age of 10, when he had expressed concerns to his mother about being a boy, wars and not wanting to kill people. But now it would surely have smacked of cowardice to an old Marlburian, and, besides, his country needed him. The German dictatorship had to be stopped. John did not like authority for authority's sake, and he believed in people's freedom of thought and action. He had seen the trenches both his uncles had been stuck in and had imagined the awful conditions and dreadful slaughter in the First World War. John was not going to follow them.

Having a growing fascination for aeroplanes and flying, and needing a new challenge, John decided that the Royal Air Force was the place for him. Thus John Vere Hopgood left home on 31 July 1940 to join the RAF and train as a pilot; his age was 18 years and 11 months. In the following letters, you will see not only how John developed his love of flying (in Tiger Moths, Cadets, Ansons, Hampdens and Oxfords) but also how, at an extremely young age, he quickly grew in maturity and responsibility.

1st August 1940
1182427 X

My dearest Mummy,

Well here I am still up at Cardington, with nothing to do, so have plenty of time in which to write letter. As I have not been stationed anywhere yet I cannot give an address. The majority of us ie the chaps who came up with me, are all going off up to Norton tomorrow morning – lucky blighters, they are going to have private billets out. The minority left are mostly Air Crew chaps – so I expect we are bound to some other destination soon – lets hope the South coast where we can get healthy! However we may be here for another week or so.

I have now got all my kit and uniform, which of course is very stuffy in this hot weather. Yesterday we were vaccinated and inoculated – against what no-one knows – anyway it caused pretty nasty after effects. Half of the chaps first fainted and/or were ill, and all of us had stinging headaches for the rest of the day, plus stiff right arms. However we were not allowed to rest in peace, as we had to spend the whole afternoon in hot sun, standing in queues waiting to collect equipment. Altogether it was hell. Fortunately I did not actually faint, though had to sit down on many occasions. However today we are all much better but pretty weak, and my arm is still stiff – which may account for this scrawl.

The food might be quite good, but they ruin it all and quite take away one's appetite by swamping it all in various different tasting pig swills.

There is no-one of my own sort here, but most of the chaps are very nice. Some of them are very humorous indeed because they grumble at everything.★ I have had to do a good many fatigue duties, and shall probably have many more worse ones if I stay here long.★★

Another parade soon, so I had better stop.

Much love to all.

Your loving Son.

★ It is interesting that John had noticed their grumbling attitudes; having come from a spartan public-school background, not only was he used to much worse conditions but he had apparently learnt to put a good face on things and be positive. This attitude is quite significant as to be a 'good squadron type' it was very important that men were able to keep their morale high. John was apparently already on the right track.

★★ Fatigue duties were manual work, such as emptying bins, cleaning, peeling potatoes and maintenance work.

John at early training in Torquay, 1940

J. V. Hopgood
AC/2 1182427
No 14 Flight
No 1 Receiving Wing
Babbacombe
Torquay
Devon
4.8.1940

My dearest Mummy,

   As you can see from the rather long addressing above, I am at Torquay, and about to
start training. Talk about luck – I have certainly had it. I arrived here yesterday afternoon
and it's certainly a first class place – lovely scenery, plenty of fun and sun. Of the 500 who
started with me at Cardington, only 6 others beside myself have been sent down here – we
are all pilots, and what is more we have been sent down here because, we surmise, we have
been recommended for commissions. And still better we are starting flying training straight
away. All the chaps down here and in Torquay are 75% public school and varsity types,
and all pilots. They are all very nice, and I certainly ought to have a good time.

   Babbacombe is just outside Torquay, about 3 miles along the coast. It's a lovely spot
with a funicular down to the beach. We are in a hotel with H and C water, someone to
sweep out our bedroom, marvellous food, eating place and eating arrangements, and very
nice corporals, sergeants and officers. In fact after Cardington, it is almost like being in
civvies again – though of course we haven't had any drilling etc yet. Everybody agrees that
Cardington is the worst dump and Torquay the best.

   We got most of today off, so we went into Torquay and then on to Paignton. Then we
came back and bathed. ★ The water was very warm, and it looks as though I may be able to
bathe quite a lot. So I should much appreciate it if you could send me my bathing trunks
– they are in my wardrobe – I think. Also could you please send me a weekly allowance.
All the chaps here have private allowances, and it will be impossible to do anything with
them, go to dances etc on my pay. There are also little things such as bus fares stamps
and cleaning materials which alone eat up my pay. I am trying to give up cigarettes, and
cut down smoking with a pipe. ★★ I am trying to be fair so hope you will understand,
especially as I am with a lot of chaps of my own sort. I hope you will be able to send 10/-
a week. It is no good trying to do it through a bank, as I shall never get time off in the
middle of the day, except Sundays when the banks close, to cash any cheques.

   Could you please send me my tennis racket, and 1 pair of white shorts (one of the
smaller kind), and 1 pair of white socks, also white tennis shoes and a tennis shirt (the
largest with buttons all the way down).

On my way down here, I tried to ring up Oliver at his office at about 10.15 – but got no reply – what a slack office – you might tell him. Supper parade now so must stop.
   Love to all,
   Your loving Son.

* See John in the middle of the photograph, with costume and towel in hand.
* This is a turnaround for John and shows his serious attempt to save money for his family, whom he knows are in a difficult financial position.

From 10 July 1940, daily dogfights took place over the water and the south coast between the Luftwaffe and RAF fighter planes. The Luftwaffe focused on the ships bringing vital supplies to Britain and tempted RAF fighters out over the Channel to test their defences.

John and fellow trainees setting off for a swim, Torquay, 1940

On 1 August the dogfights and bombing increased as Hitler ordered the obliteration of all RAF flying units, ground units and supply organisations, as well as the destruction of the British aircraft industry.

Although John was away from the worst of the bombing raids, he refers to many 'wounded RAF Officers' as a result of this in his letter below, and had to give blood.

Torquay
Devon
24th August 1940

My dearest Mother,

Many thanks for the 10/-, letter and bundle of tennis kit, all of which arrived safely. I understand about the money, and as I did remember to bring my cheque book, I will send a cheque once a month. Could you please send me the weekly 10/- at the <u>beginning</u> of each week. I enclose cheque for £2.00, which I think, should square up for what I have received so far plus next week's 10/-.

I was very glad to hear you hadn't actually been bombed, as I rather feared you might have got in for a few bombs. I wish I had seen those dogfights overhead. I should like to hear that Uncle Elliot and Aunt Sylvia, etc are OK for they must have had bombs very near them. Actually down here there is no aerodrome for about 30 miles around. However there are other interesting objectives here and round about, so that we are getting hardened to bombing and German planes. When we first came here we had at least one air raid per day, and German planes were flying overhead night and day. Now they have stopped having air raids though the planes and bombs still continue. As a matter of fact no bombs have fallen actually inside Torquay, though a fair amount of damage and death has been caused a few miles outside, which accounts for the delay in the postal service. However we are all safe and sound.

Yesterday I had to go and give a pint of my blood. A few weeks ago we had a blood grouping test, and evidently I am very strong in a special group, so I was asked if I would give them a pint of it, and as it was more compulsory than voluntary, I agreed. However it didn't hurt and I felt no worse after it. While I was having it done, I asked the MO about Harry Mile's friend, but he couldn't help me at all. I have also made other enquiries, but have drawn blank. There are hundreds of wounded RAF officers down here, so that it really will be looking for a needle in a haystack. However I will bear his name in mind.

You asked me if there is anything special I want for my birthday. Well here's a short list:

Air Force Tobacco Pouch, Pipe, Tobacco and Cigarettes, Cake (fruit) and sweets, Soap Container, Watch Strap, Money, Shaving Razor and Blades. ★

We've been having perfect weather so that I have been bathing and playing tennis quite a lot. We also have plenty of PT which keeps us fit and also sweaty.

No more now as the all clear siren has gone.

Love John.

⋆ Notice that John's resolution to stop smoking had not been achieved.

On 24 August 1940 the first bombs fell on central London, a taste of the Blitz which was to come. The next day Churchill ordered an attack on Berlin. The Luftwaffe Attacks on RAF bases had now started and with some success, and on this same day, the small fighter command station at Manston in Kent was temporarily abandoned as there were hardly any buildings left and the airfield was littered with unexploded bombs.

On 29 August 1940 – which was John's 19th birthday – it was decided, having been projected since 1936, to form the first Manchester aircraft squadron base at Lindholme. It was intended that eventually the whole command would be equipped with these two-engined heavy bombers, the precursor to the Lancaster.

John wrote a letter to his sister Betty on 3 September in appreciation of the birthday present she had given him:

> *Torquay*
> *Devon*
> *3.9.40*

My dear Betty,

Great Scott – was I amazed when I opened your present! At first, before I had unwrapped it I thought you were being funny and had sent me some hair grease, and could hardly believe my eyes when I beheld intoxicating liquor. I need not tell you how much it was appreciated, as I see you know my tastes! Thank you very much indeed. It certainly came in useful, as I was put on guard the whole night on my birthday and got very cold, so that it was just the stuff to cheer us up, especially as we were forbidden to go outside and get a drink. Actually I very nearly got put on a charge for it, but as my sergeant had also had a sip, he smoothed things over, and the officer went away.

Your letter also amused me very much. Would it not be better if you looked up some of those words again in a dictionary? – Some of them were rather out of place. However your picture of me after RAF drill was no exaggeration. I can assure you, except that we wear thick uniforms and heavy kit when doing it, not just a pair of pants!

I have quite a good time here, and get up to quite a lot of mischief – as you would call it. Its rather fun being in uniform as everybody is very nice to one. I get lifts and drinks free whenever I like. Last night I was asked out to dinner with a naval officer whom I met in a pub, and who had met Clive Lowe. He gave me a marvellous meal plus cigars and drinks in a very posh hotel. He was very interesting and told me a lot about the Navy.

The other night we had a marvellous scrap with some matelots and beat them good and proper, but all had to scatter on the approach of an officer.

I am glad to hear you like the officers who come up to tennis on Sundays! But you shouldn't run away – it's undignified – you can always slap his face!

Well I must now prepare to go out with a certain party, and comb the glamorous locks, which I am sorry to say are almost no more.

Many thanks once again for your marvellous present,

Love John.

On 7 September the London Blitz began; this month 6,954 civilians were killed in Britain. Convinced that the German invasion of Britain was imminent, the country was put on the highest alert; the code word 'Cromwell' was sent to military units and church bells rang amidst the storm not only of the Luftwaffe but also of wild weather in the guise of thunder and lightning. 'Cromwell' remained in force for twelve days, but no invasion by sea happened, and Fighter Command remained almost intact.

So John was now giving Betty brotherly advice on how to deal with men, and it sounds as if he was enjoying life, particularly the variety and excitement; the words 'dull' and 'boring' are certainly not mentioned any more.

Although John had received several communications for his birthday, his mother's letter and monetary gift had still not arrived:

Torquay

Devon

11.9.1940

My dearest Mummy,

Still your letter and 30/- has not come. I will start making further inquiries, if you will let me know what you have found out about it at Guildford or wherever you posted it.

I sincerely hope that you have escaped damage from Air Raids at Shere. From what little news we get here, it appears that London has had some nasty smacks. I trust all relations and friends are safe?

We have noticed nothing unusual in the air here, and Jerry comes over as usual, but doesn't drop anything, which is very kind of him. However we had a pretty good invasion scare on Sunday and were all kept in and we really thought we were off. However it was a mere false alarm. But now things are stiffening up and we are getting better prepared to meet Jerry when he really comes.

Great thrill last week when we were issued with our flying kit.★ It's grand stuff, marvellously warm and well made. Another fortnight or so, and I hope I shall be using it. We had a sprinkling of rain last weekend – the first lot since I joined up. However the weather has not broken and we are still sweating all day. Unfortunately we cannot bathe now as the beach has been closed to all.

I'm afraid there isn't much news as I haven't done much of late except a spot of work, as we have a few exams coming off soon just before we leave here.

Much love to all,

Your loving Son.

★ Maybe John was referring to the £50 government allowance given to RAF officers, usually towards the end of their training, that they spent on the purchase of individually tailored uniforms (less scratchy than the sergeants' uniforms), which included a dark blue shirt to be worn with a black tie, black socks and shoes, and their field service cap bearing a black mohair band with gold embroidered insignia.

Flying kit, however, consisted of flying jackets lined with sheepskin and often electrically heated, the leads of which went down inside the trouser legs to heated slippers/flying boots made of thick sheepskin. Most of the crew wore rollneck pullovers, thick woollen or silk long johns and knee-length stockings; some wore heated gloves which clipped to the sleeves of the jacket, whilst others experimented with wearing several layers of gloves in silk, chamois leather and wool. Then there was the Mae West life jacket, a parachute harness and flying helmet with oxygen mask and goggles attached.

What they wore also depended on whereabouts in the aircraft they were situated; it certainly wasn't as cold for the pilots and other crew in the front of the aircraft, beside the warm, throbbing engines, as it was for the rear gunner at the back only protected from the full force of the elements by thin Perspex (and this was often removed for clearer vision). I don't know what John wore, as there were no hard rules and individuals adapted the dress using anything of their own that made them feel comfortable. We will read in one of John's next letters (22 September 1940) that he asked his mother to send his black leather shoes to fly in, to give him more ankle manoeuvrability than the cumbersome flying boots which restricted him using the foot controls.

John's sister, Marna in the ATS, wrote from No. 2 Bramham Gardens, London, on 12 September:

My darling Mummy,

… Things are pretty hot round us every night but so far our house is still standing. I will try to come down on Sunday, but if I can't don't worry because all the lines will have been put out of action.

If I don't come, could you please send me a rug and my lilo as I have to spend the night on the floor now and it's a bit hard.

At this time John's half-sister Joan, who was also experiencing hardships, was a factory inspector in Wolverhampton by day and working for Air Raid Precautions (ARP) by night, helping out at the Report Centre every third night from 11 p.m.–7 a.m. She says, 'We manned the phone, sounded the siren and dossed down on camp beds when things were quiet. Although we got many alerts we got only one short night of bombs.' Joan was also a co-founder of the Wolverhampton

Voluntary Land Corps, who organised groups to tend and harvest crops in the evenings and at weekends, to help local farmers.

Meanwhile, John is busy doing exams, with a sprinkling of community singing:

Torquay
18.9.40

Dear Mother

… This week's going to be a busy week as we have all our Navigation, Morse etc exams to do, and if we fail we get chucked out and remustered as Air Gunners. So I shall do my best to pass. We had a Maths exam about 2 weeks ago and I passed with 91%. When all the exams are over and we are waiting to be posted I might have got 2 days or 3 days embarkation leave, but owing to this confounded imminent threat of invasion all leave and passes have been cancelled so there's no chance of leave for a long time now especially if I am posted abroad. What I hope is that I am posted to an aerodrome near London, but I don't suppose now that they are sending any more near town, with all this bombing going on.

By the way, if you listen in on Thursday evening (it may be Friday) you will hear us Broadcast! 5 I. T.W. are community singing so you may hear a few good yells. Last night I went to a very good dance. It was full of senior officers and the Mayor, etc, and there were plenty of prizes. It finished up with a rugger scrum in the middle of the floor over a packet of cigarettes!

If this invasion comes off soon I shall be very annoyed as there is little chance of us doing much fighting. I rather wish I was still in the L.D.V [Local Defence Volunteers, or Home Guard]. I must be off to lunch now,

Love to all,

Your loving Son.

By now John was progressing well in his training but feeling frustrated at not doing something more active and practical to help those caught up in the Blitz. John was thus aware that night after night there had been a constant bombardment of London, and to have been on the ground, experiencing it in the tough blackout conditions, would have been a kind of glamour for John.

R.A.F.WATCHFIELD
NR SWINDON
WILTS
22.9.1940

My dearest Mummy,

   I hope you got my telegram to say I was moving from Torquay. As you can see from the above I have not actually got posted nr Reading but nr Swindon and Marlborough.

   Many thanks for your last letter and 20/-. I was getting quite anxious about Marna as well, and was glad to hear she is OK. I was also beginning to wonder if your letter had gone astray again, as it came rather late. I only hope Jerry doesn't land any bombs on any member of the family.

   Luck again seems to have come my way, for again we have all been rushed forward. I am now at the Elementary Flying Training School, at a fairly large and new aerodrome. Tomorrow, at last we start flying — so naturally I am thrilled. This place has a very gloomy and concentration camp appearance after Torquay and the barracks are cold and damp and we miss many of the comforts of hotel life on the coast, such as hot water and good food. We are also miles from anywhere, surrounded by hundreds of cadet Army Officers. However the advantage of commencing flying, slacker discipline etc. definitely outweigh the disadvantages as far as I'm concerned. ⋆

   The last week at Torquay was a pretty sweaty one. We had quite a few exams, but as we were posted so soon, we missed one or two. On Friday morning we had our Navigation Exam, which I passed with 90%, and no sooner had we taken it than we were ordered to stand by and get packed. Of course we were thrilled, as 9 times out of 10 one has to hang around about a week or fortnight, waiting to be posted. And eventually we got here last night after travelling all day Sat.

   Here I shall get 48 hours leave every other week-end all being well. So next week-end I hope to come home. If I can manage it I should arrive rather late on Friday night — about 9–10 pm — so don't wait — I'll just hop into bed. However I may not be able to get leave next week-end, so that I may have to wait until the following week-end — I'll try to let you know beforehand.

   By the way, could you please send me my pair of black walking shoes as soon as possible. You see we more or less have to have them for flying, as boots restrict the manoeuvrability of our ankles, and hence makes it difficult to move the foot controls quickly. There are several other things I want, but they can wait 'til I can collect them myself.

Trusting all are safe and well, and looking forward to seeing you all soon,
Much love,
Your loving Son.

★ 'Slacker discipline' probably actually meant less imposed discipline; it was very important that RAF officers were capable of self-discipline. Indeed, a special characteristic of No. 5 Group was to encourage the spirit of individual initiative. This would have suited John as he hated authority for authority's sake, but he did like order.

From September 1940 onwards the monthly total of sorties by aircraft of RAF's No. 5 Group were reduced, leading to an important change of tactics mainly in the light of photographic analysis showing poor accuracy in hitting targets. So, with the approach of winter when visual identification of the target was more difficult, instead of aiming for small targets, using small numbers of aircraft and relying purely on the skill of the navigator, it became increasingly the rule for more aircraft to bomb a more general target, covering a greater area.

On 23 September 1940 John was given his Pilot's Flying Log Book. Note his name in capital letters across the leaves to enable him to pick his log book out easily from the shelf where it was kept alongside everybody else's in the officers' mess.

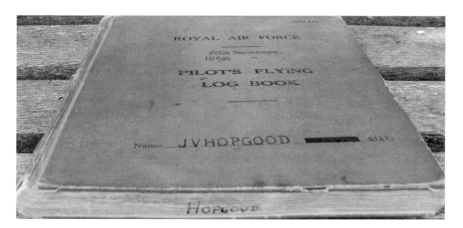

John's log book (notice the book edge)

YEAR 1940		AIRCRAFT		PILOT, OR 1ST PILOT	2ND PILOT, PUPIL OR PASSENGER	DUTY (INCLUDING RESULTS AND REMARKS)	SINGLE-ENGINE DAY	
MONTH	DATE	Type	No.				Dual (1)	Pilot (2)
—	—	—	—	—	—	— TOTALS BROUGHT FORWARD		
SEPT	23	CADET	G. ADAN	F.O. HOLLAND	SELF	1. AIR EXPERIENCE		15
						1a. FAMILIARITY WITH COCKPIT		
SEPT	24	CADET	G.ACCK	F.O. HOLLAND	SELF	2. EFFECT OF CONTROLS		35
						4. STRAIGHT AND LEVEL FLIGHT		
						5. CLIMBING. GLIDING. STALLING.		
SEPT	25	CADET	G.ACCK	F.O. HOLLAND	SELF	2. EFFECT OF CONTROLS		25
						4. STRAIGHT AND LEVEL FLYING		
						5. CLIMBING, GLIDING AND STALLING		
						6. MEDIUM TURNS		
SEPT	25	CADET	G.ACCK	F.O. HOLLAND	SELF	6. MEDIUM TURNS		40
						7. TAKING OFF INTO WIND		
						9. GLIDING APPROACH AND LANDING		
SEPT	25	CADET	G.ACCK	F.O. HOLLAND	SELF	6. MEDIUM TURNS		50
						7. TAKING OFF INTO WIND		
						9. GLIDING APPROACH AND LANDING		
SEPT	26	CADET	G.AEAR	F.O. HOLLAND	SELF	6. MEDIUM TURNS		30
						7. TAKING OFF INTO WIND		
						9. GLIDING APPROACH AND LANDING		
				GRAND TOTAL [Cols. (1) to (10)] 3 Hrs. 15 Mins.		TOTALS CARRIED FORWARD	34 15	

No. 3 E.F.T.S. WATCHFIELD

First page of John's log book

RAF WATCHFIELD
NR SWINDON
WILTS
25.9.1940

My dearest Mummy,

I have got leave for this next weekend, Friday night until Sunday night. Of course if there's another of these invasion scares the leave will be cancelled, so pray it won't happen. Look, don't wait up on Friday night as I may be very late. Transport facilities from here are very bad, so I am relying on a hitchhike as far as Reading and from there I shall train I hope. So you see I shan't probably arrive until perhaps midnight. I expect I shall be sleeping in the passage, dining room or west room — so I shall grope around and expect what I find.

I am now flying. It's absolutely grand, and I am getting on quite successfully.

In haste. Much love to all,

Looking forward to seeing you on Sat.

Your v. loving Son.

On 27 September Germany, Italy and Japan signed the Tripartite Pact in Berlin, with the aim of ensuring the United States had no active involvement in the war; in fact, the pact had the opposite effect and the United States now became resolved to aid Britain and the Allies.

On 27 September, Marna wrote to her mother from her London digs (mainly intent on her own practicalities and restrictions, rather than on the world picture), but ends her letter by saying, 'The office is becoming rather an objective, the last three nights they have been bombing round it, I wish they would hurry up and hit it and then we should have to be moved out of London.'

John did his first solo flight on 1 October, only one week after receiving his log book, and his log book shows some of the technical instruction he underwent on the same day. John must have been too busy (and too happy) to write frequently at this point.

John has progressed from a Cadet to a Tiger Moth

RAF Watchfield
Nr Swindon
Wilts
8.10.40

My dearest Mummy,

So sorry to have snaffled your ration book last week-end! I hope you haven't unduly starved. I must also apologise for not having written sooner but life has been very hectic just lately what with more exams and being billeted out. I do hope all are well – how's Marna? I hope to get back again home as last time this Friday, but, of course, I can never say definitely until I arrive!

The flying is definitely going well. I did my first solo after 6½ hours, which is the best for this course. I now do a lot of solo flying and have just started doing aerobatics which are really thrilling. I have changed my instructor and have now got a very pleasant young chap who is doing his best to get me into the fighters.★ To-day we did a lot of low flying – just hopping over trees, and running along the railway line right in front of trains and just skimming over them. This week we are doing more exams, which is very tedious; however if we don't pass them we get slung out, whether we can fly or not.

We are now all billeted out about 7 miles from the 'drome. It means getting up very early and catching busses etc which is exceedingly tiresome. Actually another chap and I are billets in the vicarage!! It is very nice and homely there, if it is rather stiff going!

No more now, looking forward to seeing you all this next week-end.

Much love,

John.

★ It seems that John wanted to be a fighter pilot, probably so that he could take revenge directly on those implementing Hitler's orders.

On the subject of her brother's leave visits, Betty says:

> It was very difficult for us at home, and John and Marna, to make plans for their leave as things kept changing, and of course we didn't have deep freezes or anything, so we had to set to, to dig up lots of vegetables and prepare things in readiness, and then if they didn't come back we had a glut!

On 7 October 1940 the German Army moved into Romania. Hitler wanted this as part of his strategy to create an unbroken Eastern Front to menace the Soviet Union and to 'defend' Romania's oilfields. On 8 October John received his first instruction in low flying in a Tiger Moth.

By 25 October 1940 the British Air Ministry had announced that they were deploying and training airmen from Poland, France, Belgium, Holland and

John and Marna in front of Hurstcote, 1940

YEAR 1940		AIRCRAFT		PILOT, OR 1ST PILOT	2ND PILOT, PUPIL OR PASSENGER	DUTY (INCLUDING RESULTS AND REMARKS)	SINGLE-ENGINE DAY	
MONTH	DATE	Type	No.				Dual (1)	Pilot (2)
—	—	—	—	—	—	—— TOTALS BROUGHT FORWARD	11.30	5.20
OCT.	7ᵗ	T. MOTH	T.7129	SELF		7. TAKING OFF INTO WIND		65
						8. POWERED APPROACH AND LANDING		
						9. GLIDING APPROACH AND LANDING		
						13. PRECAUTIONARY LANDING		
						17 FORCED LANDING		
						22. ACROBATICS		
OCT.	8ᵗ	T. MOTH	N.9382	SGT. BOWKER	SELF	7. TAKING OFF INTO WIND		75
						9. GLIDING APPROACH AND LANDING		
						10. SPINNING (2 RIGHT).		
						14. LOW FLYING		
						15. STEEP TURNS		
OCT.	8ᵗ	T. MOTH	R.4833	SELF		6. MEDIUM TURNS		44
						7. TAKING OFF INTO WIND		
						8. POWERED APPROACH AND LANDING		
						9. GLIDING APPROACH AND LANDING		
						15. STEEP TURNS		
						22. ACROBATICS		

John's first attempt at low flying on 8 October

Czechoslovakia. Meanwhile, John's sister, Marna, was in the thick of things in
London. On 27 October, having heard there had been intensive bombing of
London and returning to her ATS work from Shere in Surrey to Bramham
Gardens in South West London, Marna wrote:

My darling Mummy,
  I've got back ok; it took me 3 hours!
  Everything seems very much the same as I left it; thank goodness we still have glass
windows to our room.
  Thank you very much for making my leave so refreshing, I feel like work again.
  Love to E.,
  Marna

Meanwhile John is progressing with his flying: his first full monthly assessment
in his log book showed him to be 'average' and with 'no apparent faults in his
flying which needed to be watched'.

On 31 October 1940 the Battle of Britain ended. This day marked the end of
the continuous Luftwaffe raiding campaign. However, if you read John's letter

John's first full monthly assessment

below, the bombing didn't tail off gradually but ended with a day of constant air raids. And John was beginning to live it up.

> *Royal Air Force College*
> *Cranwell*
> *Lincs*
> *31.10.1940*

My dearest Mother

As you can see I am now at Cranwell. You can't think how glad we all are to have left Watchfield and have arrived at the Sandhurst of the RAF. To think that in peacetime it would have cost about £300 to be here, and that now it costs nothing and that we get paid into the bargain cheers us all up considerably.

It is simply marvellous here – the food is equivalent to that served in the best London restaurant and we have it in the officers' mess; which of course means that we are waited on hand and foot and have our own batmen! We have the full use of the officers' mess and all that goes with it, so of course it is going to be very expensive here. However I will do my best to make ends meet.

You will gather we are all going through our officers training so the prospects of commission are very bright, but nothing like all of us will get there. I share a very respectable size room with another chap, and the whole place is an orgy of luxury after Watchfield.

We had a terrible journey getting here. We started at 10 in the morning and arrived here on the Thursday morning i.e. to-day, at 4 o'clock! We missed our connection in London and I had a good look around & went along to Oliver's office, but he was out. Then having got another train from Kings X the fun started. We had air raids the whole way; the train broke down, the brakes refused to function properly on another, etc, etc. We were just flying about from one train to another & from one platform to another & back again. And moving about like that with full kit and kit bags is not my idea of a joke.

I will write again soon when I have some more flying. We are going to fly airspeed Oxfords which are much bigger than Tiger Moths & have twin engines.

I trust all are well, & hope you are getting the Punches ok.

Much love,

Your loving Son.

John continued his training at the RAF College, Cranwell, but now in a two-engined Oxford.

Cranwell College, near Sleaford, Lincolnshire, having been a naval aviation training centre during the First World War, became the world's first air academy in 1919. During the Second World War the college was closed and its facilities were used as a flying training school.

F.T.S. RAF College Cranwell

YEAR		AIRCRAFT		PILOT, OR 1ST PILOT	2ND PILOT, PUPIL OR PASSENGER	DUTY (INCLUDING RESULTS AND REMARKS)	SINGLE-ENGINE AIRCRAFT				MULTI-ENGINE AIRCRAFT
MONTH	DATE	Type	No.				DAY Dual	DAY Pilot	NIGHT Dual	NIGHT Pilot	Dual
—	—	—	—	—	—	— TOTALS BROUGHT FORWARD	21.45	22.25			
Nov.	1	OXFORD	9684	SGT. BROWN	SELF	1. AIR EXPERIENCE 2. EFFECT OF CONTROLS 3. TAXYING 4. STRAIGHT AND LEVEL FLIGHT 5. CLIMBING GLIDING STALLING 6. MEDIUM TURNS.					1.00
Nov.	3	OXFORD	P.1838	SGT. BROWN	SELF	6. MEDIUM TURNS 7. TAKING OFF INTO WIND 8. POWERED APPROACH AND LANDING					1.05
Nov.	6	OXFORD	1882	SGT. BROWN	SELF	6. MEDIUM TURNS 7. TAKING OFF INTO WIND 8. POWERED APPROACH AND LANDING					0.10
Nov.	7	OXFORD	P.6811	SGT. BROWN	SELF	6. MEDIUM TURNS 7. TAKING OFF INTO WIND 8. POWERED APPROACH AND LANDING					0.55
Nov.	8	OXFORD	N.4835	SGT. BROWN	SELF	6. MEDIUM TURNS 7. TAKING OFF INTO WIND 8. POWERED APPROACH AND LANDING SINGLE ENGINED FLYING 13. ACTION IN EVENT OF FIRE.					0.20
				GRAND TOTAL [Cols. (1) to (10)] 47 Hrs. 40 Mins.		TOTALS CARRIED FORWARD	21.45	22.25			3.30

Cranwell College with John now flying Oxfords

The British people were optimistic. They had withstood the wrath of Hitler, who had promised to invade and had missed his chance. The great British class system dissolved as more young men, from every corner of Britain and the Empire and from every social class, joined the RAF wanting to become bomber pilots and wreak their revenge on Hitler for bombing London. It is said that Hitler had been the best recruiting officer for the RAF! Those already in the RAF, like John, were pleased they had joined and were ready to give payback to Germany. As Churchill said, 'The fighters are our salvation, but the bombers alone provide the means to victory.'

If Britain was to remain British and be rid of the Nazis it had to fight. And with France fallen, the RAF was the only force in the world which could attack the Germans on their own ground. Churchill was adamant that 'We must be united, we must be undaunted, we must be inflexible. Our qualities and deeds must burn and glow through the gloom of Europe until they become the veritable beacon of its salvation.'

There was indeed gloom that autumn as the weather was particularly foggy. And young RAF recruits, having joined in a wave of glamour, found life in the

RAF tough, relentless and often tedious. With its tradition of institutionalised bullying, those who had not been through the public school system and a similar regime found it hard to withstand; John, of course, had been conditioned to it.

On 14–15 November, as it happens just days after the death of former British Prime Minister Neville Chamberlain, German planes bombed Coventry and Birmingham, destroying a great portion of these cities; hence John's reference in the next letter to thinking his sister safer now that there were target cities other than London.

This picture shows John at Cranwell RAF College.

Cranwell, 1940

Detail of John

RAF Cranwell
Lincs
5.12.1940

My dearest Mother,

Many thanks for your letter and sports gear. Glad Elizabeth's confirmation went off all right to everybody's satisfaction. Have you any news of Joan because I expect she must be mainly in the bombed zone these days.

Please thank M.J. for her letter & also for getting Lady Portal on the warpath re Watchfield. I will write to her soon.★

Glad to hear all are well and safe. I expect Marna gets a little more sleep now that Jerry is bombing further afield. Jerry came over here one morning, but failed to do any damage at all and was shot down.

The flying is going quite well nowadays, and I am getting a better hold over the Oxford. When the weather permits we put in as much flying as possible. I have just done two cross-country solo flights, and on the first, went over to Oxford and back. It was quite interesting, in spite of the fact that I got quite lost going there owing to the fact that the sun was dead in front the whole way. My second cross country was yesterday, this time on a triangle to Moreton- in-the Marsh and Wolverton. I was with another chap and we struck foul weather with thick cloud from 400ft to 2,000ft so we flew above the clouds, sat back and hoped we would get somewhere. After about 20 minutes we found a clearing & found ourselves nearly dead on our track. We both heaved sighs of relief because forced landing in an Oxford, except on a drome, is not at all funny, especially in bad weather.

Cross countrys are not quite so simple here as they were at Watchfield, for we have to work out wind speeds & directions, and estimated times of arrival in the air, which is decidedly difficult at first, as it is a full time job to fly the machine straight.

I have done a bit of formation flying, and in a few days start night flying which is quite tricky. I hear it is rather uninteresting, and invariably interrupted by air raids. I have no instructor at the moment, as the chap I had, a very pleasant but rather timid Sergeant, has gone to deal with another course. One of my old school friends has turned up on one of the new courses – funny how one keeps cropping up against friends.

The other day I went for a little trip over to Leicester and Nottingham which was quite interesting. On Saturday afternoon I went into Lincoln to have a look around. But I arrived in the middle of a procession of the city's A.R.P.'s Fire Services and Home Guards etc, marching through the city. The place was packed, and therefore my visit was not made any too comfortable or interesting.

Only another 2 weeks before our wings exam. When you next see me I hope I shall have wings on my front as well as my back! We have just been told today that we are getting no Christmas leave but I might be able to wangle to rush home for a day or two around Christmas, but it is doubtful. It will depend a good deal on the weather and our flying hours I expect.

Charles Gardener – the BBC reporter – is here now as an officer training with us – so if I can manage to engage him in conversation he ought to have some interesting stories to tell of his experiences.

We are going to have a choice of saying what we want to fly after here. I can't make up my mind at all, as there are so many choices. I should very much like to try our twin-engine fighters, but bombers are very fascinating if rather stolid and dull.★★

Please let me know about Christmas presents – I hope it is understood I (& we?) only do family ones. Well, I must stop now & have my four-course dinner plus coffee!

Much love to all.

Your loving Son.

P.S. I have got all the sports clothes I need, so honestly there is no need to send anything else.

★ Lady Portal was chief of air staff, Lord Portal's wife, and Marna must have complained to her on John's behalf about the awful conditions the airmen had to put up with at RAF Watchfield.

★★ Once again it looks as if John fancies the excitement of being a fighter pilot rather than a bomber pilot.

On 9 December 1940 the British North African offensive began; Tobruk (in Libya) was captured and 48,000 men were taken prisoner by the British. This offensive was to last for the remaining two and a half years of John's short life and its eventual victory, coinciding with the Dambusters' raid, served as a double morale booster.

With such a lot happening on the world stage, no wonder John is frustrated when, as he writes below, night flying consists of 'staying awake the whole night, eating sandwiches and hoping for the "all clear" and better weather!'

RAF Cranwell
Lincs
22.12.1940

My dearest Mother

I've just got your last letter. I'm so sorry I never let you know that I couldn't get leave this w/end, as I gather you were expecting me more than I had meant you to. I know I did drop hints in my last letter that I might get the w/end off, but meant to add that I would let you know definitely if I could get off.

This letter must serve as a letter to all the family for Christmas, carrying with it all my best wishes for a happy Christmas, and lets hope a brighter New Year. I shall miss being at home this Christmas, but I'm afraid there's absolutely no chance of leave, at any rate for Christmas. But, as before, we have been told we may get a long w/end (Friday night to Sunday night) this next w/end. However I will let you know by wire, as soon as I can, if I am coming. I do hope it materialises – and I only wish I could be more definite – but it all depends on such a lot of things. We have been doing very little flying lately owing to bad weather – icing up, fog and low clouds, with a very probable result that our posting, and consequently our 7 days leave will be postponed for an extra 2 weeks – meaning we shall not get away from here until about the end of Jan, in order to get the proper amount of flying hours.

I have been night flying now – at least not flying – it merely consisted of staying awake the whole night, eating sandwiches and hoping for the 'all clear' and better weather! It really is pathetic how behindhand we have got with our flying here, and it's holding everything up. At any rate, though, the exams are over, which is something in the way of progress, and although we do not get the results until to-morrow, I don't think I have failed. From now on all we do here is have interviews with various big noises, and fly.

I had a very nice dinner with Nove the Saturday before last. Last night I went to a dance in Lincoln which was quite good fun, and incidentally met Ralph Richardson – the famous film star who was in the Fleet Air Arm!

By the way it is getting colder here everyday, so I shall much appreciate Betty's scarf, if it is ready yet.★ Most mornings now we have to scrape the ice and the frost off the wings before we can fly, which at the best of times is no warm job.

I hope you will go on getting the Punches weekly, as I have asked Betty to make the necessary arrangements. I'm afraid I have been able to do nothing about anybody outside the immediate family, but hope to be able to write all round, either in time for Christmas, or if not by then, for the New Year.

I don't quite know what I shall be doing on Christmas Day, but we are getting the day off and I think we shall make up a party and go into Nottingham for the day – if there is anything doing there. Anyway I shall be thinking of you all and wishing you a very happy Christmas.

With love to all,

Your loving Son.

P.S. I have sent a parcel addressed to you with a few oddments in it for the family – please distribute them as marked. Have heard that I have passed the wings exam with an average of 82½ %, which is only 5% less than the 1st. I came 14th.

★ Betty had offered to knit things for John but was a very slow knitter; the scarf took her forever to finish because it was so long!

The next letter from John, after probably his first Christmas spent away from the family home, shows his disappointment at not perhaps showing the RAF at its best to some 'big noises from Canada'.

RAF Cranwell
Lincs
1.1.41

My dearest Mother,

Many many thanks for the book, the pencil and the writing case. I have started to read the book and find it very interesting, while the pencil and writing case are both in daily use and invaluable. Thank you so much.

As usual my letter will arrive late, but all the same it carries with it all my best loving wishes for a happier and lets hope victorious New Year.

We are not due to leave here until round about Jan 22nd so no leave until then. The weather has brightened up considerably of late and we have been able to get on with the flying; but it has just started to snow, which will completely stop us flying for as long as it remains.

Yesterday a lot of big noises from Canada – Air Vice Marshals, etc – came and made themselves unpopular by looking round and interfering generally. We had to stage various things for them & everybody was feeling furious. They came in to see us when we were supposed to be having a lecture – only half of us were there, and 2d thrillers were lying all over the place much to their surprise and annoyance.

I wonder what sort of Christmas you had ... I didn't do much. They staged a pretty good lunch here – turkey, xmas pudding, stilton, etc. and then we all went into Lincoln to somebody's friend's house. However we never got back until late early morning as the old (very) Trojan,★ which we had borrowed from somebody for the day, broke down and we got perished putting it right again.

Once again many thanks for your presents, and wishing you a very happy new year. Please thank E for her postcard asking what I want knitted. My suggestions are mittens, scarves, socks and long-sleeved pullovers (but that's a rather big job I should think).

We are more or less snowed up today after another heavy fall. Lately we have been having good fun in the air – shooting up the barges and ships on the Humber.

Love to all,

Your loving Son.

★ The Trojan Utility Car was supposed to be cheaper and more economical than wearing out your shoes walking.

John had now qualified as a first pilot, and his assessment has improved to 'above average', so he was on his way to being excellent! Now that he was used to the excitement of real flying, he was getting restless just doing theory, so his independent spirit took him flying over the Welsh mountains.

Log book report shows first
'Above Average', 1941

Certificate of Qualification as First Pilot

My dearest Mother,

Many thanks indeed for sending on those shoes and also for your letter.

As I said in my P.C. this place is a 'dump' – a week's stay has confirmed that first impression. We are absolutely miles from anywhere – about 15 from Crewe and 25 from Manchester. The rather smaller but nearer towns are all about 10 miles away and are terribly dull spots. Living quarters are far from pleasant and there is absolutely nothing to do after duty hours. However the good things are, one, the food which is excellent (at the moment) and two, there's a good crowd of chaps here and when we can find transport to get away from this place we manage to have quite a good time.

The really depressing thing is the course, which we are on. We are here on a 6 weeks advanced navigation course just doing solid navigation all day and every day. It is very dull and monotonous, and is rather revisionary. What is more, when we fly, which is very occasionally, we only go up as navigators and are not supposed to do any piloting. However I had a very good time last time I went up as I managed to get round the pilot and he let me do all the flying. I spent hours 'shooting up' Snowdon and all around the Welsh mountains and thoroughly enjoyed myself.

I am indeed sorry to hear about Marna and her commission. Personally I think it is a damn poor show, but is so typical of any of the services – they just don't know their own minds and get all tied up in their beloved red tape and various documents. It must be most disappointing for her – and I'm so sorry. Surely she can chew their heads off, or do something about it. Do let me know what happens.

After our 6 weeks here (which of course may be longer owing to weather) we are going to an operational training unit – probably in Huntingdon or perhaps near Oxford. That course will take about 2 months I suppose, and from there we shall go on to Hampdens (medium bombers), which will probably mean I shall be stationed somewhere up in Lincoln or Yorkshire.

I got half of last week off, so managed to get a lift into Chester, about 30 miles away, where we all had a very good time. It is a very beautiful town, full of quaint old houses, and crowded out with people and the army.

Hoping you are all well,

Much love to all,

Your loving Son.

You can see from John's next log book page that, his flying trips having tailed off, he went 'joy-riding' using an Anson (built in 1935 as a multi-purpose, twin-engine aircraft used for taking passengers, training and coastal reconnaissance).

YEAR 19 4 1		AIRCRAFT		PILOT, OR 1ST PILOT	1ST NAVIGATOR 2ND PILOT, PUPIL OR PASSENGER	DUTY (INCLUDING RESULTS AND REMAR
MONTH	DATE	Type	No.			
—	—	—	—	—	—	— TOTALS BROUGHT FORWA
FEB.	28	ANSON	L.4.	SGT. SLEIGH	SELF	EX. P1.
MARCH	5	ANSON	Y.2.	F/O LAWSON	SELF	" P2.
MARCH	21	ANSON	K.1	F/O DUNNE	SELF	D.R. EXERCISES
MARCH	31	ANSON	M.2	F/L HUNT	SELF	"
APRIL	6	ANSON	Y.2	SGT BROWN	SELF	"
APRIL	8	ANSON	T.3	SGT. STRANKS	SELF	"
APRIL	9	ANSON	A.1	SGT. SAUNT	SELF	"
APRIL	10	ANSON	F.4	P/O HUMPHRIES	SELF	"
APRIL	15	ANSON	U.2	F/O STEVENS	SELF	"
APRIL	16	ANSON	V.3	SGT. AUCHINVOLE	SELF	SM.EX1.
APRIL	16	ANSON	Q.3.	P/O HUMPHRIES	SELF	D.R. EXERCISE

Note a reduction in John's flying, but when he does fly it is in an Anson

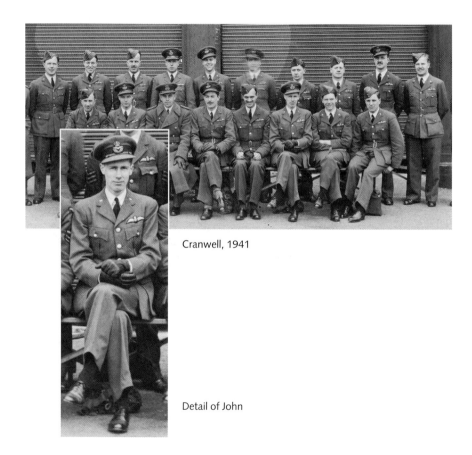

Cranwell, 1941

Detail of John

On 1 March 1941 Nazi extermination camps began full operation, including Auschwitz, where over 12,000 Jews were killed daily. John, along with most of the world, being unaware of these particular Second World War horrors, knew enough to want to get on with the fight against the Nazis, showing his frustration yet again in the following letter:

Cranage
Cheshire
20.3.41

My dearest Mother,

Many thanks for your last letter. I do hope Marna manages to get into the transport section, if there really is no chance of her getting a commission.

This place gets worse and worse. We haven't done any flying for a long time now, with the result that we have spent all day and every day in the class-rooms listening to various lectures, which is incredibly dull. We have finished our syllabus as regards ground subjects and so there is little for us to do except hang around waiting to fly. We have had some quite nice weather of late, but they seem to be scared of flying in anything but absolutely perfect weather.

Our mess held a public ball last week at a large country club near here, and it was great fun. We had a first class band composed of celebrities from various well-known dance bands, who had joined the RAF. It was supposed to finish at 1 o'clock but I don't think anyone left much before 3 am.

I get quite a lot of bridge games now in the mess as there is little else to do. There are some quite good players so it is quite good practise. There are also some pretty bad players, who think themselves very good and will persist in criticizing every move and analyze every hand after a game – a very annoying habit.

Hoping all are well,
Much love,
Your loving Son.

Marna wrote to her mother on 26 March from 'F' Company, Queen Elizabeth Camp, Chilwell, Nottinghamshire. She had been trying to get into the transport section of the ATS, and the following letter shows how unlucky she was but also what tough stuff she – a typical Hopgood – was made of.

My darling Mummy,

… I had a job finding this place, I seemed to walk miles before reaching the right office. I was feeling very tired and dirty and hungry. At about 4 o'clock it was sprung on me that I was to have a driving test then and there. I was given a 30 cwt truck to drive. I thought I got along fine but for a few scrapings of gears, which were jolly difficult to get in. But evidently I failed.

… I had a most amusing journey up here with three sailors, all of whom had fought at Narvik and Dunkirk; they told me some very interesting stories about them; they said Narvik was worse than Dunkirk.★ It seems hard to believe that, but no doubt they knew best. We chewed carrots most of the way!

The lights are just going out so I shan't be able to write any more. 'Scuse this dreadful scrawl but bed isn't the best place for letter-writing.

Will write again as soon as I know anything definite,

Your loving Daughter,

Marna

★ The Battles of Narvik were naval battles in Northern Norway. Narvik was important for its iron ore (transported here by train from Sweden), which both sides needed for weapons.

On 31 March Marna, still in Chilwell, wrote, this time very concerned about her mother's health (Grace had suffered a heart attack) and willing to give up all for her mother:

Please, please mummy do be wise, after all prevention is better than cure … but if you really think E. is enough help and she can manage all right I will be satisfied to stay here. Otherwise I will come at once. I do hope you are already feeling a bit better.

Your loving Daughter, M.

And Marna wrote again from Chilwell on 5 April 1941:

My darling Mummy,

Please don't worry about my future and getting good jobs etc. It is entirely my own fault that I was a waster at school; I was too d–ed lazy to work and no excuses will hide it. I am determined to work my own way up, and I don't want any influence – if I can't it would make no difference having push from other people because I should hate to do a job or hold a position I am not fitted for. The only way to do it is to feel one's own feet and to know what one is capable of. I don't want to run before I can walk if you see what I mean. I like going my own way about things so don't discuss me with anybody; you know how I hate it.

So Grace had clearly been known to pull strings for Marna, who was now keen to forge her own way. And in the end Marna did manage to get into the transport division.

In the following letter from John, who was also very concerned about his mother, we can see that he had now completed his theory and was flying; he must have been a lot happier once again.

Cranage
Cheshire
8.4.1941

My dearest Mother,

Many thanks for your letters. I am sorry to have been so late in writing my last one. Do hope you are really better now and taking things <u>easy</u>. Very glad to hear about Marna and her driving – I wish her all the best and hope that she will pass her various tests and such like as I'm sure it's going to be a far more interesting job than just sitting indoors all day in an office. I hope Betty likes school again and that it's a good school.★ I don't suppose I shall ever be nearer to that town than I am now, as in future I shall probably be in Lincoln or Yorkshire.

We have finished our exams now, and were supposed to have gone on to O.T.U. last weekend, but have now got a fortnight's extension in order to get in some more practical navigation in the air. Yesterday we did a very nice trip, practising some rather more advanced navigation over the sea. We went to Anglesey and then over somewhere to the East of the Isle of Man and back again the same way. I got back OK but had rather a hectic time dodging balloon barrages coming home.★★ Today we were supposed to be doing much the same sort of thing but the weather has stopped it all.

Living conditions are becoming worse and very much more cramped. At last they have rationed butter and we now get no more than civilians, which is a good thing, but we get a lot of eggs, meat and fish still. The mess is overcrowded now with a lot of schoolteachers, who are just a damn nuisance and thoroughly scorned and resented by every other member of the mess as far as I can see. They seem to get promotion too damn easily right above chaps who do far more work and have been in the RAF for years. However that's merely my impression. Anyway they certainly help to make the mess very crowded.

Last Friday we had a marvellous party in the mess. The excuse for it was that the C.O. was leaving and it was supposed to be a farewell 'do'. However nobody seemed to care about that but was far more concerned with the fact that the drinks etc were free and came out of mess profits. The C.O. was quite forgotten in a very short time and we eventually went on to a dance at Mere Country Club and continued to enjoy ourselves.

We have just started to learn something about Astro navigation – a very complex but interesting study. It consists of taking shots (or sights) on the stars or other heavenly bodies and by means of a sextant, and lots of tables, finding out your position on the ground, or above the ground.

It seems pretty definite that I shall now be posted somewhere near Melton Mowbray which is quite near Loughborough, so if I am I may be able to get over to see Oliver before he leaves there.

Much love to all and please do take it easy until you are quite fit,
Your loving Son.

* From 1941–42 Betty was at a finishing school called Onslow Hall near Shrewsbury. In their free time, students tried to earn money for the Red Cross.

** Barrage balloons were used against low-flying aircraft, forcing them to fly higher and thus into the range of anti-aircraft guns. By the middle of 1940 there were 1,400 balloons, a third of them over the London area.

John was now getting itchy feet and very impatient to get on with his training so that he could actually do his bit in the war. He was, in fact, posted to RAF Cottesmore to continue his training. The building of Cottesmore began in 1935 in response to heightened tension in Europe and the re-armament of Germany. The airfield had opened on 11 March 1938.

> *Officers Mess*
> *RAF Cottesmore*
> *Rutland*
> *27.4.1941*

My dearest Mother,

Well I have arrived OK after a very long journey trying to find this place as it is hidden away in the wilderness as usual.

However, having arrived we were very well received and told to hurry up and get ready for a party. We did so and got in for a marvellous dance and party in the mess of a rather posh nature. It is quite a luxurious mess in a large building of a permanent nature, which is a change after small, scattered, wooden huts. The refreshments last night were such as one rarely sees even in peace time, and combined with a very nice dance floor and free drinks, helped the evening to go with a swing.

However as the main mess is full up we are sleeping in Exton Hall an enormous countryseat of the Earl of Gainsborough. The grounds are lovely and so is the building. It seems we are going to be worked pretty hard, and we shouldn't be here for more than 6 weeks.

Do hope you will take things quietly and get better soon. I really did enjoy my leave – the week went all too quickly.

Much love to all,

Your loving Son.

The dates 8–9 May 1941 saw a great increase in RAF air attacks on Germany, with a total of 359 bombers, of which 317 went to Hamburg and Bremen.

On 24 May 1941 John, now at Cottesmore in Rutland, started flying Hampdens; these two-engined medium-sized fighter-bombers, modelled on the Wellington, were first used in 1936 and last used in the Battle of Britain. They were fast and manoeuvrable and were to become John's favourite aircraft, probably partly due to their cockpits resembling those of fighter planes. Despite their gunners having the best view of approaching fighter planes of any bomber, enabling evasive action, the guns on Hampdens were mainly fixed, so could not be aimed effectively at fighter planes. Also, heavy casualties were caused because at this point no British bombers had self-sealing fuel tanks. These imperfections led to the development of the next generation of bombers.

On 26 May John was tested for solo Hampden flying by Flt Lt Nettleton, who, eleven months later, would lead the epic daylight raid against the MAN diesel worksat, Augsberg, and be awarded the VC:

Officers' Mess
Cottesmore
Rutland
2.6.1941

My dearest Mother,

This'll have to be a short letter as I haven't much time in which to write it … Last Saturday we had another big party and dance in the mess, which went off as well as if not better than last time.

We've been having bad weather lately, which threatens to hold us up a bit if it continues for long.

News isn't good these days – however it'll have to get better sooner or later. What do you think of this clothes rationing. It's going to be very hard luck on Marna, as I suppose she doesn't get any coupons at all. Fortunately I think I shall get as many coupons as a civilian since I have to buy all my clothes and uniforms.

Must rush off now,

Much love,

From your loving Son.

On the subject of clothes rationing, Betty says, 'During these years we had to use curtains and bed spreads etc. to make imaginative clothes and barrage balloons cut up came in very useful for underwear. The gardener at Hurstcote kept rabbits, so I used the rabbit skins to make fur mittens.'

From about this time in 1941 censorship became rigorous, particularly overseas mail. Letters would be trashed completely if they even hinted at military locations or plans. In addition, the media were subject to censorship and had to work with the government to counter propaganda from the Nazis, also not printing things likely to offend the Soviet Union or encourage anti-Soviet feeling. There was even talk of Parliament taking over the BBC.

In the following letter, John, having just clocked up the grand total of 160 hours 25 minutes in flying time, wrote that he had about three more weeks of training left before he would be ready to go on active service, i.e. bombing raids:

Cologne raid men of Bomber Command, Guy Gibson is front centre

In the following letter, John wrote that he had about three more weeks of training left before he would be ready to go on active service, i.e. bombing raids. It seems that he had had two letters 'go astray' and thus decided it was 'just as well not to say much'.

Officers' Mess
RAF Cottesmore
Rutland
Monday
16.6.1941

My dearest Mother,

Well, I wonder what sort of holiday you had with Betty in Shropshire and Wales. Do hope you enjoyed it, and also feel all the better for it.

I'm sorry I can't sort of tell you much about what we do here, but as I've already had two letters go astray in the post since I've been in the RAF I think it's just as well not to say much. Of course we do a lot of flying, sometimes for quite a long time. We practise bombing and gunnery etc. and really I enjoy it all very much.

I managed to nip into Leicester one night last week and got Marna's present. If it isn't what she wants do get her to send it back to me and I can change it quite easily for something else.

Last week the Duke of Kent★ came and visited this station. I didn't actually see him as I was up in the air most of the time.

... We have had some marvellous weather just lately – almost too hot and sunny. As a result we have been on duty all day and every day and very busy with very little rest. We have been getting on so fast that providing the weather holds for another 2 or 3 days I shall be finished here, and should be able to get home on a week's leave either at the end of this week or the beginning of next! It'll be grand to get home again and have a rest – I've only had a day and a half off since I've been here! Is there any chance of Marna and or Oliver being on leave sometime next week? I will let you know as soon as I can when exactly I am coming home.

We managed to get off yesterday evening, and first of all went into Uppingham to watch a cricket match there against Cranwell. We met several of our old Cranwellian instructors, which was very pleasant. We then went on to Leicester, and had a very enjoyable time there. Another 2 weeks should see us finished here, so my week's leave will come at the end of this month or beginning of July. As always it depends on weather.

Well, I'll keep all the news 'til later.

Much love to all

Your loving Son.

★ The Duke of Kent, fourth son of George V and Queen Mary, was in the Royal Navy, but at the start of the Second World War he returned to active military service and for a short time served on the Intelligence Division of the Admiralty. In April 1940 he transferred to the Royal Air Force and became Air Commodore at RAF Training Command; he was killed in an air crash in 1942.

John, still flying a Hampden Bomber, in the last of this bout of training, was doing more night practice and learning air firing and bombing.

Meanwhile, Marna wrote from Chilwell on 30 June 1941:

My darling Mummy

I had a letter from John this week about his leave, this morning I went to the officer with a good story to get some leave. The best they can do is to put me on a convoy going near home and then let me have 48 hours. If I am not so lucky I can have three days, come down by train and the time will be deducted from my next leave.

Marna did get leave, and so did John.

At this time, life was comparatively mundane for the rest of the Hopgood family, who were thankful for Marna's letters containing down-to-earth and sometimes frivolous ramblings from the ATS; they welcomed her leaves, when she was pleased to change out of her smart khaki uniform, forget the war and simply relax.

(*4690—117) Wt. 51983—5030 48,500 4/40 T.S. 700   FORM 414 (A)

SUMMARY of FLYING and ASSESSMENTS FOR ~~YEAR COMMENCING 1st~~ PERIOD AT 14 O.T.U. *19.41.

[* for Officer, insert "JUNE ". For Airman Pilot, insert "AUGUST".]

		ANSON		HAMPDEN		TOTAL	GRAND TOTAL
		Day	Night	Day	Night	AT 14 OTU.	All Service Flying
DUAL		1·15	—	1·00	—	~~~~	219.05
PILOT	1st / 2nd	4·80 / 14·00	— / 6·15	14·36 / 21·55	— / 7·20	} 60·40	~~222·15~~
PASSENGER							

ASSESSMENT of ABILITY

(To be assessed as :—Exceptional, Above the Average, Average, or Below the Average)

    (i)   AS A...M.B. † PILOT _____ _Average._

    (ii)   AS PILOT-NAVIGATOR/NAVIGATOR _____ _Above Average._

    (iii)   IN BOMBING _____ _Above Average_

    (iv)   IN AIR GUNNERY _____ _Average_

† Insert :—" F.", " L.B.", " G.R.", " F.B.", etc.

ANY POINTS IN FLYING OR AIRMANSHIP WHICH SHOULD BE WATCHED.

Date...1.7.41.   Signature ___ _R.R.Christie_   W/Cdr

Officer Commanding TRAINING WING, No. 14 O.T.C., COTTESMORE.   COMMANDING,

Log book Assessment Summary, July 1941

Marna wrote on 8 July:

My darling Mummy,

I am just waking up out of a wonderful dream, the dream lasted 2½ days and I really thought I had jumped back two years and it was peace all over again.

… I spent last night in Swindon and was amazed to find it quite a tiny place. There was a bit of a raid but nothing fell, the only noise was the blowing of policemen's whistles and motor horns, I can't think why!

Poor little John; this is his last night of leave, I expect he is feeling rather low, but I guess he is like a giant refreshed after lots of sun and good food.

I can't see to write more – thank you for all the good things in life. I hope we didn't leave you tired. It will be your turn for a holiday next.

Your loving Daughter.

Marna certainly shows appreciation of her mother's hospitality and good food at Hurstcote when on leave, and the description of John as 'a giant refreshed' shows her admiration of him; it is very touching.

In this, John's last training report, he was assessed as 'above average' for 'pilot navigator' and also for 'bombing' ('MB Pilot' probably means Medium Bomber Pilot).

John had finished his training and was now ready to be launched 'full on' into the war. What was he thinking at the time? If you recall, Marna had previously said that 'John would never do anything to hurt anyone or anything' and had related how 'distressed John was when he shot a green woodpecker in mistake for a pigeon'. There are also references in other books and write-ups about the Dambusters that John 'wept openly when he accidentally shot a pigeon whilst doing target practice with some bottles and his Webley revolver'.

However, I dispute Marna's quote that John would not 'hurt anything', and find it very unlikely that John would have 'wept openly' shooting a pigeon. Betty reports that as a teenager in Shere he had enjoyed the chase of Beagling, even if he wasn't too keen on the brutal ripping apart of the innocent hare at the end by the excited dogs. He had also enjoyed, until he happened to mistakenly kill the green woodpecker, shooting with his airgun, when he had often killed pigeons, squirrels and rabbits. The Hopgoods, and especially John, were nature lovers, but they were not sentimental about animals. Perhaps the original statement made by Marna about the woodpecker went round a little like Chinese whispers and resulted in a different story with the same theme. Or perhaps John did weep openly in the pigeon scenario, not for the pigeon but perhaps for himself.

John was still only 19 years old, and under increasing strain in the face of considerable responsibility, danger and loss. The dead pigeon may just have triggered an emotion that he had been keeping under wraps, maybe of carefree days in Shere, maybe of his mother – who knows or will ever know?

Whatever the case, Bomber Command would prove to be John's ultimate challenge.

5

And so to Bomber Command

Why did John join No. 5 Group Bomber Command? Despite being a deep thinker and sensitive by nature, John had no scruples now: Hitler was a maniac who needed to be stopped at all costs. Fighter pilots were a direct way of doing this, coming face-to-face with the enemy (and for John the mechanics of this would have been faintly reminiscent of his shooting pigeons and squirrels at home in Shere). John was now up for the challenge: he considered being a fighter pilot as glamorous and exciting, and the job would have suited his competitive nature.

But John had no choice, and it wasn't to be. At this stage in the war they needed bombers and therefore bomber pilots. Tactics under Winston Churchill had changed from defence to attack. The situation which needed addressing urgently was the constant destruction of our Merchant Navy and convoys by German U-boats, mainly in the Atlantic but also in the Mediterranean, preventing food supplies reaching our ports and preventing military personnel and equipment reaching their destinations. Having failed to invade us, or destroy our air force, the Germans were now trying to starve us into surrender and destroy our mobilised troops.

So what special qualities were required of bomber pilots? Not only did they need skill and guts in the face of all weathers but they needed iron discipline too. They were responsible for their crew and it was vital that they could imbue them with good morale. Stoicism, efficiency, order and pride were important attributes; John, a perfectionist at heart, had all these and had learnt to shoulder responsibility.

Bomber pilots also needed to be sociable, as Guy Gibson wrote:

In a squadron the boys live eat sleep and face death together … the only plan is to go out with the boys, drink with them, lead them into thinking they are the best, that they cannot die … be polite, listen, advise; this keeps high morale and a keen team spirit … Hoppy [John] was a good squadron type.

The qualities required did, in fact, fit very well with John: the competitive comradeship of Bomber Command would be very much like that which he had experienced at Marlborough College, and he loved partying.

Currently there was still theoretically a policy not to attack civilian targets, so bombers were to be used in precision bombing on industrial targets and U-boats; this suited John, who would not have wanted to target innocent civilians. So John, not quite 20 years old and still up for glamour and fun, had to act with a maturity and responsibility unbelievable for someone of his young age; no wonder he was appreciative of his leave, as shown in the following short note:

> *Officers Mess*
> *Lindholme*
> *Nr Doncaster*
> *Yorks*
> *9.7.1941*

My dearest Mother,

Arrived safely after much longer journey than I expected and after a lot of trouble in finding out where this place is. Everything is very different here and everybody is very friendly. It all seems very nice. Today we have been very busy settling in and collecting all our stuff. It's a pity but we shall all have to move very soon to another station near Lincoln, as the squadron is moving.

I did enjoy my leave so much. It was a great relaxation and so nice all the family getting together like that combined with good weather.

This is only just a line – will write a longer letter later,

Much love to all,

Your loving Son.

So John, having had a week's leave, was now in 50 Squadron, part of the No. 5 Group of Bomber Command. The motto of 50 Squadron was *Sic fidem servamus* (Thus we keep faith), and its badge insignia read 'From Defence to Attack'; this is amazingly appropriate as on John's first sortie with 50 Squadron he started his role in the war in earnest, going on his first bombing mission, attacking Bremen in a Hampden Bomber. On this sortie he acted as navigator/bomb aimer to Pilot Flt Officer Abbott, as was the norm for a second pilot; he says his bombs fell 'On Target'. Instead of returning to RAF Lindholme, they were diverted, due to inclement weather, to RAF Docking in Norfolk, which was a satellite airfield for RAF Coastal Command. According to him it was 'great fun', but it seems extraordinary that his first flight with 50 Squadron was a bombing operation.

The reason John was so needed may have been because he was a proficient Hampden pilot; Manchester aircraft, which had been most widely used by 50 Squadron for their recent bombing raids, had been deemed as unfit for

YEAR 1941		AIRCRAFT		PILOT, OR 1ST PILOT	2ND PILOT, PUPIL OR PASSENGER	DUTY (INCLUDING RESULTS AND REMARKS)
MONTH	DATE	Type	No.			
—	—	—	—	—	—	Totals Brought Forward
				50 SQUADRON.		
JULY	12	HAMPDEN	AD 844	F/O ABBOTT	SELF	OPERATIONS — BREMEN
					SGT. GREY	DIVERTED TO DOCKING
					SGT. WELFORD	1 × 1000 2 × 500 ON TARGET.
JULY	13	HAMPDEN	AD 844	F/O ABBOTT	SELF SGT. GREY SGT. WELFORD	DOCKING — BASE
JULY	14	HAMPDEN	A.D. 854	P/O SMITH	SELF + CREW	N.F.T.
JULY	14	HAMPDEN	A.D. 954	SELF	CREW	CONSUMPTION TEST
JULY	15	HAMPDEN	A.D 854	P/O SMITH	SELF + CREW	N.F.T.
JULY	15	HAMPDEN	A.D. 852	SELF	CREW	CONSUMPTION TEST
JULY	15	HAMPDEN	A.D. 854	P/O SMITH	SELF	OPERATIONS — HAMBURG
					SGT. PETRIDES	4 × 500 2 × 250 ON WILHELMSHAVEN
					SGT. WELFORD	HAZY
JULY	16	HAMPDEN	AD. 852	P/O SMITH	SELF	OPERATIONS — COLOGNE
					SGT. PETRIDES	4 × 500 2 × 250 ON TARGET
					SGT. WELFORD	HIT BY FLAK
JULY	19	HAMPDEN	AD. 158	SELF	P/O CANN + 2 CREW	To SWINDERBY — FORMATION
JULY	20	HAMPDEN	AD. 854 231	SELF	P/SGT. GROSE	N.F.T.
JULY	20	HAMPDEN	AD. 854	P/O SMITH	SELF	OPERATIONS — COLOGNE
					SGT. PETRIDES	4 × 500 2 × 250 BOMBS BROUGHT
					SGT. WELFORD	BACK. HAZE
JULY	22	HAMPDEN	AE. 115	P/O SMITH	SELF	N.F.T.
					SGT. WELFORD	
JULY	22	HAMPDEN	AE. 115	SELF	SGT. WELFORD	LOCAL
				GRAND TOTAL [Cols. (1) to (10)] 221 Hrs. 05 Mins.		Totals Carried Forward

NFT stands for Night Flying Training Consumption Test: presumably a fuel usage test on the aircraft

operations due to their lack of power when loaded and their unreliability. On 1 July 1941 all Manchesters were grounded by No. 5 Group and were temporarily replaced by Hampdens. This caused a serious delay to the expansion of the whole command but led to the development of the Lancaster. However, you will see that from January 1942, in 106 Squadron, John would be trained on Manchesters and from March carry out eleven operations flying Manchesters whilst awaiting the production of the Lancaster. But for the moment, John was still flying Hampdens.

JULY 12th TARGET BREMEN, DIVERTED TO DOCKING
ON TARGET. Bombs dropped:1 x 1,000, 2 x 500

Lindholme
Doncaster
Yorks
14th July 1941

My dearest Mother,

… Well, I did my first trip the other night. All went very well and we found the target and hit it. It was great fun and as we were the first there they didn't shoot at us much and we got away from a fighter ok. There were a lot of thunderstorms en route and plenty of lightening, but we got round them ok.

This is a very good squadron – a very nice set of blokes and a very good spirit, also a very nice C.O. This is a very comfortable place, but unfortunately (or fortunately) we are moving out from here at the end of the week to a place called Swinderby near Lincoln, so when you write next that will be the new address. Yesterday we had a sort of farewell party. It was a great success, but I missed some of it, as I didn't get back in time for the beginning of it.

There's a bloke here, actually the chief engineering officer of the squadron which is coming here instead of us – called Dowson – John Dowson. He has heard of the name Hopgood, so I take it he must be a distant cousin of some sort.★ His father comes of a very large family (I think he said 11 children). Do you know much about that side of the family?

By the way, a bundle of washing may arrive at home addressed to me from Cottesmore. Could you send it on immediately if it does arrive, because what with leave and all this moving about, my washing is going all astray and I have very little clean stuff to wear.

Much love to all,

Your Loving Son,

PS One of the boys has just got back after 3 months having escaped from Germany after being shot down – great celebration ahead!★★

★ Later in the war Oliver worked for Hopgood and Dowson Solicitors.
★★ Note John's PS and then refer to dinghy search in his log book of 16 August. Was this 'boy' perhaps J.A. Whitecross?

At this stage, John seems to have been treating his entry into Bomber Command as a great game, with Germany as his competitive opponent; he was enjoying the excitement and challenge.

JULY 15th: OPERATION HAMBURG ON WILHELMSHAVEN,
HAZY. Bombs dropped: 4 x 500, 2 x 250

JULY 16th: OPERATION COLOGNE
ON TARGET. HIT BY FLAK. Bombs dropped: 4 x 500, 2 x 250

When on operations at night, the crew were given caffeine and Benzedrine tablets (nicknamed 'wakey-wakey' pills), and Betty remembers John telling how one of the trips to Cologne or Essen was cancelled due to the weather breaking, resulting in a very sleepless night for the cancelled crew members. However, maybe these tablets were not distributed when on the operations described in his next letter, John writes, 'coming back we nearly all went to sleep'.

Officers Mess
RAF Station
Swinderby
Nr Lincoln
19.7.1941

My dearest Mother,

Many thanks for your last letter which I found waiting for me when I arrived here. My washing has arrived at last after chasing all round England.

I've done two more trips now – in two nights running which was a bit fatiguing. In fact coming back on the second one we nearly all went to sleep. The first one was not such good fun as my very first trip, as we couldn't find the exact target owing to dense haze and cloud. However we cruised around for nearly two hours and eventually found something to hit, which we did. We were fired at a bit but otherwise it was rather dull. The second one was again rather dull though we got fired at quite a lot and got picked up in searchlights several times. Again the target was covered in haze and although we went down to 4,000 ft, we couldn't find it well enough to bomb. We then cruised around everywhere for hours but couldn't find anything much so came back feeling tired and browned off.

We moved here yesterday. The mess isn't so comfortable and we are rather cramped for room. However we reckon we can organize things a bit so that the mess will be better.

Last night we went into Lincoln and I met a lot of blokes in the RAF whom I know.

This squadron has been doing ground work and the C.O. has just got the D.S.O. for it and his own personal efforts. We had a terrific party when it came through.

Much love to all,

Your loving Son.

This is typical of the RAF forced bravado, and as John's Hampden was hit by enemy flak, I think he now understands the full meaning of Bomber Command.

The German city of Cologne was bombed in 262 separate air raids by the Allies during the Second World War, including thirty-one times by the Royal Air Force (RAF). However, the first actual bombing took place on 12 May 1940 and these two attacks that John went on were not the most notable ones.

JULY 20th: OPERATION COLOGNE.
HAZE. Bombs BROUGHT BACK: 4 x 500, 2 x 250

Marna wrote on 21 July from Chilwell:

My darling Mummy,

I hope you have not been worrying why no letter has come from me recently, there is no excuse except working and enjoying myself after work.

The other evening we had a company picnic to discuss things with our C.O. as there is no chance when we are all over the country. The place chosen was a weir on the Trent; as soon as we got there some of the girls dashed in amongst stinging nettles to change for bathing. I didn't risk weir bathing so I watched. Evidently the water was very warm and not deeper than the waist, this was too much for the girls who hadn't brought costumes, again the nettles started quivering, in two minutes the river bank was swarming with little Venus' in vests (in some cases not even that) and pants! There was only one person who didn't seem to enjoy it, that was a fisherman on the opposite bank, I guess he thought his fly didn't stand a chance with so much competition! I did not exhibit myself to hungry trout …

If you have John's address I wish you would jot it down for me, I suppose he has been too busy to drop me a line.

The other day I enjoyed myself towing 3-6 ton lorries, I had never driven them before and to have to tow a breakdown of its own tonnage or more was a good game. When I said it was the first time I had ever towed anything at all and driven those things they thought I was telling a lie, but it was the truth!

I suppose E. will be home this week or is it next; I hope she will help you all right and give you a rest. I just have time to post this before I go to bed.

Keep well,

Your loving Daughter.

PS Di 'opes yer got a yellah thin' in a poice of breown poiper!!!!

Whilst Marna was driving lorries and mocking her colleagues' dialect, John continued being thrown right in at the deep end, although not as first pilot; he completed five bombing operations in his first two weeks in Bomber Command.

JULY 23rd: OPERATION FRANKFURT.
Bombs carried 4 x 500, 2 x 250 Dropped Deckars and Pamphlets on an Aerodrome

Year		Aircraft		Pilot, or	2ND Pilot, Pupil	Duty
MONTH	DATE	Type	No.	1ST Pilot	OR Passenger	(INCLUDING RESULTS AND REMARKS)
—	—	—	—	—	—	— TOTALS BROUGHT FORWARD
JULY	23	HAMPDEN	AD.854	P/O SMITH	SELF	OPERATIONS — FRANKFURT.
					SGT. PETRIDES	4 × 500 2 × 250 DECKARS AND
					SGT. WELFORD	PAMPHLETS. ON AN AERODROME.
JULY	25	HAMPDEN	AD.854	P/O SMITH	SELF	OPERATIONS — HANOVER
					SGT. PETRIDES	4 × 500. 2 × 250 DECKARS AND
					SGT. WELFORD	PAMPHLETS. ON TARGET.

SUMMARY FOR Period ending July 31st 1941
UNIT "A" Flight 50 Squadron
DATE 31.7.41.
SIGNATURE gw.Hopford P/O

1. HAMPDEN.
2. ....
3. ....
4. ....

O.C. "A" Flight 50 Squadron.

This is the beginning of John's operational flying

RAF Station
Foss Way
Swinderby
Lincs
24.7.1941

My dearest Mother,

I have done another two trips [Cologne and Frankfurt] since I last wrote. The first one was not so much fun as the weather wasn't good and we developed engine trouble. Actually the engine trouble looked worse than it was, but as it developed 200 miles inside German territory, we were a bit upset – blue flames and sparks kept flying out and we thought it was going to blow up and catch fire any minute. However it didn't, and we managed to bomb the target and get back safely.

The latest trip was really good fun and was the longest I have done. We couldn't find the exact target owing to bad weather, so came down to about 1500 ft and managed to find an aerodrome and a railway station both of which we bombed very successfully. Actually we nearly blew ourselves out of the air by our own bomb bursts as we were so low. On the way back we walked straight into a hot bed of searchlights and 'flak' and all felt we had 'had it' (as they say). The stuff was bursting only a few feet away and we could hear the bangs and also the stuff clanging against the aircraft. We thought we'd been hit many times, but fortunately we weren't, and got back ok.

I have been into Lincoln several times and met a lot of my friends and had a very good time. I also met Mr Nove who has promised me dinner any time I like. He is still there but is expecting to move to some other place in England (I don't know where) quite soon.

Much love to all,

Your loving Son.

John's mother, Grace, must have been worried witless by the letters she was now receiving, and she must have begun to prepare herself for the possibility, if not likelihood, that her beloved son one day might not return.

JULY 25th: OPERATION HANOVER
Dropped Deckars and Pamphlets, Bombs carried 4 x 500, 2 x 250 ON TARGET

John, it seems, if weather conditions had been right, could have borrowed an aircraft to 'fly south' for a friend's wedding; that would have been quite a perk!

John experienced all sorts of hazards, which he describes in this next letter:

RAF Station
Foss Way
Swinderby
Lincs
30.7.1941

My dearest Mother,

I'm a bit late in writing this letter I'm afraid, as I have just had a 48 hr pass and only got back yesterday.

I managed to get the week-end off and was going to come home – but unfortunately my plans fell through. I was going to a friend's wedding down at East Grinstead on the Saturday and was going to fly down there and then come on home. But the weather on Sat. was lousy and I couldn't fly that day. On top of which I was operating Friday night [Hanover], so I had to cancel everything, as trains these days are so bad I got as far as Leicester and stayed there where I had a very good time and met several RAF friends. It was a pity I couldn't get down South as I wanted very much to get to the wedding and see you all.

The trip on Friday went very well but it was not very exciting. We had quite a tough target and a well-defended route to get to it but nothing much seemed to happen. We saw another fighter, but it didn't see us which was a good thing. We had one rather bad scare when a fire started in the fuselage just as we were coming back over England and all of us nearly asleep. However our A.R.P. [Air Raid Precautions] organization proved to be very effective and we had it out in no time.

We are getting the mess more organized now and it is getting quite comfortable; we are going to have our own poultry farm, so that we can have more eggs. I get plenty of chocolate now, and fruit occasionally.

Please thank E. for her long letter, which I got this morning.

Much love to all,

Your loving Son.

So John had already managed to cheat death, having had a fire in the Hampden's fuselage. Meanwhile Germany had been advancing across Eastern Europe, and other countries, e.g. Finland, Hungary and Slovakia, were joining the war.

YEAR 1941		AIRCRAFT		PILOT, OR 1ST PILOT	2ND PILOT, PUPIL OR PASSENGER	DUTY (INCLUDING RESULTS AND REMARKS)
MONTH	DATE	Type	No.			
—	—	—	—	—	—	TOTALS BROUGHT FORWARD
AUG.	1	HAMPDEN	AD.908	SELF	SGT. WELFORD	N.F.T.
AUG.	2	HAMPDEN	AE.231	SELF	SGT. PEACE	LOCAL.
AUG.	3	HAMPDEN	AE.250	SELF	SGT. WELFORD	N.F.T.
AUG.	4	HAMPDEN	AE.250	SELF	SGT. WELFORD	N.F.T.
AUG	5	HAMPDEN	AE.250	SELF	SGT. WELFORD	N.F.T.
AUG.	5	HAMPDEN	AE.115	P/O SMITH	SELF	OPERATIONS — KARLSRUHE
					SGT. PETRIDES	1 x 1,000 2 x 500. NEAR MANNHEIM
					SGT. WELFORD	ICED UP. NO HEATING.
AUG.	7	HAMPDEN	AD.977	SELF	F/SGT. CASEY	To CONNINGSBY
AUG.	7	HAMPDEN	AD.977	SELF	SGT. LITTLE	FROM CONNINGSBY
AUG.	8	HAMPDEN	AE.115	P/O SMITH	SELF	OPERATIONS — KIEL
					SGT. PETRIDES	1 x 1,000. 2 x 500. ON TARGET
					SGT. LAWSON	
AUG.	12	HAMPDEN	AE.250	SELF	SGT. WELFORD	N.F.T.
AUG.	12	HAMPDEN	AE.115	P/O SMITH	SELF	OPERATIONS — MAGDEBURG
					SGT. PETRIDES	2 x 500 2 x 250 2 SBC.'s ON TARGET
					SGT. WELFORD	LANDED AT DIGBY.
AUG.	13	HAMPDEN	AE.115	P/O SMITH	SELF + CREW	FROM DIGBY
AUG.	15	HAMPDEN	AE.115	SELF	P/O PEACE SGT. LAWSON	N.F.T.
AUG.	16	HAMPDEN	AD.839	W/C WALKER	SELF	DINGHY SEARCH. FOR JIM WHITBROOK
					SGT. ROPE	NO JOY. IN FORMATION.
					SGT. SCEVILLE	
AUG	17	HAMPDEN	AD.977	SELF	P/O PEACE SGT. WARE	N.F.T. TO COTTESMORE + RETURN

GRAND TOTAL [Cols. (1) to (10)] ....27.2... Hrs. ....15... Mins. TOTALS CARRIED FORWARD

Note that John is now flying Hampdens

AUG 5th KARLSRUHE: NEAR MANNHEIM. ICED UP. NO HEATING.
Bombs dropped:1 x 1,000, 2 x 500

The beginning of August saw a frustratingly inactive week for John, due to inclement weather, however on the very day he wrote the following letter, his operations restarted:

RAF Station
Swinderby
Lincs
5.8.1941

My dearest Mother,

Many thanks for your long letter. I'll certainly see if I can fly down that week-end but having just had 48 hrs and also a long stand off from ops lately, I very much doubt if I shall be able to manage it.

Yes I haven't done a thing now since I last wrote in fact for about 10 nights, we have been 'on' several times but the weather has cancelled it every time. So we have all had a good rest and are now looking forward to getting cracking again.

This last week has consequently been rather dull with very little to do. I have been into Lincoln quite a lot where we always have a good time.

In rather a hurry – will write again in a few days time when I hope there will be more to write about.

Much love to all,
Your loving Son.

Meanwhile Marna was making the best of any situation and experiencing life to its full; she wrote from Toton Beeston on 8 August:

My darling Mummy,

Would I like any tomatoes or grapes, I shall say I would, I had not dare suggest it before as I thought transport would be impossible. ★ *Anything else you can bung in please do, I have had hardly any fruit since last leave. Now and again we get a rhubarb pudding and that is all.*

… I can't imagine why John went to Leicester on his 48, I wish he had let me know he had leave then as I'm sure I could have amused him in Nottingham with some of my friends, but I dare say there were other attractions!★★

… I have made rather a disheartening discovery since working in the office and that is one can't get a commission these days without having a stripe first, unless under exceptional circumstances … It looks as if for the present I am stuck, but I hear the C.O. wants to see me on Monday so I will sound her on the subject and see what she thinks and can do. Look here mummy dear, because I am telling you of my troubles it does not mean that I can't solve them for myself, as I can; please don't start telling everyone and writing letters to people of influence – thank you!★★★ *Xxx uuu*

Keep well Mummy,
Your loving Daughter.

* Betty says that when she was in the Lake District she craved fruit, which was impossible to get locally, and because they had apple trees at Hurstcote her dear mum used to package them up and send parcels of them to her. She was always hungry and so protected these with her life. Did Betty share these apples with others? She admits that she probably did not.

** Attractions of the non-feathered type? Certainly not merlins or vultures.

*** It is rather significant Marna tells her mother in no uncertain terms not to interfere or use her influences, which presumably she has done in the past to further the interests of her children.

AUG 8th: OPERATION KIEL
Bombs dropped: 1 x 1,000, 2 x 500 ON TARGET

From 9–13 August 1941 US President Franklin D. Roosevelt and British Prime Minister Winston Churchill met at Placentia Bay, off the coast of Newfoundland, and signed the Atlantic Charter, a document outlining the Allied war aims, one of which was for 'freedom of the seas'. Many of the attacks John mentions in his next letter are against U-boat pens to promote this, which he seems to be enjoying despite icing up.

Swinderby
Lincs
10.8.1941

My dearest Mother,

How are you all? Life here still goes on much the same. The station is gradually getting more comfortable and things are getting organised.

I have now done my 7th [Karlsruhe] and 8th [Kiel] trips. Our working nights have slackened off considerably owing to consistent bad weather, which is a pity as we are missing the best of the moon period. The 7th trip was anything but enjoyable. To start off with our heating system packed up quite early on, and the temperature was between -27° and -30°C, on top of which none of us were dressed for such cold. Several other gadgets packed up due to the cold, and we got iced up 3 times, with ice forming all over the aircraft and ice being flung off the propellers against the fuselage. However we found the target, bombed and got back without meeting much trouble. The 8th trip was much more fun. It was a long trip (not as long as the 7th) but it was worth it when we got there. Perfect visibility with a full moon all round the target helped us a great deal. However the target was very well defended and we met a lot of very heavy flak etc., but nothing hit us, and we had good fun dropping bombs accurately. The place was well 'pranged' as we say, and we left enormous fires behind us.*

My best friend, Jim Cumming, who lives at Bletchworth, is missing. It's a great shame, but I hope to hear soon he is a prisoner of war – one never knows!

I ought to be going on a 'conversion' course soon as I am about due for it. It's a short course, mostly flying which one does before becoming 1st pilot and captain and having one's own aircraft and crew.

Must stop now, Much love to all,
Your loving Son.

★ The target referred to here is Kiel; during the Second World War Kiel was severely bombed because of its shipyard which produced submarines. The bombing destroyed most of the historic city.

AUG 12th: OPERATION MAGDEBURG
Bombs dropped: 2 x 500, 2 x 250, 2 x SBCs ON TARGET, LANDED AT DIGBY.★

★ SBC stood for 'Small Bomb Container'. Each SBC held 236 x 4lb incendiaries.

Swinderby
Lincs
15.8.1941

My dearest Mother,
*   … I did another trip the other night and it was probably the most successful that I have done. We were one of the only 3 who managed to get there and also find the target near Berlin [Magdeburg]. It was a long trip with bad weather all the way and especially for the return over England. But as I said we found everything and although there was plenty of accurate flak we hit the main target plum in the centre and started 2 or 3 fires – one quite juicy one. We all enjoyed it very much.*
*   By the way when you come back from Seaford could you possibly send me off my golf club, and also stuff my grey flannel bags [trousers], green sports shirt and golfing sweater in the bag as well? There is a golf course near here and it is a good opportunity to get some exercise.*
*   Much love to all,*
*   Your loving Son.*

John was enjoying the excitement of his trips, especially the ones where his crew succeeded and others didn't; this is the competitive nature we have seen in him from a young age. Then comes a period of relative inactivity as far as operations are concerned, but notice that on 16 August that John and W/C Gus Walker★ go out in a Hampden searching for the dinghy of F/O J.A. Whitecross and crew, who are presumed lost over the North Sea, shortly after signalling at 1530 the day before that the engines were failing. It seems that F/O Whitecross had only recently returned to the squadron following his successful evasion from France, where he had landed following a mining sortie on 28–29 April 1941. It can be seen from John's log book page below that John continues this search as first pilot. I wonder if F/O Whitecross was the 'boy' referred to, whose safe evasion from enemy hands caused 50 Squadron to have a 'great celebration', in the PS of John's letter of 14 July 1941? If so, it seems that his clever escape was to little avail as he and his crew were now lost. John mentions these searches in the next letter:

Swinderby
Lincs
24.8.41

My dearest Mother,

I'm so sorry all my letters have missed you. The last one I wrote, I posted to Shere as I did not get your letter telling me to address it to you at Seaford until too late. I'm so sorry as you must have been a bit worried. I have been holding this letter up in order to tell you all about the next trip, but owing to bad weather it has been cancelled and we are getting pretty browned off.

So, this last week there has been very little to do. Round about last week-end I went on two dinghy searches – ie searching for dinghies with their crews of bombers which had had to land in the North Sea. Unfortunately we found nothing, but of course, the enemy may very likely have picked them up. The first search took us just off the Dutch coast in broad daylight – however we had a fighter escort. However it is very tiring work, as the sea is a very monotonous and a glaring thing to look at for hours on end.

Today I went over to see Oliver and have only just got back. Fortunately he was in, and there to meet me. I took him up for a little flip around but I don't know how he liked it as I had to push off again as soon as I had dropped him.★ He says he expects to be in Shere round about Sept 3rd when Marna has leave.

I don't see any prospects of leave in the near future, although I am overdue for a week. We are supposed to get one week in every 6, as well as odd 48 hr passes every now and then. So it looks as though I shall not be able to get home for the 29th.★★

I went into Notts last night, but as I only got a lift in at the last moment, I couldn't arrange to meet Marna as she is not on the phone, which is a great pity.

I must finish this now as the post is just going.

Much love to all,

Your loving Son.

★ John takes his half-brother Oliver for 'a little flip around' in an aircraft, perhaps in a Hampden.
★★ John's 20th birthday.

Marna wrote on the same day from Toton, Beeston:

My darling Mummy,

… You know you are in no fit condition to run two homes and so far apart, it will only mean another illness and in these times that must be avoided if possible.

The last two days of this week Ailsa and I have been recruiting in Derby, and by the time I have my leave I shall make a good tout, it wouldn't be surprising if I don't try selling hoovers after the war. Don't get alarmed if I try recruiting you and E!

I don't know what to give John for a birthday present, I have asked him but naturally there has been no reply!

Love to E.

Your loving Daughter.

In the letter below, John, apart from his training, is playing golf, but he has sore tonsils:

Swinderby
Lincs
31.8.1941

My dearest Mother,

Many thanks for so many things. For your letters and present and golf clubs – all of which have arrived safely. I have already had a game of golf – in fact the day they arrived – with my C.O. and two other chaps one of whom is a golf pro. We had a very enjoyable game. The book is grand – I've already started to read it and find it very interesting. Thank you so much.

Life has been pretty dull this week. I have done nothing, since my pilot went sick and there was no-one else to fly with. And for the last 3 days I have been suffering with an ulcer on my right tonsil, which has put me off flying for a few days. I am really perfectly all right except that my throat is very painful – but it is getting better by degrees. I'm glad you liked 'Target for Tonight' – I haven't seen it myself yet but hear that it is something like the real thing. ★

Please tell E that I have got her letter and will write in thanks pretty soon.

Much love to all,

Your loving Son.

★ *Target for Tonight* was a documentary film about the Royal Air Force and was filmed in 1941 whilst they were under fire; it revolves for the most part around one crew in a single Wellington aircraft.

In his next letter, John was in hospital but luckily not for an accident or anything connected with flying.

RAF Hospital
South Rauceby
Nr Sleaford
5.9.1941

My dearest Mother,

Please don't let the address alarm you. You remember I mentioned something about a sore throat in my last letter? Well it's that what's put me in here.

They think it's a 'vinsence' or something like that. Anyway it got no better and got so painful that I couldn't swallow that I had to complain about it, and after a few days they sent me here for treatment as they couldn't do it so easily on the station. I was furious about it and tried to refuse to go as I felt absolutely ok (except for the throat), but it was no good. So I was pushed off here – its near Cranwell – and immediately shoved into bed where I've been kept for 2 days now, without having any treatment. All the time I am perfectly fit and have no temperature. Naturally I am almost choking with fury and have every intention of walking out if they don't get on with the treatment very soon.★ However I shan't be here more than another week at the outside.

If I go on writing I shall only go on moaning about being in bed so unnecessarily, so I shall stop now.

Much love,

Your loving Son.

★ John was certainly not looking for excuses to shirk bombing activities; he was a driven man! And in the next letter he was very annoyed that his mother had been concerned enough to ring the hospital. (Rauceby Hospital, formally known as No. 4 RAF Hospital, had been a lunatic asylum since 1902, but in 1940 it was taken over by the RAF, mainly as a crash and burns unit for aircrew injured on operations.)

RAF Hospital
Sleaford
Lincs
9.9.1941

My dearest Mother,

Have just got your letter. How silly of you to ring up – I said I was perfectly fit and still am and there is nothing wrong with me. My throat is very much better and is clearing up quickly – it's a Vincents Angina (last word spelt phonetically) and is supposed to be slightly infectious.★ However it really is much better and the doctor says he is going to send me off on leave for a few days in 2 or 3 days time, so expect to see me probably at the end of the week.

They kept me in bed for 3 days all by myself but I got so fidgety and sulky that they at last let me get up and go out – so I damn nearly cleared right out but thought better of it.

Anyway I am still kept apart from all the others, as I have to have my own crockery to eat with because of infection – but it's not a breathing infection. But the doctor has taken another swab and says providing there are no more infectious germs left, I can go on leave. I actually asked to go straight back to my squadron, but he won't let me – you see I haven't done any 'operations' since the middle of last month, and I feel I have had quite a long enough rest and don't really deserve leave – however he says I must have leave as this throat trouble would only start again if I went straight back to my job.

So I am now looking forward to seeing you at the end of the week – I will wire you when I am coming. It's a pity, but I suppose I shall have missed Marna? Anyway I haven't seen Betty for months and months and I am longing to see how she looks with her hair off.

This is a terrible place and I find it intensely dull – I hope I never have to go near a hospital again – I should be only too glad to bomb it! It used to be a mad house before the RAF took it over!

Well, well I will wire you when I am coming home.

Much love to all,

Yr loving Son.

★Vincents Angina is also commonly known as 'trench mouth', an infection often occuring in patients who are heavy smokers and undernourished.

Swinderby
Lincs
27.9.1941

My dearest Mother,

What a grand leave that was – I'm sure you must be very tired after all that cooking – anyway I feel very much better for it all (and that's a compliment!).

I got back here on time but found nothing doing after all. So on Monday I went to the medical board at Rauceby and after much blowing up of mercury etc. I was passed fit again.★ Since then I have done nothing.

My pilot has just gone on a week's leave, much to my dismay and the possibilities of going on this captain's course are not so good. Things have got held up and it looks as though I shall have to wait some time – perhaps several weeks – before going on it. It's a nuisance as I have got rather fed up with all this hanging about. However I am getting a good deal of day flying in which is always useful.

I don't think there is anything to say except repeat how much better I feel for those 10 days.

Much love to all,

Your loving Son.

★ 'Blowing up of mercury' was a fitness test for lung capacity.

Officers Mess
RAF Station
Swinderby
Lincs
4.10.1941

My dearest Mother,

… Well I am still hanging about and naturally getting very impatient and annoyed about it all. Of course the weather lately has been all against operating and I am getting pretty 'browned off'. ★ *They are expecting any moment now to send me off on this conversion course (to be a captain) but things have all got held up and one way and another it looks as if I shall go on hanging about for quite a long time.*

However I have played quite a few games of squash and golf and am just going off to golf now.

There have been quite a few parties round here lately and we went into Notts one night, but no sign of Marna.

I am sorry there is so little news,

Much love to all,

Your loving Son.

★ The weather during the autumn of 1941 and the following winter was the worst flying weather recorded for fifteen years.

50 Squadron, August 1941. John is seated, sixth from the left

John's impatience to get back to operations was clearly building up, but he did see action again, at last.

OCT 12th: OPERATION HULS RUBBER FACTORY
Bombs dropped: 2 x 250, 4 SBCs ON TARGET

Swinderby
Lincs
13.10.1941

My dearest Mother,

Well at last I have got cracking again and did my 10th trip [Hüls was near Krefeld N. Germany] – hence I am not feeling so browned off as I was. It was a grand trip – successful in every way, although it was a very difficult target to find and well-defended. We all went in very low and had great fun in spite of opposition. I went with my C.O. who's a grand little man.★

I got your letter OK – many thanks. This 'blowing up mercury' is a dreaded thing. One has to blow up a column of mercury in a glass tube and keep it at a certain pressure for over a minute – I believe its to test ones lungs and blood pressure reactions or something.

(Continued next morning) Your latest letter with E's enclosed has just arrived. I am so sorry to hear that U. Mocar is still ill – I will write to him. I liked E's letter very much – she certainly seems to get on well at school. No I have not heard Marna's news which

you suggested I had – what is it? You sound as if you must be tiring yourself with all this cooking – do hope you get away and have a rest.

We had a very instructive practise the other day with a dinghy.✶✶ We got one out on a little pond and four of us got in it (myself included), while everybody looked on. Things went badly from the start. We got out in the middle of the pond and tried to find everything in it rations etc. – but all the time there was a horrid hissing noise – but we couldn't find the leak and anyway we were busy trying to find the rum! However suddenly there was an awful long hiss and the damn thing started to deflate very quickly – immediate panic by everybody and water coming in fast! We all got soaked – I fell half in the water and managed to get the thing near the side where we scrambled out much to everybody's amusement. One chap however stayed in it to the last until he had found the rum! It was all very instructive and now we know what we did wrong we shall be able to manage things better if ever the occasion arose.

Am just going off to golf, I hope, so must stop now.

Much love to all,

Your loving Son.

YEAR 1941		AIRCRAFT		PILOT, OR	2ND PILOT, PUPIL	DUTY
MONTH	DATE	Type	No.	1ST PILOT	OR PASSENGER	(INCLUDING RESULTS AND REMARKS)
--	-	—	-	—	—	— Totals Brought Forward
OCT.	10	HAMPDEN	A.E. 231	W/c WALKER	SELF	A/c TEST
OCT.	11	HAMPDEN	A.E. 231	W/c WALKER	SELF.	N.F.T.
OCT.	12	HAMPDEN	A.E. 231	W/c WALKER	SELF	OPERATIONS — HULS RUBBER
					F/LT UNDERY	FACTORY. 4 SBC's 2×250
					F/SGT. HOBSON	ON TARGET. DIVERTED N LUFFENHAM
OCT.	13	HAMPDEN	A.E. 231	W/c WALKER	SELF + CREW	N. LUFFENHAM To BASE
OCT.	16	HAMPDEN	A.E. 380	SELF	4 CREW	To LITTLE RISSINGTON
OCT.	16	HAMPDEN	A.E. 380	SELF	1 CREW	FROM LITTLE RISSINGTON
OCT.	20	HAMPDEN	P. 1152	SELF	—	FROM WADDINGTON
OCT.	20	HAMPDEN	A.E. 427	P/O SMITH	SELF + CREW	To WADDINGTON
OCT.	21	HAMPDEN	A.E. 427	SELF	P/O FORD P/O STONEY	To UPPER HEYFORD
OCT.	21	HAMPDEN	A.E. 427	SELF	P/O STONEY	To BASE
OCT.	24	HAMPDEN	P. 1202	SELF	SGT. BOWNTON	TEST
OCT.	26	HAMPDEN	A.E. 747	P/O SMITH	SELF. SGT. PETRIDES	To FINNINGLEY

SUMMARY FOR Period Ending Oct. 26⁵ 1941
UNIT "A" Flight 50 Squadron
DATE Oct. 26⁵ 1941.
SIGNATURE W. Hopgood S/o

AIRCRAFT TYPES
1. HAMPDEN
2. ....
3. ....
4. ....

October saw the last month of John consistently flying Hampdens

* Wing Commander Gus Walker.
** A practice to make sure they survived if their planes crashed in the sea and they transferred to their onboard dinghies.

John had now found out that he was leaving his favourite little Hampden aircraft to be trained for the big bombers; in his letter he says, 'What Ho!', apparently glibly, but a note of doubt creeps in when he writes, 'I don't really know whether I like the idea or not.'

He must have been very aware of the tasks likely to be ahead of him with such a large aircraft, carrying massive bombs and therefore with huge killing potential. And killing was not, as we have already explored, in John's nature. But he had no choice: this was war and he was an RAF pilot.

John's original letter, below, is an important one, which it describes a turning point in John's life – and which also indicates that his throat is playing up again:

Lincs
19.10.1941

My dearest Mother,

… I at last have news of my course and I am going to Finningley, Nr Doncaster some time this week. It's not quite what I thought as it's a new course and I shall not come back on to Hampdens unless I can wangle it. I am going to learn to fly Manchesters – our biggest 2 engined bombers – and then after that I shall go on to 4 engined bombers – what ho! I don't really know whether I like the idea or not as I have a great affection for our little Hampdens and should very much like to finish my ops. on them. On the other hand 4 engine bombers seem to be the thing for the future. Anyway it remains to be seen how these things handle.★

Bad news for the squadron has just come through, our Wing Commander has been posted.★★ It'll be difficult indeed to find another man like him – he has done wonders for the squadron and no man could have been better liked.

My throat is giving trouble again, but I hope with plenty of Milton gargling it will go down again. Anyway it's certainly not going to interfere with my posting this time.

I will write to you when I get to this new place.

Much love to all,

Yr loving Son.

★ The Hopgood motto is 'Good Hope gives Strength'. In full it is *Spes bona dat vires, animum quoquc spes bona firmat. Vivere spe vidi qui moritorus erat,* or 'Good hope gives strength, good hope also confirms resolution; him who was on the point of death, I have seen revive by hope'. What could be more appropriate for John, a Hopgood, faced with a situation where he has no choice and must proceed with fortitude no matter what?
★★ Wing Commander Gus Walker was the popular one that John refers to. In 1941 Walker commanded 50 Squadron at Swinderby, and it was while flying Hampdens with the squadron

that he was awarded firstly the Distinguished Service Order and then the Distinguished Flying Cross (DFC). (See also earlier reference re dinghy search August 1941 and later references related to John's letters in October 1942.)

Finningley became a Military Airport in 1915. In the Second World War it was used for the final training of Bomber Command crews. In 2005 it became Doncaster & Sheffield's international airport and is called 'Robin Hood Airport'.

Meanwhile John was piloting Ansons and Oxfords, awaiting his training on the big bombers.

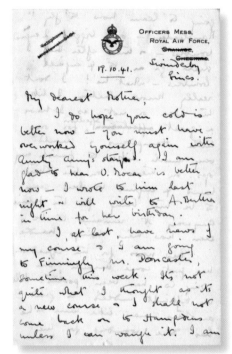

Letter from John,
October 1941

Finningley
Doncaster
Yorks
28.10.41

My dearest Mother,

I am so sorry this letter is so late, but I have been very busy moving and flying just lately. I hope you got my telegram last week. Will you please tell me of something you would really like as a present.

Well, I moved here on Sunday – it was very hard to break away from the squadron, and the other bloke who came with me was of the same opinion so we came 3 days late. At the moment we are acting as staff pilots until our own course here starts. We just fly around while pupils navigate by day and by night and also give them instruction. It is a change but very dull. However in a week or so's time we shall get on a course and learn to fly Manchesters. ★ We shall be here some time and I hope to get leave soon and then I can tell you all about it. The prospects are rather gloomy as it looks as though it will be a long time before we get on to ops. again and also it looks as though we may have to go to another squadron, which will be terrible after getting settled down in our own squadron. However we are moaning in a big way and hope to get things changed a bit. We have to get up terribly early here – ½ past 6 – in order to fly these pupils around which is a great change after rolling out of bed somewhere in the region of 9 o'clock!

We went into Doncaster last night – it is quite a pleasant sort of place but the dialect is very monotonous.

Well please let me know what you would like for your birthday and once again very many happy returns of the day.

With much love to all,

Your loving Son.

★ Avro Manchesters picked up a bad reputation due to their Rolls-Royce Vulture engines being unreliable. The Lancaster Bomber, which John was to fly in the dam raid, was an adaptation of the Manchester; its wingspan was increased and the two Vulture engines were replaced with four Rolls-Royce Merlin engines.

In the following letter, written from Finningley, we can see that John was finding 'ordinary flying rather tame now' but was enjoying 'blind' flying:

Finningley
Doncaster
4.11.41

My dearest Mother,

No letter from you has arrived for nearly a fortnight now – I do hope everything is ok and that you are well …

Life here is not nearly as exciting as at Swinderby – ordinary flying seems rather tame now. We have been working pretty hard and I have done quite a lot of flying. At the moment I am doing a week's course on Blind Approach – landing an aircraft without being able to see the ground. It is very interesting and very good practise in flying on ones instruments and not just visually. There seems little chance of getting back on to ops. until Christmas – the programme has got rather held up as usual owing to weather mainly. I still hope to be able to get back to my old squadron eventually, but it may be some time.

There is still a chance that I may be able to get a few days leave soon probably next week, but it is only a 50:50 chance.

How is Uncle Mocar now? ★ *I do hope he is really better.*

Much love to all,

Your loving Son.

★ Uncle Mocar refers to Grace's brother Harold, who had fought in the First World War. He was nicknamed Mocar as he had been influential in the early British motorcar industry.

Marna, who was not an academic, was clearly finding all the college work and assessment for her commission very stressful, as she wrote on 6 November to her mother:

My darling Mummy,

It was marvellous being home once again, although not such a long time, I could well do with a week or two. I feel very small here and like a grain of sand among a cart of it; there are over 200 cadets, and it is just like going back to school or rather college.

Meanwhile, John was now flying Oxfords again, as he had at RAF Cranwell for four months a year before; no wonder he was getting impatient to move on to the big bombers.

Finningley
Doncaster
8.11.41

My dearest Mother,

At last your letter has arrived. I was beginning to get a bit anxious – thank you very much. The 4 letters you posted on have not yet arrived here but I expect there has been some delay in posting them on from Swinderby and I expect to get them on Monday.

I have just finished a week's course on blind landings, and immediately applied for leave as they don't seem to want any of us very much yet. But no! As soon as I mentioned leave they stalled and immediately organised something for us to do. This time we have got to attend lectures for a week – you can imagine what we feel about that. So at the end of next week I shall again see about getting some leave – I am well overdue for it now. This place is very depressing after Swinderby and of course we have to work considerably harder and our hours are much longer.

Another chap (who came from Swinderby with me) and I, had great fun one night last week. The weather began to get very thick in the afternoon one day, so we immediately volunteered to fly, and having got permission, we promptly went over to Swinderby, waited until the weather really clamped down, then landed and rang up here and told them we couldn't possibly come back until the following day. We had a grand party that night – my pilot, Smithy, had just been made a flight lieutenant and so we had a great celebration, and it was a shame to have to drag ourselves back here the following morning and face all the music here. We plan to do the same sort of thing whenever possible in the future, as it is well worth it.

I do hope Marna has some luck with her commission now – she deserves it if anyone does and I do hope she's not disappointed. I haven't heard from her or been given any news of her since I was last home and was beginning to wonder how she was getting on. I am planning to play golf tomorrow, fortunately there is a course just next door, and they say it is a very good one.

Much love to all,
Your loving Son.

On 13 November 1941 aircraft carrier HMS *Ark Royal* was sunk by U-boats, which were wreaking havoc to the British Fleet in the Eastern Mediterranean. However, in John's letter below the incident is not mentioned:

Finningley
Doncaster
Yorks
16.11.41

My dearest Mother,

I am so sorry to hear that A. Bertha has died, yet I suppose really that it would have been terrible if she had gone on living and suffering, more or less bed-ridden.★ All my sympathies are with Uncle Edwin. Is there any need for me to write to him? I expect he has quite enough letters to deal with already. I am sorry I cannot get to the funeral – it is quite out of the question just now.

The question of leave is rather washed up just now. The authorities that be are just beginning to decide what they want to do with us, and in order to get on I must get in a lot more flying – so I am now busy flying whenever the weather allows. There is every chance of going back on 'ops' as a captain/1st pilot on these new Manchesters – it will be a very good thing if I can make it, as so far, only chaps with much more experience than me have been allowed to go as captains. And it will also help me to get back to my old squadron on 4 engine machines, which is what I am aiming at. So I feel that leave must be sacrificed.

Once again all my sympathies to U Edwin,

Much love to all,

Yr loving Son.

★ Aunt Bertha was Grace's sister.

In his next correspondence, we can see that John's low boredom threshold is being taxed again, and life for him at this point was 'dull':

Finningley
25.11.41

My dearest Mother,

Many thanks for your last letter. There is no more news of leave for me yet. At the moment they are very stingy with it but I think I will wait and try and get some round about Christmas when Marna gets hers, and I believe Oliver is going to get some round about then as well. The only trouble is that everybody wants leave for Christmas and of course not everyone can get it.

Life goes on here just the same: lots of flying but nothing really interesting. I have been trying my hardest to get back to my squadron but haven't met with any success yet. We went over to Swinderby for a night last week, this time with permission, and had a grand time with everybody there. It's good to know a place like that where one can always go and have a good time.

There is so little news these days as every day is just the same, which makes things very dull.

Much love to all

Yr Loving Son.

And John's time at Finningley continued to be dull. He couldn't go home for Christmas, and, according to his logs, he spent time taking photos on trips in an Anson, and once in an Oxford, presumably for reconnaissance. The log also records a trip in a Tiger Moth when he did some aerobatics, perhaps to break the monotony. However, things were about to change.

On 21 December John wrote home to wish his family a happy Christmas.

On 7 December 1941 Japan attacked the United States' naval base at Pearl Harbor. Britain declared war on Japan and the United States entered the war on the side of the Allies.

Finningley

21.12.41

My dearest Mother, Marna and Elizabeth,

Here's wishing you a very happy Christmas and many more of them to come. I only wish I could get home for the 25th but it is now definitely off the cards, as all leave has been granted and I am not included since I have only just had some. It's a shame as there is nothing important to do here. However there it is, and I send all my best wishes and love.

I went into Doncaster the other day to try and do some shopping, but came to the conclusion after about 2 hours that it is anything but a shopping centre. So I think the best thing is to wait until I can get into Leeds or Nottingham or even London and see if I can get the presents you suggest. I am so sorry they will be late.

I wrote off to V. Heads immediately and gave him my measurements and fixed up about the coupons.★ It's going to be a lovely present Mummy, thank you so very much.

I ought to have a good time here at Christmas as a big party and dinner are planned but all the same I'd rather be at home. I am hoping to get over to Swinderby and spend the day with all the boys there.

Well done Marna, congratulations on the commission.

I have left all my Christmas letters to the last minute and so am in a rush of course, and must stop now.

Much love and best wishes to all,

John.

PS I am giving this to a friend to post in town so as it may arrive in time – I hope he remembers.

Marna ATS,
January
1942

*Vincent Head Outfitter 1929–42 was a clothes shop in Marlborough, and it seems John's measurements and coupons were to be for a sweater, his Christmas present from his mother.

John's log book shows that at this time he was mainly flying Ansons for his daily or twice daily flight exercises. Now and again, to break the boredom, he took a Tiger Moth and did some aerobatics or went for a personal local visit.

31.12.41

My dearest Mother,

In all the Christmas activities I'm afraid this letter got delayed. I am sorry as I wanted this one to arrive in time for New Year's Day. However here are all my best wishes and love for 1942, and may it be a more victorious year as far as the war goes.

I haven't been able to get my photo taken yet, but will have it done as soon as possible.

The sweater arrived from Marlborough just before Christmas — it is grand and just what I wanted — thank you very much for it. I wore it the other day with great satisfaction.

Christmas Day here was great fun and everything went off very well. In the morning we had to go and serve the airmen's lunch — an old custom. It was good fun. We then had our own dinner and party later on in the evening. It all went very well and the meal was very good. However I wish I had been at home for it.

Since Christmas there has been little to do as the weather has been contrary.

I can't write any more now as I have a lot of letters to write. Once again many, many, thanks for the sweater, and very best wishes and love for 1942.

Your loving Son.

John, now training on Manchesters, was desperate to return to real action, but he was nostalgic about his Hampdens and would have liked to have been involved in strategic operations, such as the Norwegian one mentioned in his letter below. Surely the thought of heavy bombing with huge Manchesters should have been filling him with trepidation, as it would anyone, but John seems to have relished the challenge.

Finningley
8.1.42

My dearest Mother,

Oh dear I do seem to be getting behind hand with all my letters, and yours has got very delayed. Many thanks for your last letter, also Betty's very long letter which I hope to answer soon.

Life goes on just the same here. I am expecting to move to another aerodrome — a satellite of this — in a few days time and get cracking on these Manchesters, in which case I hope to get back on to 'ops' in about a months time — Hooray!

I saw a very interesting newsreel of this Norway raid — the one before the very latest. ★ The Hampdens all came from my old squadron — picked because it is one of the best.

Today I got hold of a Hampden again — the first time I have flown one for several months, and thoroughly enjoyed myself and convinced myself that I want to get back onto them again.

I still haven't been able to get my photo taken — actually I was confined to camp for a few days for borrowing the C.O.s car! — and so wasn't able to go outside the camp. However now I am free again I will see what I can do about it.

Much love to all,
Your very loving Son.

⋆ John clearly thinks he has missed some excitement. 'This Norway raid' refers to Operation
Archery, on 27 December 1941, the raid on Vaagso and Maaloy which aimed to quash the
German troops in Norway and so hamper the advance on the Eastern Front, towards Russia.
Whilst British troops disembarked from destroyers and submarines, low flying Hampdens of
RAF Bomber Command dropped smoke bombs to obscure the path of the advancing troops
as they landed on the beaches. At the same time air cover was provided by Beaufighters and
Blenheims to ward off the German Luftwaffe. This broke new ground with the provision of
air cover, using RAF Hampdens, as an integral part of a raid.

Bircotes,⋆
Doncaster
Yorks
15.1.42

My dearest Mother,

*Many thanks for your last letter. It must have been very annoying for other people in
the cinema! Sorry to hear about Marna getting chickenpox – I have written to her.*

*I don't seem to be able to get into any town before closing time (shop's closing time!)
with order to get my photo taken – so I may have to wait until I can get leave. I expect
leave in about 3 weeks time.*

*As you can see from the address, I have moved aerodromes again, and am now getting
on with these Manchesters. This is quite the worst place I have ever been to – it is brand
new and therefore lacks any form of comforts – no baths, heating, carpets (just concrete),
electricity, etc – and I have to do a 5 minutes walk to get even a wash! However I
shouldn't be here more than about 3 weeks, I hope. But it is very cold at the moment.*

*I ought to get pretty fit here owing to the absence of transport and cars. I reckon I walk
about 5 miles per day – which is quite unusual for me …*

Much love to all,
Your loving Son.

⋆ RAF Bircotes opened in late 1941 and was used by OTUs (Operational Training Units)
Nos 25 (John's) and 82, from nearby Finningley, for their Ansons, Vickers, Wellingtons and
Manchesters. It was situated next to RAF Bomber Command HQ (at Bawtry); it consisted of
a grass strip, connecting perimeter tracks and blister hangars. The airfield is currently farmland
after being decommissioned on 13 July 1948 with little of the perimeter track left.

John had very much taken to heart the Hopgood motto 'Good Hope gives Strength' and was even enjoying the daunting next step as he moves onto the heavy Manchester bombers.

Bircotes
Doncaster
Yorks
28.1.42

My dearest Mother,

Still here and very cold, but it looks as though I should finish off my course here in about a week's time and then a few days leave.

Many thanks for your letter. Glad Marna got over her chicken pox so quickly – I expect she is glad to get back to her job again.

Things progress here – I have done quite a bit of flying on these machines and they are quite nice. But, I think, I am now definitely going on to even bigger stuff very shortly and I am looking forward to this very much.

It has been terribly cold just lately, as it has been everywhere, and we shall be glad when it gets a bit warmer. We were more or less isolated for a day, and everything got iced up, which made this place most unpleasant.

Still last night we made the best of it and held a sort of opening night party, which went off very well.

Am looking forward very much to seeing you again and getting home. I will drop you a telegram when I know which day.

Much love to all,

Your loving Son..

As the cold weather continues, John worries about his mother's health:

RAF
Bircotes
Doncaster
Yorks
6.2.42

My dearest Mother,

Just received two of your letters and also one from E. – yes, they must have been held up by the snow, etc – I do hope you have got my last letter by now.

Poor you getting ill like that by yourself. I hope you will get a bit of sunshine soon and get better quickly. I was getting a bit worried as I had no letter from anybody for some time and I suppose the same thing has happened vice versa – very annoying.

The weather seems to have been bad everywhere just lately. It has been bitterly cold here every day without exception – so I suppose we are getting quite acclimatised, as it doesn't seem so bad now. I have only seen the green grass 3 times in 4 weeks now! However it is all a great nuisance – all this snow – as it is holding me up a good deal. I expect it will be another week now before I finish here and before leave. My prospects now look much better and I expect to be a captain on a big bomber fairly soon.

Great excitement now as we are getting electric light laid on soon.★ At the moment we only have two oil lamps for the whole of the ante-room – and they are invariably smoking away happily shrouding everything in a nice thick layer of soot.

Yes I read about the Hampden that experienced a bit of cold without much heating – but they had it 30° colder than we did. I am enclosing a picture from the DT (Daily Telegraph) of one of our machines, which I have flown several times, though not on ops.

Am looking forward so much to my leave,

With much love to all,

Your loving Son.

★ Squadron conditions were usually very primitive and spartan, often in prefabricated buildings with no comfort, privacy or basic services, not unlike Marlborough College!

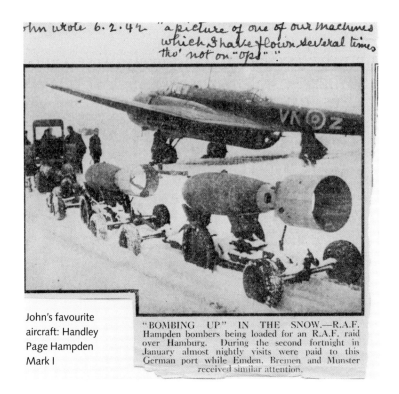

John's favourite aircraft: Handley Page Hampden Mark I

"BOMBING UP" IN THE SNOW.—R.A.F. Hampden bombers being loaded for an R.A.F. raid over Hamburg. During the second fortnight in January almost nightly visits were paid to this German port while Emden, Bremen and Munster received similar attention.

On 12 February 1942 the German warships *Scharnhorst*, *Gneisenau* and *Prinz Eugen* sailed up the Channel, under cover of dense clouds, and RAF Bomber Command were powerless to stop them. This caused the increase in minelaying, of which No. 5 Group had the monopoly.

Marna, who was now running a platoon, was feeling her way nervously in the formal situations and having ideas for suitable activities to amuse 'the girls' in their leisure time. She was also struggling to find basic necessities and wrote, on 14 February, from Chesterfield:

My darling Mummy,

Thank you very much indeed for the eggs; they all arrived intact much to my surprise. I had one for my breakfast this morning, it was such a change from the shop soiled one I had last week! I will send the box back 'returned empty' on Monday, I am too late now to go to the post office.

I have come to the conclusion that the Midlands are very poorly stocked as compared with Guildford and district. I can hardly get a thing I want, so if you see any of the following would you mind buying some for me: light tan boot polish, soapless shampoos, face flannel. I am in no hurry, but if you did happen to see some of each going begging, remember me.

I held a Platoon meeting on Wednesday, I quaked in my shoes and my knees bumped together all the day before; the Company Commander opened the meeting and introduced me but she said most of the things I had thought of to say, which caused my knees to knock more furiously as I wondered what I should gabble about. When the time came, I gulped, opened my mouth and a few incoherent words came out. I then asked them if they had any complaints or suggestions. They looked at each other, sniggered, looked at me as if I was something out of the ark and sniggered again. I was quite unprepared for this muteness, I expected to be showered with knotty problems. I then suggested we should do something as a platoon, the question was what? Well after several ideas had been extracted from my dumb crowd I found them quite voluble on the subject of a 'whist drive'.

Last night I went to a social evening of the units (men); I played badminton with a large audience. I think the chief attraction was my trousers and bright blue shirt as everyone else was dressed in khaki! I started the evening with the intention of doing PT but only the sgt instructor turned up, we waited some time and still no one else came; so he escorted me to this social to play badminton. We had a grand time with all the lads, there being no male officer present.

I can hardly believe that I have been here nearly 3 weeks, the pea soup fog is gradually lifting and my feet are coming to earth – I can't say I am very thrilled with the job, but I may like it better as time goes on, if not I shall ask to be reposted.

*At last it is time to lock the cupboards and stroll home to mend some stockings which
are full of holes, caused by my 5 miles a day round.*

I hope you are all right now; is John home yet? If he is give him my love.

Your ever loving Daughter.

In reaction to this particular letter from Marna, Betty says:

Marna was 3½ years older than myself so I wasn't really in her world. I remember
she always had a tidy bedroom. She was a terribly shy girl; I would never have
imagined her playing a leadership role.

Everything was in short supply; we used rags as flannels, and anything we
could get just making do the whole time. You couldn't just go to the shops
to get whatever, but then it was nearly the same before the war; everything
was economy!

On 16 and 17 February 1942 John received his assessments for flying Manchesters,
which showed him to be 'above average'. This was to be his passport to flying

(*6391—117) Wt. 39210—2791 33,000 1/41 T.S. **700**   FORM 414 (A)

SUMMARY of FLYING and ASSESSMENTS FOR ~~YEAR COMMENCING 1st~~ Period at 25 O.T.U. 26/10/41 & 16/2/1942

[* For Officer, insert "JUNE" ; For Airman Pilot, insert "AUGUST."]

	S.E. AIRCRAFT		M.E. AIRCRAFT		TOTAL for year	GRAND TOTAL All Service Flying
	Day	Night	Day	Night		
DUAL			4.20	2.05	6.25	52.10
PILOT	18. 29	1.10	51.00 16.45	19.20 3.35	77 .30 20.20	195.10 183.35	436.50
PASSENGER	—	—	—	—		7.55
					103.15	

ASSESSMENT of ABILITY

(To be assessed as :—Exceptional, Above the Average, Average, or Below the Average)

(i) AS A M.B. † PILOT *Above the Average.*

(ii) AS PILOT–NAVIGATOR/NAVIGATOR

(iii) IN BOMBING

(iv) IN AIR GUNNERY

† Insert :—"F.", "L.B.", "G.R." "F.B.", etc.

ANY POINTS IN FLYING OR AIRMANSHIP WHICH SHOULD BE WATCHED.

Signature .... w/cdr

Date 17. 2. 42

Officer Commanding .... CHIEF INSTRUCTOR.

heavy bombers in operations as first pilot. He was immediately transferred to 'B' Flight 106 Squadron in Coningsby, Lincolnshire.

All might have been frugality of the Home Front but not now for our airforce. At the end of February 1942, Harris (later to be known as 'Bomber Harris' or even 'Butcher Harris') took over as Commander-in-Chief of Bomber Command, and the RAF were cranked up a gear with their new heavy bombers and new strategy of attack. Now with the backing of both Russia and America, Britain, by means of the RAF, was ready to outdo Hitler and the Nazis. And John was ready trained and one of the better pilots, full of audacity and pluck, raring to go.

6

106 Squadron, Together with Wing Commander Guy Gibson

On Friday, 17 May 2013, to mark the 70th anniversary of 617 Squadron RAF, a service of commemoration and thanksgiving was held at Lincoln Cathedral. Everyone stood for the Act of Remembrance taken from the Funeral Oration of Pericles (429 BC):

> Take these men for your example. Like them, remember that posterity can only be for the free; that freedom is the sure possession of those alone who have the courage to defend it.

It is significant to note that the 106 Squadron motto is *Pro libertate* (For freedom), which is certainly one of the reasons John joined the RAF, to fight for freedom and against oppression by the Nazis.

As yet not having befriended nor even met Guy Gibson, John is hankering after his old squadron:

RAF Station
Coningsby
Lincolnshire
4.3.42

My dearest Mother,

I feel very guilty about not writing sooner to say I had arrived safely, etc. However I have really been very busy getting moved and settled in and also meeting everybody.

Now that I have got here and have begun to get settled, I hope I shall be moving again as there is a chance of getting back to my old squadron. We went into Lincoln two evenings and the second time, the party never finished until well on into the morning! Of course I met all my old friends from the squadron and learned that they wanted me back and could use me as a first pilot pretty soon. … I think everything is more or less fixed up, and I shall be going back pretty soon perhaps tomorrow.

This place here simply doesn't compare with my old squadron – one notices the lack of friendliness and greeting when one arrives, and the blokes seem to be a bit duller. So I shall be pretty glad to move again, and also because they can't use me here as a first pilot for some time and are not really very sympathetic with my wishes!

Well, I expect you are pretty tired after all the trouble you went to cook those lovely meals when I was on leave. I really did enjoy my leave and thank you very much. After I left home on Tuesday I got up to town ok and met my friend and wife as prearranged. After lunch we saw an excellent revue called 'Rise Above It'. It was terribly funny all the way through and well worth seeing again. We eventually got back to Doncaster in the early hours of the morning and then moved to here that same day – a bit of a rush.

Next time I write I hope it will be from a different address nearer Lincoln – but as I am not sure of it I won't give you the address now.

I got an airgraph* from Richard Hope** the other day – the first I have heard from or about him for over a year. He's still out East somewhere and very hot!

Thank goodness the weather is not so cold now – I knew it would change soon after I had finished leave.

I did my best to get on the Paris 'do' but no luck. *** It was a marvellous success – the best ever.

Much love to all,

Yr loving Son.

---

* During the war, the GPO introduced the Airgraph Service for messages between servicemen and civilians. The message was written onto a special form that was then given an identification number and photographed onto microfilm.

** The same friend from Marlborough College.

*** John was clearly still very much missing operations and wished he had been on the Paris 'do', in which, on 3 March 1942, during the night, the RAF carried out a treacherous air raid on the residential quarter of Paris. As a result of this more than 600 people were killed and 1,000 wounded. Two hundred and thirty-five aircraft were despatched, including twenty-six Manchesters, though mainly not from No. 5 Group, who, at this stage in the war, were busy converting from medium to heavy bombers.

It seems that John had blanked his mind now to the human tragedy of such an operation, which was important in enabling him to carry out the next chapter of his RAF career. It was also at this point that John was transferred from 'B' Flight 106 Squadron to 'A' Flight 106 Squadron, for the first time under Wing Commander Guy Penrose Gibson.

Guy Gibson, aged 23, was three years older than John – still amazingly young – and had joined the Royal Air Force in 1936. By the outbreak of the Second

John V Hopgood   David Shannon

Picture of a Manchester aircraft

World War he had become a bomber pilot with 83 Squadron. Gibson won the DFC in July 1940 on Bomber Command's first raid of the war. He was fast-tracked to Fighter Command, where he won a Bar to his DFC. At the age of 23 Gibson was promoted to the rank of wing commander, and by April 1942 he had been posted back to Bomber Command, leading 106 Squadron; he had flown 172 sorties before taking over the 617 Squadron.

Of his first impressions of John, Gibson wrote the following:

There was John Hopgood, Hoppy they call him. He was a fair-haired chap about medium height, rather good-looking, except for one prominent tooth. The boys seemed to be always taking him off about this, but he took it good-naturedly. He was a serious fellow at heart though, even though he spent most of his time with the boys. As soon as I saw him I thought, 'what an ideal squadron type. I like that chap.'

Betty says that both John and Marna had slightly protruding front teeth and that her mother paid for them to have orthodontic treatment; this was on their first teeth, and when the second teeth came through they grew over the top of the brace and so were even worse. Marna had one front tooth removed and John ended up with one protruding, so never smiled naturally as he was always trying to cover it up.

John's flying career was to become permanently linked with that of Guy Gibson, and they were to become firm friends and highly skilled colleagues, greatly respecting each other's capabilities and sharing their skills and tips on how to fly the heavy bombers. Guy Gibson, best known as the leading Dambuster but also for his other activities in Lancasters (and in Mosquitos), started his career in Hampdens (John's favourite aircraft), and his book *Enemy Coast Ahead* contains many details of the aircraft and its operations. He had been involved in laying the first sea mines dropped from a Hampden; these special weapons, weighing about 1,700lb, were virtually sweep-proof. Known as 'vegetables', Gibson eased new crews into operational flying with minelaying which he codenamed 'Nasturtium training'. Intended to be dropped in deep water, these mines contained so much explosive that even if a ship was some way off, the force of an explosion would lift it out of the water. Thus anything in the log book which refers to 'Gardening' or 'plantingVeg' is code for placing mines. Names of particular fruit or vegetables refer to the position where the mines were to be placed and it seems that 'Nectarine' was off the north coast of Holland. Weighing 1,500lb, the mine was dropped by parachute in a depth of water between 30ft and 75ft. The aircraft's airspeed at the time of release had to be below 200mph and at an altitude of between 400ft and 1,000ft. The magnetic mine would lie on the seabed until a passing ship distorted the Earth's normal magnetic field enough to detonate the mine.

MARCH 20th OPERATION NECTARINE
4 VEGS CRASHED OK

On 20 March, the very day that Gibson assumed command of 106 Squadron, John did his first operation in a Manchester as second pilot to Flt Off Whamond. Happening in thick cloud, it only took twenty minutes; they realised the hydraulics had stopped working, the under-carriage of the Manchester being stuck, and so they returned to Coningsby still carrying a heavy bomb load (mainly mines), crash-landing, presumably, on the runway. Hoppy wrote 'we spread ourselves out a bit'; the plane must have been quite badly damaged but, miraculously, did not blow up.

Note that John's log book records, about once a month, John taking a local flight in a Tiger Moth; this has become the normal way for John to get about the country for his private trips!

MARCH	8	MANCHESTER	7418	P/O WHAMOND	SELF + 5 CREW	H.L. BOMBING + N.F.T.
MARCH	8	MANCHESTER	7418	P/O WHAMOND	SELF + 5 CREW	X. CROUNTRY
MARCH	17	MANCHESTER	5840	S/L NELMS	SELF + 6 CREW	WADDINGTON, HORSHAM ST. FAITH + RETURN
MARCH	18	MANCHESTER	5839	P/O WHAMOND	SELF + 5 CREW	N.F.T.
MARCH	18	T. MOTH	T.6309	SELF P/O WHAMOND	—	LOCAL.
MARCH	20	MANCHESTER	5839	P/O WHAMOND	SELF P/O FINLAYSON SGTS. KIELL, HANSON CLARKE, PARSONS.	OPERATIONS – NECTARINE. 4 VEG's. CRASHED O.K.

GRAND TOTAL [Cols. (1) to (10)]
....440....Hrs. ....45....Mins.
TOTALS CARRIED FORWARD

Flying Manchesters for minelaying and a private trip in a Tiger Moth

Tiger Moth

Conigsby
Lincolnshire
23.3.42

My dearest Mother,

So sorry to have delayed writing this letter for so long. Each day lately there has been quite a lot to do and I have not been able to catch the post – so put it off till the next day (lazy).

I really did enjoy those few days leave – thank you very much for all those delicious meals. I got to Swinderby on Sat ok and the party went off very well indeed. I managed to speak to several people in command and think that I shall eventually be able to get back there – anyway they are still trying to get me back. I went over there again last night and met everybody again.

Life certainly got a bit more interesting during this last week, as we nearly got cracking again. One day we did actually take off with a heavy bomb load in order to do a daylight mission, but unfortunately we crashed (no-one hurt). It was a shocking day, cloud base only 100 – 200 ft and visibility only 1,000' which is very bad indeed for any flying, let alone a heavy machine. However we managed to get down again ok but as our trouble was hydraulic, the undercarriage packed up and we spread ourselves out a bit.

Well now I must hurry off and do some flying,

With much love to all,

Yr loving Son.

John was proving to be a very competent pilot, and on a postcard of 30 March he wrote:

Excuse this brief epistle, but written in a hurry – a letter is to follow. I have been away from base for a few days and have been very busy – hence delay in writing.

I have got my F/O through now. ★

Have done some very interesting trips and had plenty of excitement, being hit quite badly (not my personal self).

Lots of love,

John.

★John has been confirmed as a flying officer and now has the potential to be first pilot. Note Guy Gibson's signature on the next log book page.

YEAR 1942 MONTH DATE	AIRCRAFT Type	No.	PILOT, OR 1ST PILOT	2ND PILOT, PUPIL OR PASSENGER	DUTY (INCLUDING RESULTS AND REMARKS)
— —	—	—	—	SELF,	— TOTALS BROUGHT FORWARD
MARCH 22	MANCHESTER	7317	P/O WHAMOND	7 CREW	N.F.T.
MARCH 23	MANCHESTER	7485	P/O WHAMOND	SELF + 5 CREW	N.F.T.
MARCH 24	MANCHESTER	7515	P/O WHAMOND	SELF + 5 CREW	N.F.T.
MARCH 24	MANCHESTER	7515	P/O WHAMOND	SELF. SGT.'S CHAPLIN, JORDAN, HANSON, CLARKE, PARSONS	OPERATIONS – GARDENING LORIENT. 4 VEG.'s. O.K. LANDED EXETER. S'LIGHTS AND G SHOT OUT. 500 f
MARCH 25	MANCHESTER	7515	P/O WHAMOND	SELF + 5 CREW	TO BASE.
MARCH 26	MANCHESTER	7391	P/O WHAMOND	SELF + 4 CREW	N.F.T.
MARCH 26	MANCHESTER	7391	P/O WHAMOND	SELF, P/O FINLAYSON SGT.'s JORDAN, HANSON, CLARKE, PARSONS	OPERATIONS – GARDENING BORDEAUX. 4 VEG.'s UNSUCCESS LANDED BOSCOMBE DOWN. FLAK HIT ST
MARCH 27	MANCHESTER	7391	P/O WHAMOND	SELF + 5 CREW	TO BASE.
MARCH 28	TIGER MOTH	T.6309	SELF	P/O YOUNG	LOCAL
MARCH 29	MANCHESTER	7485	P/O WHAMOND	SELF + 5 CREW	N.F.T.
MARCH 30	MANCHESTER	7485	P/O WHAMOND	SELF + 5 CREW	N.F.T.

SUMMARY FOR March 1942.
UNIT "A" Flight 106 Sqn.
DATE 31.3.42.
SIGNATURE N Hopford P/O

AIRCRAFT TYPES
1. MANCHESTER
2. TIGER MOTH
3. ....
4. ....

OC. "A" Flight 106 Sqn.

OC. 106 Sqn. W/C

GRAND TOTAL [Cols. (1) to (10)]
457 Hrs. 50 Mins.

TOTALS CARRIED FORWAR

This is the first appearance of Guy Gibson's signature in the log book

24th MARCH: TO LORIENT SUBMARINE BASE
4 VEGS SEARCHLIGHTS AND GUNS SHOT OUT

Lorient was the location of a German U-boat base during the Second World War. The base was capable of sheltering thirty submarines under cover. Although Lorient was heavily damaged by Allied bombing raids, as we see in John's next letter, this naval base, due to excellent defences, survived through to the end of the war. John was flying very low (at 500ft) and says he could see 'the blokes on the ground'. He must have been becoming hardened, because connecting his bombing with real people would have very much disturbed him in the past.

John rarely talks about feelings or emotions in his later letters; his inner thoughts always added interest in his early letters and in his Marlborough College diary, but now he had to avoid emotion, or too much analysis of his thoughts, or he might have wavered in his resolve and courage. Apparently, in squadron messes men didn't talk of war and death but of women and beer; mental amnesia and small talk protected them from fear.

YEAR 1942		AIRCRAFT		PILOT, OR 1ST PILOT	2ND PILOT, PUPIL OR PASSENGER	DUTY (INCLUDING RESULTS AND REMARKS)
MONTH	DATE	Type	No.			
—	—	—	—	—	—	— TOTALS BROUGHT FORWARD
APRIL	1	MANCHESTER	7317	SELF	4 CREW	LOCAL
APRIL	3	MANCHESTER	7461	P/O WHAMOND	SELF + 5 CREW	N.F.T.
APRIL	5	MANCHESTER	7515	P/O WHAMOND	SELF + 5 CREW	N.F.T.
APRIL	5	MANCHESTER	7515	P/O WHAMOND	SELF, F/O FINLAYSON, F/O COMBIE SGTS HANSON, CLARKE, PARSONS	OPERATIONS – COLOGNE. 1 x 4,000 4 x 500. ON TARGET
APRIL	7	MANCHESTER	7515	SELF	3 CREW	LOCAL + BEAM FLYING
APRIL	8	MANCHESTER	7319	SELF	4 CREW	LOCAL + BEAM FLYING
APRIL	8	MANCHESTER	7515	P/O WHAMOND	SELF + 5 CREW	N.F.T.
APRIL	8	MANCHESTER	7515	F/O WHAMOND	SELF F/O FINLAYSON F/O COMBIE SGTS HANSON CLARKE PARSONS	OPERATIONS — HAMBURG. 3 x 2,000. NEAR TARGET ? 10/10 5's Cb.
APRIL	11	MANCHESTER	7485	SELF	5 CREW	DUSK + DARK
APRIL	13	MANCHESTER	7319	SELF	6 CREW	N.F.T.
APRIL	13	MANCHESTER	7319	SELF	SGT.'s HOGG, BATES GIBSON, HOBSON, FERGUSON, CLARKE	OPERATIONS – GARDENING. HELIGOLAND. 4 VEG's. O.K.
APRIL	15	MANCHESTER	7319	SELF	6 CREW	N.F.T.
APRIL	16	T. MOTH	T.6309	SELF. F/O PRESCOTT- DECIE		LOCAL
APRIL	17	MANCHESTER	5796	SELF	6 CREW	N.F.T.
APRIL	17	MANCHESTER	5796	SELF	SGT.'s HOGG, BATES GIBSON, HOBSON, FERGUSON, FELTHAM.	OPERATIONS — HAMBURG. 114 x 250 OIL BOMBS. ON TARGET. 11,000 ft.

GRAND TOTAL [Cols. (1) to (10)]
491 Hrs.   05 Mins.

TOTALS CARRIED FORWARD

Note the heavy schedule of operations

Coningsby
Lincolnshire
3.4.1942

My dearest Mother,

I seem to have got very behindhand with my correspondence lately – for which I am very sorry. Thank you for your last letter.

I am very well and have been very busy lately, though much of the preparations have been in vain owing to last minute cancellations. However I have got in two more trips both of them very interesting. The first one was mine laying which we did with accuracy, and had a few very hectic minutes when we stayed over a very heavily defended town at only 500 ft. However we shot out many guns and searchlights – we could actually see the blokes on the ground – and got safely away without undue damage to the aircraft.

The second trip was unsuccessful as regards results but had plenty of excitement. We had to return early – but before getting clear we again strayed a bit over another heavily defended place this time at only 1,000 ft. Again we inflicted damage to the defences, but not before we had been hit. A shell exploded inside our wing just next door to our engine (luckily), and made a large hole and sprayed about a bit – but all was well and we got back ok.

I hope you got my p.c. ok. The F/O has come through at last.

In a hurry again, much love,

Your loving Son.

MARCH 26th: TO BORDEAUX
4 VEGS UNSUCCESSFUL

It can be seen that having had two disasters in three operations, John's life was constantly hanging by a thread, even when planting 'VEG' (mines). His mother and the rest of the family must by now have been painfully aware of that fact.

APRIL 5th COLOGNE,
Bombs dropped: 1 x 4,000, 4 x 500

Just look at the size of the bombs John was carrying: 4,000lb is about 2 tons. He referred to his bombs as 'eggs'. And look at the temperatures and conditions under which he was flying (see next letter). The Hamburg bombs may not even have been dropped on target, although the flak indicated he was near.

APRIL 8th HAMBURG
Bombs dropped: 3 x 2,000

On 8 April 1942, in one of the most intense air raids of the war, the RAF attacked Hamburg, Germany, with more than 270 bombers. At around this time John wrote:

Coningsby
Lincolnshire
10.4.42

My dearest Mother,

Many thanks indeed for your last letter. I do hope you enjoyed your stay at Seaford and that Uncle Edwin has bucked up a bit. I got a letter from Marna and she certainly seems to be getting on all right.

I have done two more trips now. The first one was very successful and with one of these new big bombs we started a large fire, which we could see from 80 miles away. It was a lovely night and everything went very well. But the second one was a bit of a bind. The weather was filthy all the way and over the target large towering thunder clouds causing extreme cold (-35° C) static (crackling on our internal telephone and blue flames all over the aircraft) and also causing some of our flying instruments to pack up which made things very tricky.★ The target was a very hot one but cloud obscured it – however we must have dropped our eggs more or less over it, as we were fired at very accurately and for a long time.

At last I have been made a captain/1st Pilot, and have now got my own crew, so from now on I have to make all the decisions.

Am expecting leave either on the 17th or the 23rd; I can't say which yet.

Much love to all,

Your loving Son.

★ Note 10/10ths recorded 8 April on the log page; it is a measure of sky cloud cover, hence 10/10ths equals total sky cover by C6s (Cumulo Nimbus Clouds responsible for thunderstorms). John hopes they were near the target, but even optimistic John puts a question mark in his log. As he writes, it is significant that John is first pilot for all minelaying and bombing operations from now on.

TO HELIGOLAND
4 VEGS [i.e. mines]★

Heligoland, meaning 'Holy Land', is an island off Germany which been part of the British Empire for eighty years; it sat on one of the busiest shipping lanes in the world, from Hamburg and the mouth of the Elbe to the Straits of Dover and the

English Channel. So it was of huge strategic importance and the British needed
to keep hold of it, not just to allow their warships safe passage, but also to prevent
the Germans seizing it and using it for their anti-aircraft guns. By the end of the
Second World War the civilian population had fled, leaving just British military
personnel and on 18 April 1947 British engineers attempted to destroy the
entire island in what became known as the 'British Bang'. Roughly 4,000 tons of
surplus Second World War ammunition were placed in various locations around
the island and set off. The island survived, although the extensive fortifications
were destroyed. Apparently the energy released was about 3.2 kilotons of TNT
equivalent. When it was restored to German ownership in 1952, the land needed
extensive mine clearance before it was habitable.

APRIL 17th TO HAMBURG
Bombs dropped: 14 x 250 oil bombs. ON TARGET

The RAF claim to have sent 173 aircraft, including five Manchesters, one of
which was lost (luckily not John's) on this particular mission to bomb Hamburg.
John writes that bombing this large target was 'fun', but remember he is still only
20 years old, not much more than a boy.

Coningsby
Lincolnshire
18.04.1942

My dearest Mother,
*… We have really been working pretty hard during this last week and tonight is our
first stand off for 10 nights. I have only done another two trips since I last wrote but then I
have been busy converting from 2nd to 1st pilot. I did both these last trips as a captain / 1st
Pilot and they were both very enjoyable and successful. The first one was reviewing which
was very uneventful but successful. The second one was on a big target and we had plenty
of fun again, but managed to hit the place ok in spite of a lot of opposition.*
*Good news (providing it comes off) – my wing commander told me the other day he
was going to make me a Flight Lieutenant. It hasn't come through yet and may take
anything from a week to a month to do so as it all depends on how soon somebody is
posted away. However it's a good thing – I shall have to run a flight every time the
squadron leader is away.*
No more news now until I see you next week,
Much love to all,
Your loving Son.

Unbeknown to John, perhaps as he was writing this very letter, something was being investigated which was to be crucial to his future.

On 18 April 1942 the Road Research Lab, under Collins and his team, had been working on two 1:10 scale models of the Nant y Gro Dam in the Elan Valley, Wales trying to find the best way to demolish it. Having been built in the 1890s as a temporary dam to supply water and power to the workers building the main Elan Valley Dams (to supply drinking water to Birmingham), it was no longer needed. A scientist, Dr Barnes Wallis, had become aware of this, and in 1941 he had received permission from Birmingham Corporation Water Works to stage some demolition experiments.

On 1 May 1942 an underwater charge was set several metres behind the dam wall and did not blow up the dam. However, the next test, on 24 July 1942, where the charge was suspended by scaffolding in contact with the dam itself, proved successful. The explosion caused a huge spout of water and then revealed a large breach in the dam wall. It so happened that this dam, complete with small power station, was a one-fifth scale version of the Möhne Dam. This pointed Barnes Wallis towards his bouncing bomb.

Meanwhile, John was in the thick of RAF operations and assuming more responsibility as first pilot. Marna was also taking on more responsibility in the ATS. She wrote from No. 45 Cobden Rd, Chesterfield on 20 April 1942:

My darling Mummy,

Don't be too surprised if I fail to turn up on Friday because – your funny little daughter has been put in command of the whole company while the C.O. is on a course. I was quite thrilled when I was suddenly told on Sunday morning, I never thought I should have to do it, being 1. the most junior officer in the company 2. by far the baby of the party! I was astonished when today I was told by our Group Commandant that I was to have full disciplinary powers! That is quite an honour and responsibility.

Well my duties started by having a general buzzing round this morning, fortunately everyone was very good and we were congratulated on our smartness. I felt most awfully small during the inspection as the party consisted of a General, a Brigadier, a Colonel, 2 Majors, an Adjutant our Group Commandant (Lt Col) and me! I was thankful for my height because that helped to redeem my inferiority complex. I must not be too pleased with life as this is a whole week of trials and tribulations to get through.

Your loving Daughter.

APRIL 23rd: OPERATION ROSTOCK (HEINKEL WORKS)
Bombs: 6 x 1,000 ON TARGET 4,000ft

YEAR 1942		AIRCRAFT		PILOT, OR 1ST PILOT	2ND PILOT, PUPIL OR PASSENGER	DUTY (INCLUDING RESULTS AND REMARKS)
MONTH	DATE	Type	No.			
—	—	—	–	—	—	— Totals Brought Forward
APRIL	19	MANCHESTER	7378	SELF	8 CREW	A/C TEST
APRIL	21	MANCHESTER	7378	SELF	6 CREW	N.F.T.
APRIL	23	MANCHESTER	7378	SELF	6 CREW	N.F.T.
APRIL	23	MANCHESTER	7378	SELF	Sgt.'s HOGG, BATES, GIBSON, HOBSON FERGUSON, MATHISSON	OPERATIONS – ROSTOK. (HEINKEL WKS 6 x 1,000. ON TARGET. 4,000 ft

Summary for APRIL 1942.   1. MANCHESTER
Unit 'A' Flight 106 Sqn. Aircraft   2. TIGER MOTH.
Date 24/4/42.
Signature J. Hopgood F/o

OC. 'A' Flight 106 Sqdn.

I. Gibson w/c
OC. 106 Sqdn.

GRAND TOTAL [Cols. (1) to (10)]   TOTALS CARRIED FORWARD
501 Hrs 15 Mins.

April is signed off by Guy Gibson after a month which included taking part in five operations

The RAF sent 143 aircraft to bomb the town of Rostock in North Germany, a port on the Baltic Sea. John was part of an added small force of eighteen bombers targeting the Heinkel factory, which made aircraft and was on the southern side of Rostock. Bombing conditions were good but the results of the raid were disappointing.

Despite John's log entry 'ON TARGET', this factory was not hit and most of the main bombing intended for the Altstadt fell between 2 and 6 miles away; in fact, it was rare for bombs to land 'on target' as navigation aids were still very primitive. Four aircraft were lost, including one Manchester. It was the first of a series of four raids here.

MAY 4th HELIGOLAND
OPERATION GARDENING, 4 veg.'s. OK 500ft

Note in John's log page that on 5 and 6 May he did his first familiarisation flights as second pilot in an AVRO Lancaster, with two crew, and then on 6 May he also flew solo as first pilot in one. From now on John was to trial the Lancaster more and more often; from this time on, flight engineers were to take the place of second pilots to reduce the need for as much pilot training.

Merlins take over from Vultures: The Avro Lancaster, with its four Rolls-Royce Merlin engines, was the RAF's most successful heavy bomber of the Second World War. Known by Harris as his 'Shining Swords', they dropped 608,612 tons of bombs in 156,000 sorties in the period 1942–45. Despite these new Lancasters being a huge improvement on the two Vulture-engined Manchesters, they were still fraught with teething difficulties; having cost the equivalent of £6 million each to build, they were very flimsy machines, made of aluminium skin just a couple of millimetres thick and with the only substantial piece of metal being the armour-plating behind the pilot's head. Although the first Lancs had front, mid and rear gunners, it was 'soft-bellied', i.e. fighter planes could come up underneath this huge heavy bomber and easily finish it off by firing at it from below.

According to the *Pilots Notes for LANCASTER*, produced by the Air Ministry, the pilot had to do a routine of over 200 checks (before take-off, during flight or after landing) on his plane on each trip. John, with his perfectionist nature, became very proficient at these and, as you will soon read, used his knowledge to train other pilots, including Guy Gibson. Indeed, it can be said that Flt Lt John Vere Hopgood showed Wing Commander Guy Gibson how to fly the Lancaster Bomber.

MAY 8th WARNEMUNDE
6 x 1,000. ON TARGET, intense Flak and Searchlights

John was, at this point, still flying Manchesters on operations. Although, according to his log book, his bombs fell 'ON TARGET' for the Warnemünde Raid and the nearby Heinkel aircraft factory, the attack was, after reconnaissance, shown to be only moderately successful. Of the 193 aircraft that went, nine were Manchesters, one of which was lost. John describes this raid as 'quite the worst [for flak and searchlights] he has experienced and probably ever likely to in the future'.

Lancaster (courtesy Josh Thorpe)

Coningsby
Lincolnshire
9.5.42

My dearest Mother,

What a grand leave. I really feel much better and brighter for it. Lets hope we can all manage to get leave again at the same time in June or July. Thank you too for all your hard work in the kitchen, its good to get food like that.

I got back here on Sunday OK, though travelling was very slow and tedious. I had lunch in town, but it wasn't very exciting.

By the way I am now a Flight Lieutenant; it came through about 3 or 4 days ago. In the absence of a new Flt Commander I am now running a flight and like it very much as there is plenty of work, which is a change from having to hang about.

I have done another two trips since my leave. The first one was very successful but quite uneventful, except that I flew out for 2 hrs in tight formation, which is very hard work and tiring. The last one was really very exciting and we managed to do very well in a low-level attack in intense and dazzling opposition. It was a very long trip, and when we got there the flak and searchlights were terrific – it is quite the worst I've experienced and probably ever likely to in future. There didn't seem to be a way through it all. However we went in very low down under 2,000 ft and succeeded in hitting our objective and also in getting away again without being hit at all, though why we weren't I don't know as they sent up everything at us for about 5 minutes. We could hear it whistling past the aircraft and also hear it sizzling as it burned.

Tonight I am going over to see Oliver and join in the party in his mess. It ought to be good fun. I certainly feel like a party after my last trip!!

Much love to all,

Your loving Son.

John deserved a party with his half-brother Oliver, in which to let off steam after that raid which assaulted all his senses.

YEAR 1942		AIRCRAFT		PILOT, OR 1ST PILOT	2ND PILOT, PUPIL OR PASSENGER	DUTY (INCLUDING RESULTS AND REMARKS)
MONTH	DATE	Type	No.			
—	—	—	—	—	—	— TOTALS BROUGHT FORWARD
MAY	4	MANCHESTER	7319	SELF	6 CREW	N.F.T.
MAY	4	MANCHESTER	5769	SELF	SGT's HOGG, BATES, GIBSON, HOBSON, LEWIS, HALLAM.	OPERATIONS – GARDENING HELIGOLAND. 4 VEG's. O.K. 500 ft.
MAY	5	LANCASTER	5485	S/L STENNER	SELF + 2 CREW	FAMILIARISATION
MAY	6	LANCASTER	5485	P/O HEALEY	SELF + 2 CREW	FAMILIARISATION
MAY	6	LANCASTER	5485	SELF	3 CREW	SOLO
MAY	6	MANCHESTER	7378	SELF	3 CREW	DUAL INSTRUCTION
MAY	7	TIGER MOTH	T.6309	SELF	P/O CHURCHER	TO PETERBOROUGH + RETURN
MAY	8	MANCHESTER	7488	SELF	5 CREW	N.F.T.
MAY	8	MANCHESTER	7488	SELF	SGT's HOGG, BATES, GIBSON, HOBSON, LEWIS, HALLAM.	OPERATIONS – WARNEMUNDE 6 x 1,000 ON TARGET. 2,000 ft. INTENSE FLAK + S'LIGHTS.
MAY	9	OXFORD	152	W/C GIBSON	SELF	TO CASTLE CAMPS
MAY	10	OXFORD	152	W/C GIBSON	SELF	TO BASE
MAY	10	MANCHESTER	7488	SELF	6 CREW	N.F.T.
MAY	12	MANCHESTER	7417	SELF	SGT. HOGG, HOBSON	DUAL INSTRUCTION
MAY	14	MANCHESTER	7457	SELF	SGT. McHARDY, REES	DUAL INSTRUCTION
MAY	16	MANCHESTER	7434	SELF	5 CREW	N.F.T.
MAY	16	MANCHESTER	7434	SELF	SGT's HOGG, BATES, GIBSON, HOBSON, SGT. LEWIS, P/O FERGUSON	OPERATIONS – GARDENING HELIGOLAND. 4 VEG's O.K. 500 ft.
MAY	18	MANCHESTER	7457	SELF	SGT. CASSELS + CREW	DUAL INSTRUCTION

GRAND TOTAL [Cols. (1) to (10)]

530 Hrs. 30 Mins.

TOTALS CARRIED FORWARD

May showed a huge variety in John's flying activities. Note that Gibson is first pilot on 9 and 10 May

The log page for 9 and 10 May shows that John and W/C Gibson flew together as pilots in Oxford aircraft, possibly heralding the start of their close professional relationship. John had done about ten hours of extra Lancaster training and so was an ace at cockpit drill; this was especially important on a foggy night as it enabled the pilot to position every tap without looking down at the controls. Guy Gibson picked up many tips from John on flying these larger bombers; by this point, Guy and John were firm friends and trusted colleagues.

The next operation was to Heligoland once again.

MAY 16th HELIGOLAND
OPERATION GARDENING, 4 VEGS OK 500ft

Marna, who had obviously been reading the papers and wondering about her dear brother John, wrote on 17 May, from Reservoir House, Chesterfield:

My darling Mummy,

… Am glad J. has got his promotion; I wondered if he had been on that Vaarnemunde raid [which of course he was!] as I saw Manchesters had taken part.

In contrast, Elizabeth was pretty oblivious to the war and wrote to her mother from Onslow Hall, Shrewsbury (often using French in her letters to her mother since her schooling for those two terms in France):

LE 17 MAI (DIMANCHE)

Darling Mummy,

Another week gone by all ready – how aggravating time is! Isn't this school a terror, guess what's happened now? Matrons gone and developed German Measles! Aren't we a hopeless crowd – not a term has passed since I've been here that we haven't had <u>something</u> going by way of infectious diseases! However she's got it very slightly so lets hope it won't spread.

… In the afternoon I sat in a field with cows for companions and sketched Onslow surrounded with all her marigold flowering shrubs which were just at their best. I ended the day by playing tennis all the evening.

Oh! Dear I'd better now talk about work or you'll begin to think that I spend all my time playing which is <u>quite</u> untrue!

I've set myself to read my French books again this term, I've just finished 'Lettres de mon Moulin' A. Daudet and begin another one today though haven't decided yet which. For the first time in my life, on Tuesday, I was top in Dictée; I hope it will last, though very unlikely!

We've started doing modern artists in 'Histoire de l'art' and I'm finding it very interesting.

YEAR 1942		AIRCRAFT		PILOT, OR 1ST PILOT	2ND PILOT, PUPIL OR PASSENGER	DUTY (INCLUDING RESULTS AND REMARKS)
MONTH	DATE	Type	No.			
—	—	—	—	—	—	TOTALS BROUGHT FORWARD
MAY	19	MANCHESTER	7488	SELF	P/O COOKE, WILLIAMS P/O FINLAYSON, P/T COMBIE. SGT. HANSON, CLARKE, PARSONS.	SEARCHLIGHT CO-OP (LONDON)
MAY	21	MANCHESTER	7457	SELF	P/O WILLIAMS. CREW	DUAL INSTRUCTION .
MAY	21	MANCHESTER	7434	SELF	P/O WILLIAMS + CREW	DUAL INSTRUCTION . DUSK .
MAY	23	LANCASTER	7508	SELF	F/O YOUNG W/O YOUNG + 5 CREW	To KIRTON-LINDSEY, LYNTON AND SKELLINGTHORPE.
MAY	24	MANCHESTER	5796	SELF	P/O COATES + 3CREW	DUAL INSTRUCTION
MAY	26	LANCASTER	7579	SELF	W/O YOUNG P/O WILLIAMS P/O COATES + 3 CREW	DARK LANDINGS (3).
MAY	30	LANCASTER	5608	SELF	CREW	N.F.T.
MAY	30	LANCASTER	5608	SELF	P/O COATES SGT. BATES GIBSON HOBSON F/SGT. LEWIS P/O FERGUSON	OPERATIONS — COLOGNE. 1 X 4,000 8 SBC's BROUGHT BACK INTER-COMM. U/S. OVER 1,000 a/c
MAY	31	LANCASTER	5608	SELF	CREW	N.F.T.

Summary for MAY 1942
Unit "B"Flight 106 Sqdn. Aircraft
Date 31/5/42 Types
Signature W. Hopford F/L.

1 LANCASTER
2. MANCHESTER
3. OXFORD
4. T. MOTH

Jack Woolcroft
Flight Commander
No. 106 Squadron
S/L

W/C
O.C. 106 Sqdn.

GRAND TOTAL [Cols. (1) to (10)]
544 Hrs. 40 Mins.

TOTALS CARRIED FORWARD

Note each SBC would be loaded with 4lb or 3lb incendiaries

In English this term I am doing Othello and we are going to study it in detail, also Shakespeare's life.

In music I'm learning Debussy's Golly-Wog cake Dance (!) and a Chopin Waltz, at the moment.

The only thing I am not enjoying and that's German – their (I must use some of John's language) BLOODY grammatical rules send me quite potty – I'm in the bottom class!

Well I'm off to the Wrekin now, so Aurevoir.

With lots of love from Elizabeth.

In the letter Betty is seemingly unaware of her brother's danger, except to show her (and his) disdain for the Germans and their language!

In his next letter, John aired his views on communal feeding and his intolerance of conciliatory talk towards the Germans, both of which his mother had presumably discussed in her letters to him and both of which have probably been talked of on the British radio and in newspapers:

Coningsby
Lincolnshire
22.5.42

My dearest Mother,

I am so sorry this letter is so late. Actually I wrote one last Sunday but on turning out my pockets this morning found it still unposted. Many thanks for your last letter. Communal feeding certainly seems to be a good idea.

I have only done one more trip [Heligoland] since I last wrote. It was highly successful but quite quiet. I am now busy doing a lot of training flying. During this last fortnight I have had to run a flight but now a new squadron leader has arrived so I am only a deputy now. It has been hard work but good experience.

The party over with Oliver and Celia was a great success and I enjoyed it very much.

I quite agree with you I wish they'd get on with the war. Fancy paying a lot of self-centred blokes to talk about what they want to do with Germany after we've beaten them. 'They' indeed, as if they had an active hand in fighting. I sincerely hope the blokes who did the fighting are given a free hand to deal with Germany as she deserves and lets have none of this conciliatory talk. One can't make peace until Germany has been properly and completely crushed and invaded and made to suffer; she didn't suffer enough last time.

Much love,

Your loving Son.

Understandably, as John has witnessed many of his friends and fellow squadron members not returning from operations, he was out to make the Germans pay for it, and in no uncertain terms. His attitude echoes that of Bomber Harris after the London Blitz with his famous quote, from Hosea, chapter eight, verse seven, 'They sowed the wind, and now they are going to reap the whirlwind.'

Meanwhile, Marna had been promoted and her netball team was winning games; she wrote on 1 June 1942 from Reservoir House, Chesterfield:

My darling Mummy,

… The outstanding piece of news this week is my promotion; I now bear the weight of another pip on my shoulder! The first I knew of it was that I saw my name on a piece of paper with the new rank preceding it, I naturally made fun of it and told the CO she had better treat me with more respect in future or tick the typist off for making an error. She said she thought it probable that I actually had been promoted and so took steps to

find out. Well, anyway word through on Thursday but it dates back to – I'm not quite sure when yet! By the way you now address me as Sub M H! (Sub Lieutenant Marna Hopgood).

… I played tennis here for the first time yesterday, having found someone to play with I hope I shall get some more games. For future reference his name is Derek Buxton, a young officer who is stationed not far away, he took me out for dinner in his mess the other day and we had a very enjoyable evening at least I did!★

I do hope John is all right after these last escapades.

Your ever-loving Daughter.

★ This Derek Buxton was to become a feature of Marna's life for a good while!

7

Bomber Harris and his Thousand Bomber Raids

On 30 May 1942 the Cologne operation was the first of three Thousand Bomber Raids launched by Bomber Harris, which were of critical importance for the whole future of the bomber offensive; they involved using Lancasters and indeed every aircraft available, not only from Bomber Command but from wherever they could muster them, including Coastal Command and OTUs, to try to destroy the morale of Germany and so hasten the end of the war. It was a very successful strategy and proved that the defences of a major industrial city could be saturated, enlarging the area of damage out of proportion to the increase in the number and weight of bombs. It solved, in a single night, many of the problems of strategic bombing and demonstrated what Bomber Command could do if it were given the priorities in men and material that had been being witheld.

MAY 30th: OPERATION COLOGNE
1 x 4,000, 8 SBCs BROUGHT BACK

The operation above was John's first flying a Lancaster. Unfortunately, they returned early before completing it due to the dysfunction of their internal telephone system. You will see also, on the log book page, that it was not just the telephone systems which were not functioning on these first Avro Lancasters; note the entry for 1, 5 and 25 June, where two starboard engines failed each time, twice on the 5551 and once on an operation in the 5680. Note also the entry of 5 June, when they failed whilst 'Beating up the mess'. (Even if modern young pilots were this spirited, they never would admit to it in their log book entries!)

YEAR 1942		AIRCRAFT		PILOT, OR 1ST PILOT	2ND PILOT, PUPIL OR PASSENGER	DUTY (INCLUDING RESULTS AND REMARKS)
MONTH	DATE	Type	No.			
—	—	—	—	—	—	— TOTALS BROUGHT FORWARD
JUNE	1	LANCASTER	5608	SELF	CREW	N.F.T.
JUNE	1	LANCASTER	5608	SELF	P/o COATES SGT. BATES, HOBSON, GIBSON, SGT. LEWIS P/o FERGUSON	OPERATIONS — ESSEN. 1 x 4,000 8 SBC's ON TARGET 12,000 OVER 1,000 a/c
JUNE	3	LANCASTER	5551	SELF	P/o COCKBAIN P/o AYTOUN + CREW	DUAL INSTRUCTION.
JUNE	4	LANCASTER	5551	SELF	P/o COATES P/o MAXWELL SGT. BATES, GIBSON, HOBSON P/o FERGUSON	FORMATION X COUNTRY. FORCED LANDED HARWELL. BOTH STB. E's CUT
JUNE	5	LANCASTER	5551	SELF	P/o FINLAYSON, P/o COCKBAIN + 6 CREW	To BASE. BOTH STB. E's CUT. WHEN BEATING UP THE MESS.
JUNE	7	MANCHESTER	5796	SELF	SGT. CHURCH, BUTLER	DUAL INSTRUCTION.
JUNE	8	LANCASTER	5608	SELF	P/o COATES + 4 CREW	DUAL INSTRUCTION.
JUNE	8	LANCASTER	5608	SELF	P/o WILLIAMS + 2 CREW	DUAL INSTRUCTION.
JUNE	10	LANCASTER	7579	SELF	SGT. CASSELS + CREW	DUAL INSTRUCTION. To SUTTON BRIDGE
JUNE	16	LANCASTER	5608	SELF	SGT. CHURCH + 3 CREW	DUAL INSTRUCTION.
JUNE	21/22	LANCASTER	7579	S/L WOOLDRIDGE	SELF + 7 CREW	To NEWTON + RETURN LOW LEVEL ON BLACK BOT
JUNE	24	LANCASTER	5680	SELF	8 CREW	X. COUNTRY + TEST.
JUNE	25	LANCASTER	5680	SELF	6 CREW	N.F.T.
JUNE	25	LANCASTER	5680	SELF	SGT. LODGE, BATES, HOBSON, GIBSON, SGT. LEWIS P/o FERGUSON	OPERATIONS — BREMEN. 1 x 4,000, 8 SBC's JETTISONNED OVER HOLLAND. BOTH STB. E's CUT OVER
JUNE	29	LANCASTER	5551	SELF	6 CREW	L.L. BOMBING

GRAND TOTAL [Cols. (1) to (10)]
.....570...Hrs.........20...Mins.

TOTALS CARRIED FORWARD

Now John is nearly always flying Lancasters. Also note 'BEATING UP THE MESS'

JUNE 1st: ESSEN
Bombs: 1 x 4,000, 8 SBCs ON TARGET

This was the second Thousand Bomber Raid using the still intact bomber force, which had not yet returned to training. It was not quite so successful on this occasion as Essen, always rather hidden in the industrial haze of the Ruhr, was concealed by thick cloud, the weather being poor. Essen, containing the Krupp's Steel Guns Factory, suffered 272 air strikes through the duration of the war, resulting in the whole city being destroyed.

As we can see from his next letter, John was enjoying the huge scale of these operations, and approved of this mass bombing strategy:

Coningsby
3.6.42

Dear Mother,

I seem to have been very busy just lately so that is why this letter is a bit delayed.

I took part in the last two big raids. The first one was damn brassing off for me, as our internal telephone system packed up. As there were so many fighters and other machines around it would have been foolhardy to have gone on, so we had to come back. However the last one was grand fun and very successful. On the way out we saw two fighters, one tried to attack and got as close as 300 ft, but then I started to weave about a bit and the fighter went off after somebody else. The other one came at us too fast and went over the top of us at about 100 ft above, and we managed to elude him all right. The target was well smashed about and there were lots of fires. We managed to drop ours right in the centre of the town. This mass attacking certainly seems to be the answer to night bombing and thus quickening of the end of the war. I hope we do lots more of it; there is much more safety from one point of view in numbers as they confuse and smash up the defences, thereby allowing much more accurate bombing.

I am expecting some more leave in about a fortnight's time, or if not then definitely by the end of this month.

At last we seem to be getting some decent weather. Today it has been so hot that we have all been going about without any coats on.

Glad to hear that Marna has found some better billets. I must try and write to her soon.

The press came down here the other day and we shot our respective lines. One of my remarks was printed!!

Much love

From your loving Son.

John was clearly enjoying flying and playing 'cat and mouse' with German fighter jets. His mention of 'weaving about a bit' may have been a precursor to 'corkscrewing' (see October 1942).

John was also apparently enjoying a great social life and, as we can see from the letter below, didn't seem to mind too much that his leave had been cancelled:

CONINGSBY
LINCS
14.6.42

My dearest Mother,

Many thanks for your last letter. I'm afraid my leave has temporarily fallen through and I shan't be able to get my leave until the middle of next month. There's too much work to do and I've got to help see that it's done. However I'm hoping for a 48 hours soon though doubt if I shall be able to get home as travelling wastes so much time!

106 Squadron after the first Thousand Bomber Raid (Guy Gibson is centre front)

This last week has been good fun but I haven't done any more trips yet. I haven't had much time off but when I have we have had some excellent parties. At the end of last week we had a mess party and this week we had our squadron party: a social gathering of the squadron and all ground crews.

I was very annoyed last week as I was going to Ireland and then they scrubbed it. I was going to be in charge of the party and we had planned to have a very good time and probably nip across into peace-time Eire.

I am writing off to Marna and Betty and telling them when I expect leave, probably from July 13th until about the 22nd and see what they are likely to be doing around that time.

My friends who were missing last time I was on leave are all reported prisoner of war and we have heard from them all: grand news. Poor Jim Cumming has been reported killed now.

During the early part of the week we had some grand weather here and managed to organize some bathing outings to the nearby swimming pool.

Much love to all,

Your loving Son.

Meanwhile, Marna wrote to her mother:

56, Sheffiled Road,
Chesterfield
21.6.42

My darling Mummy,

Derek and I seem to be becoming great friends, the attraction being mutual as we have so much in common, only he is quite clever. Ex University and is hoping to go into the diplomatic service after the war!★ We hope to arrange our leave to coincide, as we are both due for it at the end of July or beginning of August. Owing to the upheaval goodness knows where we may be by then but I hope it will come off all right.

I have made tentative enquiries about gardeners and wives but the position here is as bad as at home, there just aren't any surplus bodies knocking about of that trade.

It is so hot and lovely today Derek and I are going bathing this afternoon in a private pool.

Lunch time,
Your ever-loving Daughter.

★ Note that Marna is reassuring her mother that Derek is 'suitable' to be connected to a Hopgood. Betty remembers that the family started saving up their clothes coupons for a potential wedding, and Betty even had her measurements taken for a bridesmaid's dress.

In the letter below, John had been taken to give a talk on 'Life as a Pilot in Bomber Command' to factory workers and evidently enjoyed the experience:

Coningsby
Lincs
24.6.42

My dearest Mother,

Many thanks for your last letter. Do hope your cold is better; this weather ought to have done it a bit of good.

I have had a very interesting time just lately. Last week I was chosen with another bloke to go and visit a factory near London. We had our rooms and meals paid for in London by the RAF, and so everything was very nice. We were driven out to the factory in style and when we got there we were very well looked after. First of all we were shown over by the managing director and later on by the chief boss himself. It was all very interesting and we had some long chats with everybody. Then after a superlative lunch we had to address the workers. It was a very large audience, however we both managed to find something to say mostly about our operational experiences and we were nearly mobbed at the end of it. Later on we had tea and then back to town where of course we had an excellent time. I hope to get on some more of these jobs as they really are most frightfully interesting and also a very pleasant change from everyday RAF life.

Sorry for this bad scrawl but I burnt my hand rather – a matchbox blew up in it and made a bit of a mess – however it is much better now and no pain.

My leave should definitely come off as planned – the middle of next month.

Much love to all,

Yr loving Son.

25th JUNE 1942: OPERATION BREMEN
Bombs: 1 x 4,000, 8 SBCs JETTISONNED OVER HOLLAND Both STB
Engines cut

Summer 1942 saw the Battle of the Atlantic and the German U-boat campaign in full swing. In June 1942, Bremen, on the coast and a main centre of the U-boat building industry, and also having the Focke-Wulf aircraft works, was the target for the RAF's third Thousand Bomber Raid. In all over 1,000 aircraft (472 Wellingtons, 124 Halifaxes, 102 Hudsons, 96 Lancasters, 69 Stirlings, 51 Blenheims, 50 Hampdens, 50 Whitleys, 24 Bostons, 20 Manchesters and 4 Mosquitos) were sent. The limited success was entirely due to the use of GEE, which enabled the leading crews to start marker fires through the cloud cover. GEE, devised by Robert Dippy and developed at the Telecommunications Research Establishment (TRE) at Swanage, Dorset, was the code name given to a radio navigation system used by the Royal Air Force during the Second World War. It was the first hyperbolic navigation system to be used on operations and measured the time delay between two radio signals to give a position.

Six hundred and ninety-six Bomber Command aircraft were able to claim attacks on Bremen. Five hundred and seventy-two houses were completely destroyed and 6,108 damaged. Eighty-five people were killed, 497 injured and 2,378 bombed out of their homes. It was the last night Manchesters were used on operations, and the last Thousand Bomber Raid, although the use of large numbers of aircraft at a time continued to be a strategy of the RAF.

But John, as first pilot, was not part of this raid in the end; he turned his Lancaster back due to major engine failure (both starboard engines cut), jettisoning the bombs over Holland and, against all odds, limped home. John had experienced serious functional problems with his Lancaster so far. On 4 July 1942, John's log page shows him jointly first pilot with W/C Guy Gibson when he is familiarising his Wing Commander with this latest heavy bomber (i.e. John here is actually teaching Guy Gibson how to fly Lancasters). Guy Gibson's log book shows the same event, indeed it is Gibson's only log where Hopgood is mentioned by name.

When the new Lancasters were delivered to the squadron, Guy Gibson tells:

YEAR		AIRCRAFT		PILOT, OR	2ND PILOT, PUPIL	DUTY
1942		Type	No.	1ST PILOT	OR PASSENGER	(INCLUDING RESULTS AND REMARKS)
MONTH	DATE					
—	—	—	—	—	—	— TOTALS BROUGHT FORWARD
JUNE	30	LANCASTER	5551	SELF	7 CREW	L.L. BOMBING
		Summary for	JUNE	1942	1. LANCASTER	
		Unit "B" Flight	106 Sqn	Aircraft	2. MANCHESTER	
		Date July 1st 1942 Type			3.	
		Signature		W. Aspford P/S.	4.	
		J. Oskd-Woodcuife S/L.			Guy Gibson W/c	
		OC "B" Flight 106 Sqn.			OC. 106 Sqn.	
JULY	1	LANCASTER	5551	SELF	6 CREW	H.L. BOMBING
JULY	2	LANCASTER	5604	SELF	4 CREW	H.L. BOMBING
JULY	3	LANCASTER	5861	SELF	SGT. SMITH + 5 CREW	DUAL INSTRUCTION
JULY	4	LANCASTER	5081	W/C GIBSON SELF	5 CREW	FAMILIARISATION
JULY	7	LANCASTER	5551	SELF	5 CREW	FORMATION PRACTISE (LEADING)
JULY	8	LANCASTER	5680	SELF	6 CREW	N.F.T.
JULY	8	LANCASTER	5680	SELF	P/O DOWNER, SGT. BATES, GIBSON, HOBSON, SGT LEWIS P/O FERGUSON	OPERATIONS — WILHELMSHAVEN 1×4,000 6×500 2×250. ON TARGET 12,000
JULY	11	LANCASTER	7579	SELF	P/O DOWNER, SGT. BATES, GIBSON, HOBSON, SGT. LEWIS, P/O FERGUSON.	OPERATIONS — DANZIG (DAYLIGHT) 5×1,000. FORMATION. ABANDONNED — PORT PETROL COCK U/S.
				GRAND TOTAL [Cols. (1) to (10)]		TOTALS CARRIED FORWARD

Note that 4 July is the significant day when John familiarises Guy Gibson with Lancasters

My own squadron did not have a conversion flight … We had to do our training ourselves. Hoppy … had done about 10 hours training … I asked him to show me. It was mostly a question of getting the cockpit drill dead right. All it means is getting to know the position of every tap so that you can fly the aircraft without having to look down for the controls. … I noticed the cockpit layout was much the same as that of a Manchester … only the four throttles and one or two refinements seemed to be the difference. Hoppy climbed into the driving-seat while I stood behind him. … Hoppy explained the starting–up procedure in detail … and answered the long list of checks on both equipment and crew.

When all was done, Hoppy turned round to me. 'Of course that is the complete drill, Sir. If I were you I'd do it for the first few flights, then you'll find you want to slacken off. It'll all come absolutely automatic. The next thing is the starting-up, take-off and air drill, which never varies. Most pilots do this no matter how experienced they are.'

Then came a string of orders from Hoppy … He ran up the engines to full power, one by one, each time checking the two stage blower, the airscrew pitch control and the magnetos … and then … all together, evenly until each one was showing zero boost, then released the brakes. The acceleration was terrific, and I had to grab the back of his armour-plated seat to hold myself upright … Soon the A.S.I. was showing a speed of 110 mph and the aircraft suddenly became steady. We were airborne.

… Hoppy showed me how to stop (feather) an engine simply by pressing a button, how it would fly quite well on only one … He showed me how to 'ditch' the aircraft … 'It's very important to get the landing drill wrapped up' … 'You want to keep the nose well up when landing these things', said Hoppy over his shoulder … Hoppy, with both hands on the wheel, pulled off a good landing to the accompaniment of crackling and popping exhaust stubs. When we had run about 1,000 yards we came to a stop. He pulled his oxygen mask off his sweating face and grinned. 'There, now you have a try.'

Of course John didn't mention this, what was to become 'historic', episode in his next letter to his mother:

RAF Station
Coningsby
Lincolnshire
5.7.1942

My dearest Mother,

Many thanks for your last letters. I was very glad you managed to get away for a few days holiday at Shrewsbury. I hope you didn't tire yourself too much on the bicycle rides and country rambles. Good news about Betty – it'll be a good thing for her I'm sure.

Things have been pretty hectic here just lately. I took part in that last big raid on Bremen and had rather a shakey do. Just before we got to the target we developed serious engine trouble and the machine became almost uncontrollable. However I managed to get things sorted out and set off back home at a snails pace and only just being able to keep the plane flying. It was a hell of a sweat and at one time I thought we would never make it. It was a great relief to land safely. Next day the big chief from group came down to see me and handed out a pat on the back. ★ *It was the first time someone has managed to do what I did. Since that I have been very busy getting ready for another job which has now been cancelled, which is a great shame. My leave has now been fixed for the 18th of this month. It may not be a week perhaps only 4 or 5 days, as it is difficult for me to get off for a long period just now.*

Oliver wrote and said he intended coming up here to see me one day soon and be shown around, but no sign of him yet.

Much love to all,

Your loving Son.

★ The 'big chief of the group' was probably Air Vice Marshal W.A. Coryton, who was in charge of Bomber Command's Group 5 at this time, and his approval shows that John was now excelling as a pilot.

Until now, most raids had been carried out at night when the moon was full and in clear weather, but Germany's night fighter force had been expanded and become so powerful that Bomber Command could not sustain pilot provision with the resultant increase in casualties. New tactics were needed. They would operate mainly on dark nights or in cloudy weather. GEE navigation, improved wireless, photography and eventually the Pathfinder Force all began to make this possible.

JULY 8th OPERATION WILHELMSHAVEN
Bombs: 1 x 4,000, 6 x 500, 2 x 250, ON TARGET

The dock area of Wilhelmstrasse was attacked by 285 aircraft; of the fifty-two Lancasters which went, one was lost.

JULY 11th DANZIG (daylight)
Bombs: 5 x 1,000, FORMATION ABANDONED

This operation was to bomb U-boat yards in Danzig (now Gdansk) just before dusk. The experimental plan called for the forty-four Lancasters to fly at low level and in formation over the North Sea but then to split up and fly independently in cloud (although target clear), which was forecast to be present especially over Denmark. With a round trip of 1,500 miles, it was the most distant target Bomber Command had yet attempted to reach, and the new tactics did indeed foil the German fighter planes, although their searchlights thwarted the attempt to hit the submarine-building yards.

John was leading this sortie, and it was very frustrating to him that once again there was a functional problem (port petrol cock unserviceable), which meant that for the third time he had to turn his Lancaster back; he was very cross indeed.

Notice in the last and next two log book pages a John Wooldridge has signed along with Guy Gibson as John's OC in 106 Squadron; he is John 'Dim'

106 Squadron: Gibson, Wooldridge, Hopgood (detail from squadron photo, p.207)

Wooldridge, one of Gibson's flight commanders. He became Squadron Leader of 106 Squadron when Gibson left to form 617 Squadron and was known for his charisma and leadership qualities, but he was a bit of a 'loose cannon', for instance Gibson once saw his personal aircraft being used by Wooldridge after he had himself told Gibson it was out of order! He took part in ninety-seven operations.

A man of many talents, like John he shared a love of music, writing the musical score and some of the screenplay for the film *Appointment in London*, starring Dirk Bogarde, which was an account of a Lancaster squadron operating in 1943. Tragically, Dim was killed in a road accident in 1958 at the early age of 39.

JULY 13th DUISBURG
Bombs: 5 x 2,000 ON TARGET

This was the first of a series of raids on Duisburg, an industrial city on the edge of the Ruhr. The force encountered cloud and electrical storms and reported that their bombing was well scattered.

John found the electric storm on his Lancaster 'a very pretty sight'.

On 14 July John flew an Oxford with Gibson and Flt Lt Whamond to Hendon for a CS (Capital Ship) bomb demonstration; it was a new bomb, expressly designed for use against large warships. It was claimed that one hit would sink a battleship, but at this stage it was ballistically unsound and impossible to aim; it did, however, prompt a lot of practice and preparation for its use by 106 squadron in the following weeks.

Meanwhile, Marna seemed to be in love and John had some thoughts about his sister Marna having a young man:

RAF Coningsby
16.7.42

My dearest Mother,

Many thanks for your last letter. I wonder how Marna and boyfriend are getting on – I'm all against wartime marriages – they are inclined to put blokes off the fighting spirit and give them additional worries and cares, which is obviously not a good thing.

There is quite a lot of news since I last wrote. My leave which I expected to start sometime this week has been postponed – I can't get off yet as I am much too busy – but definitely I am now getting leave from August 1st until about the 10th, so I should see something of Betty and also I hope Oliver if he can make it.

I have done 3 more trips since I last wrote. The first one was very ordinary and very successful. We saw some German fighters and got fired at quite a lot but otherwise it wasn't anything out of the ordinary. The second was the daylight raid to Danzig. I was leading our formation and we got on very well until we got to Denmark. Something went wrong with my machine and we were unable to carry on any further and much to my fury had to come home again, where I managed to get down all right. I was really furious – it is the 3rd time I have had to return early due to some sort of trouble or another. The rest of the boys had a grand time and got on very well. The 3rd trip was a very ordinary and successful trip – plenty of flak, a fighter, and lots of cloud. Coming home we got in a bad electrical storm and the aircraft was just a mass of blue sparks and flames – actually a very pretty sight.

Oliver came up here last Sunday and I think enjoyed himself – anyway we gave him a very good party. We had our first lot of new potatoes and green peas the other day – I shall look forward to those sort of things when I get my leave.

Much love to all,

Your loving Son.

John's first *M-Mother*, a B1 type Avro Lancaster with tail code R5731, now arrives on the scene.

Oliver wrote on 24 July 1942 to John's mother, his stepmother (whom he called Marna, as had his father):

Dear Marna,

… I saw John last week and found him very flourishing though a bit weary after the Danzig raid. He seems to be doing extraordinarily well and is a very popular member of his Squadron.

I hope to get home for a few nights early in August.

Yours ever, Oliver.

YEAR 1942		AIRCRAFT		PILOT, OR 1ST PILOT	2ND PILOT, PUPIL OR PASSENGER	DUTY (INCLUDING RESULTS AND REMARKS)
MONTH	DATE	Type	No.			
—	—	—	—	—	—	—— TOTALS BROUGHT FORWARD
JULY	13	LANCASTER	7579	SELF	6 CREW	N.F.T.
JULY	13	LANCASTER	7579	SELF	P/O DOWNER SGT. BATES	OPERATIONS — DUISBURG
					GIBSON HOBSON	5 x 2,000 ON TARGET. 14,000 ft
					F/SGT. LEWIS SGT. MERRICK	
JULY	14	OXFORD LANCASTER	4095	W/C GIBSON SELF	F/LT WHAMMOND	To HENDON ↑ RETURN C.S. BOMB DEMONSTRATION
JULY	23	LANCASTER	5731	SELF	6 CREW	N.F.T.
JULY	23	LANCASTER	5731	SELF	P/O DOWNER SGT. BATES	OPERATIONS — DUISBURG.
					GIBSON HOBSON	1 x 4,000 6 x 500 2 x 250 12,000 ft.
					F/SGT. LEWIS SGT. MERRICK	ON TARGET.
JULY	26	LANCASTER	5731	SELF	6 CREW	N.F.T.
JULY	26	LANCASTER	5731	SELF	P/O DOWNER SGT. BATES	OPERATIONS — HAMBURG.
					GIBSON HOBSON	1 x 4,000 6 x 500 2 x 250. 11,000 ft.
					SGT. MERRICK P/O REES	ON TARGET.
JULY	28	LANCASTER	5731	SELF	6 CREW	N.F.T. To SYERSTON
JULY	31	LANCASTER	5731	SELF	P/O DOWNER SGT. BATES	OPERATIONS — DUSSELDORF
					GIBSON HOBSON	1 x 4,000 12 SBC's (30 lb's) 14,500 ft
					F/SGT. LEWIS SGT. MERRICK	ON TARGET. PHOTO .OF AIMING P.

SUMMARY for JULY. 1942
UNIT "B" Flight 106 Sqdn. 42 AIRCRAFT TYPES
Date 1/8/42
Sign. JW. Heyford F/L.

LANCASTER
OXFORD

JohnLoosdenidge J/L
OC. "B" Flight 106 Sqdn.

P.....? W/C
OC. 106 Sqdn.

GRAND TOTAL [Cols. (1) to (10)]
.....609.....Hrs.......25.....Mins.

TOTALS CARRIED FORWARD

Note on 23 July 1942, John acquires his first B1 type Avro Lancaster *M-Mother* with tail code R5731; he sees it as a 'lucky' plane

JULY 23rd DUISBURG
Bombs: 1 x 4,000, 6 x 500, 2 x 250, ON TARGET
In Avro Lanc R5731 ZN-M (B1)

Notice on this, John's second operation to Duisburg, the log book shows the serial number of his Lancaster Bomber to be R5731. She was a B1 (one of the first Lancasters) and was coded ZN-M (ZN being the squadron two-letter code of 106 Squadron) and M therefore being John's original *M-Mother* Lanc (but not the one he was to use in the Dams Raid because this one is recorded as one of four Lancs lost on the night of 3/4 April 1943, on a raid on Hamburg). Maybe John requested *M-Mother* for the dam raid, as this first ZN-M would prove to be a faithful friend seeing him survive many operations; he would see it as a lucky letter for him.

JULY 26th HAMBURG
Bombs: 1 x 4,000, 6 x 500, 2 x 250, ON TARGET
In Avro Lanc R5731 ZN-M (B1)

There were many attacks on Hamburg in the Second World War due to its being a large port and industrial area, with U-boat pens, oil refineries and a dynamite factory. The destruction on night of 26/27 July 1942 was minor compared with exactly a year later when, after dry weather, the RAF Bomber Command sent every plane it could muster, and the city of Hamburg went up in a fireball of destruction.

John classed it as 'one of the best trips I have done'; it provided his need for an adrenaline rush as he dodged anti-aircraft guns and searchlights. But, having done five operations in two weeks, and quadrupled his operational flying hours in July as compared with June, he is now understandably ready for, and very keen to have, his leave.

RAF Coningsby
28.07.1942

My dearest Mother,

Many thanks again for your last letter. Glad to hear a member of the family will be home at the same time I am. I am definitely getting leave on the 2nd but may not be able to get home until the 3rd as my crew want to have a party in town. I certainly feel like leave now – its over 3 months since I had any and I am looking forward to seeing you all.

I seem to have got a bit behindhand with this letter writing this last week, but we have really been pretty busy. I have done 2 more trips now. The first one was very enjoyable and although we saw fighters and encountered a lot of flak we managed to get the target ok. The second one was one of the best trips I have done and enjoyed. The visibility was

marvellous and we hit our target right slap in the centre. The flak and searchlights were
terrific all the time and held us for over 20 minutes – but no damage to us.

No more news now – will wire you giving definite time of arrival.

Much love to all,

Your loving Son.

JULY 31st: OPERATION DUSSELDORF
Bombs: 1 x 4,000, 12 SBCS (30lbs), ON TARGET

Once again a huge force of aircraft were sent out, and it was the first occasion
when more than 100 Lancasters took part in a raid. Four hundred and eighty-
four aircraft claimed successful bombing, although their photographs showed
that part of the force bombed open country. More than 900 tons of bombs
were dropped.

John's log shows that photographs were taken by someone on his Lancaster; we
know no more from him as he took his leave almost straight after this operation.

Whilst John was away, there was some alarm as to whether the battleship *Prinz
Eugen* might escape into the Atlantic, which, combined with the U-boats, would
have been very serious for our convoys. Also other German warships were causing

John with Marna

concern. With these in mind, Lancasters from No. 5 Group were sent to lay large numbers of mines in the Baltic to stop their passage.

When John returned from leave on 12 August, he was plunged straight into a very heavy bombing schedule.

AUG.15th: OPERATION DUSSELDORF
Bombs: 1 x 4,000, 10 SBCS (30lbs), ON TARGET, Hit by Flak

YEAR 1942		AIRCRAFT		PILOT, OR 1ST PILOT	2ND PILOT, PUPIL OR PASSENGER	DUTY (INCLUDING RESULTS AND REMARKS)
MONTH	DATE	Type	No.			
—	—	—	—	—	—	TOTALS BROUGHT FORWARD
AUG.	1	LANCASTER	8680	SELF	6 CREW	N.F.T.
AUG.	13	LANCASTER	5731	SELF	3 CREW	FROM WOODHALL
AUG.	14	LANCASTER	5901	SELF	4 CREW	N.F.T.
AUG.	15	LANCASTER	5901	SELF	6 CREW	N.F.T. TO SCAMPTON
AUG.	15	LANCASTER	5901	SELF	SGT. BRENNAN, BATES, GIBSON, HOBSON, F/SGT's LEWIS, MERRICK	OPERATIONS – DUSSELDORF. 1×4,000 10×SBC's ON TARGET. 80% OF TOWN VERY CLOUDY. HIT BY FLAK 14,000 ft
AUG.	16	LANCASTER	5731	SELF	4 CREW	N.F.T.
AUG.	16	LANCASTER	5731	SELF	SGT's BRENNAN, BATES, GIBSON HOBSON F/SGT's LEWIS, MERRICK	OPERATIONS – DANZIG. (GDYNIA) GARDENING. 3 MINES. O.K. 700 ft. HIT BY FLAK.
AUG.	18	LANCASTER	5900	SELF	4 CREW	N.F.T.
AUG.	18	LANCASTER	5900	SELF	SGT's BRENNAN, BATES, GIBSON, HOBSON, F/SGT's LEWIS, MERRICK	OPERATIONS – FLENSBERG. 5×1,900 1×1,000. ON TARGET. ? 9,000 THICK HAZE.
AUG.	23	LANCASTER	5551	SELF	4 CREW	L.L. BOMBING
AUG.	24	LANCASTER	5731	SELF	6 CREW	N.F.T.
AUG.	24	LANCASTER	5731	SELF	SGT's BRENNAN, BATES, GIBSON, HOBSON, F/SGT's LEWIS, MERRICK	OPERATIONS – FRANKFURT 1×4,000 10 SBC's. ON TARGET. 10,500 ft. F.W.190 DESTROYED. HIT BY FLAK.
AUG.	26	LANCASTER	5551	SELF	6 CREW	H. L. BOMBING.
AUG.	27	LANCASTER	5551	SELF	6 CREW	N.F.T. AND H.L. BOMBING.
AUG.	27	LANCASTER	5551	SELF	SGT's BRENNAN, BATES, GIBSON, HOBSON, W/O NAYLOR F/SGT MERRICK	OPERATIONS – GDYNIA (GRAF ZEPPLIN 1×5,500 C.S. Bomb. NEAR MISS ON LAND. STBD OUTER U/S. ALL THE TIME. 10,000 ft.
					GRAND TOTAL [Cols. (1) to (10)] 648 Hrs. 50 Mins.	TOTALS CARRIED FORWARD

Another month of very intensive operations and not always in 5731 (*M-Mother*)

Note in the log that Sgt Brennan has joined John's crew; he would be flight engineer for *M-Mother* on Operation Chastise as John's longest serving (and most loyal) crew member.

This was only a comparatively light raid, but two Lancasters were lost and John's was hit by anti-aircraft flak. The weather conditions were poor.

On 15 August the Pathfinder Force was formed, a new RAF marker squadron using GEE.

AUG. 16th: OPERATION DANZIG (GDYNIA)
GARDENING. 3 MINES. HIT BY FLAK
In Avro Lanc R5731 ZN-M (B1)

Gdynia was a Polish seaport city located on the Baltic Sea. It was the first city to be invaded and taken by the Nazis and so was, in effect, the starting place of the Second World War; it became, together with the rest of South West Poland, the German Reichsgau of Danzig (West Prussia). Sixty thousand inhabitants (mainly Polish Jews) were sent to concentration camps.

This minelaying operation was very tough and long (and in the area they codenamed 'Spinach'); John's rear gunman was injured by a piece of flying shrapnel.

AUG. 18th: OPERATION FLENSBERG
Bombs: 5 x 1,900, 1 x 1,000 ON TARGET ?

Flensberg, on the edge of the Baltic Sea (now an independent state on the border of Germany and Denmark), was supposed to be an easy target, especially when on this occasion pathfinders had located and marked the area with flares. However, due to thick haze and unpredicted winds, the bombs apparently landed 25 miles north into Denmark and missed Flensberg.

John puts a question mark in his log, which shows that he hadn't been convinced they had dropped their bombs in the right place.

Note also in the log that on 23 August he did one hour, ten minutes of low-level flying practice, which is interesting in the light of hindsight regarding Operation Chastise.

My dearest Mother,

   Things have been so hectic ever since I came back that I have had little chance to do much writing until today. It was a grand leave and I feel very much better for it. I know that if I hadn't had such a good leave I should have cracked up during this last week or so.

   I have worked it out that I had only 5 hours sleep a day for 7 days! Which included 3 trips in 4 nights!! The first trip [Düsseldorf] was a very ordinary one, but we certainly had a hot time. We were held in lots of searchlights and all the flak seemed to be directed against us – however in spite of filthy weather and everything else, we managed to hit the target and bring back a photo of the town – the only one to do so out of a large force of bombers! We found several flak holes on landing but nothing much to talk about, although one had gone through the petrol tank.

   The next trip [Danzig] was a very long one [nine hours, five minutes according to his log] – in fact one of the longest ever done. I was as tired as hell before we even started, as it was the second night running. Soon after take off my automatic pilot packed up and as I had no 2nd pilot I had to do all the flying – over 9 hours of it. I could hardly stand up when we got back. However we completed our mission very successfully, again in spite of filthy weather all the way there and most of the way back. Again we found a few flak holes after landing. One piece of shrapnel had gone through our rear turret missing my rear gunman by only ½ inch and causing his face to be cut a bit by flying Perspex pieces – however he didn't mind and never said a word.

   The last trip [Flensberg] was not so successful – although we think we got the target. It was a very dark night with lots of haze and therefore it was extremely difficult to see the ground at all.

   The Dieppe show was a good thing I think, though we had nothing to do with it – I only wish we had. ★

   Much love to all,
   Yr loving Son.

★ This refers to the Allied attack on the German-occupied port of Dieppe, Northern France, on 19 August. The objective was to seize and hold a major port for a short period, both to prove it was possible and to gather intelligence from prisoners and captured materials while assessing the German responses. The Allies also wanted to destroy coastal defences, port structures and all strategic buildings. There were a lot of casualties but it helped inform later attacks on similar targets.

John had done three operations in four days, no wonder he says he would have 'cracked up' were it not for his leave.

The following appeared in a newspaper, probably *The Times*, on 22 August 1942:

Act.Flt.Lt. J.V.Hopgood. R.A.F.V.R. No. 106 Squadron. Flt. Lt. Hopgood has participated in a number of successful attacks on enemy and enemy occupied country. On one occasion he made a low level attack on Rostock and also bombed Warnemunde from only 2,000 feet in face of intense opposition.

And on this exact date (22 August 1942), Wing Commander Guy Gibson was officially recommending John for his DFC. See below:

CONFIDENTIAL

RECOMMENDATION FOR A NON-IMMEDIATE AWARD.

Christian Names ... John Vere   Surname ... HOPGOOD
Rank   ... Acting Flight Lieutenant   Number ... 61281
Group ... No.5 (Bomber)   Unit ... No 106 Squadron
Total hours flown on operations ... 183hr 05mn
Number of sorties flown ... 32
Appointment held ... Pilot, Deputy Flight Commander
Recognition for which recommended ... DISTINGUISHED FLYING CROSS

Particulars of Meritorious Service:
The first of Flight Lieutenant Hopgood's operational sorties were made as navigator. He navigated successfully to such objectives as Kiel, Cologne, Hanover and Magdeburg and his bomb-aiming was very accurate – on the Huls Rubber Factory raid, he claimed direct hits.

In April he qualified as Captain and on the eighteen raids he has made he has displayed a magnificent dash and courage, pressing home his attacks whatever the opposition. He made a successful low-level attack on Rostock a few days later, in face of fierce anti-aircraft fire, bombed Warnemunde from only 2000ft. He has taken part in the 'thousand raids', bombed Dusseldorf, Hamburg and Duisburg in the recent heavy attacks and has made successful sorties, one of them Danzig.

Flight Lieutenant Hopgood has shown always the greatest enthusiasm and zest for operational flying, and his commendable initiative and determination have made him an invaluable member of the Squadron.

Signed: Guy Gibson (Wing Commander, Commanding)   Date: 22/8/42
        W.G.Aure (?) (Group Captain, No 106 Squadron, RAF)

Note that John was commended as having 'initiative and determination'. Do you remember how his mother nurtured his initiative by sending him on those trips to France and how his first school report, at the age of 5 years, commended him for his perseverance and determination?

Marna wrote from No. 56 Sheffield Road, Chesterfield, on 23 August 1942. In this letter she declines an engagement to Derek (amazingly using her head rather than her heart), is very scathing about the other men in the unit, clears out some rotten tomatoes and raises her own morale by referring to the Dieppe raid as a successful 'dress rehearsal'. She also refers to her brother John as 'his lordship' following the news that he is to receive an award:

My darling Mummy,

… You may well ask what were in those letters from Derek, actually he only wanted to publish the engagement officially and send me a ring as soon as he arrives. I suppose you want to know what I said! Well, I declined the offer graciously and thought it would be better to wait until he returns before taking the plunge as no doubt we shall be two very different personalities in a year or so's time and it would be such a nuisance cancelling it all, and anyway I don't think I am all that struck at the moment!

… I shan't be able to do any celebrating of J's 21st until after the 15th, but I think I could skip off then for a couple of days. Your description of the zip shaving compactum sounds ok; I think it should suit his lordship!

… The Dieppe raid seems to have been a great success. I must say it had a psychological effect on me, the feeling that at last we were taking the offensive and that my uniform would mean something. A feeling I had very strongly at the beginning of the war, but it has gradually diminished since we have been on the defensive. This is not the talk of a defeatist far from it, but I think it is the truth which most of us have experienced lately. We seem to be quite content to go from day to day in the same old rut of work without exerting ourselves at all to do any extras. ★ I hope that raid was the dress rehearsal and that the performance will follow shortly.

Your ever-loving Daughter.

★ It is interesting to see that Marna thinks the war has been in a rut and there should be more action.

AUG 24th: OPERATION FRANKFURT
Bombs: 1 x 4,000, 10 SBCs (30lbs), ON TARGET, F.W.190 DESTROYED, HIT BY FLAK
In Avro Lanc R5731 ZN-M (B1)

'F.W.190' refers to a Focke-Wulf Würger (Shrike), a German fighter aircraft which was single-seat and single-engine, designed by Kurt Tank in the late 1930s and widely used during the Second World War.

Two hundred and twenty-six aircraft set out towards Frankfurt on this second pathfinder-led raid, and the pathfinder crews again experienced great difficulty in locating the target in cloudy conditions; most of the bombing fell in open country north and west of Frankfurt. Local reports say that some bombs fell in the city (one of which was probably John's).

Please note that in the following log book entries # indicates raids specifically mentioned in Guy Gibson's recommendation for John's Bar to DFC.

#AUG 27th: OPERATION GDYNIA (GRAF ZEPPELIN)
1 x 5,500 C.S. Bomb. Near Miss, On Land, STB'D u/s all the time

On the night of 27/28 August 1942, Lancasters attacked the new German aircraft carrier *Graf Zeppelin*, which was reputed to be almost ready for sailing. This was a one-off operation to destroy her. Each Lancaster carried a single 'Capital Ship' bomb, a 5,500lb device with a shaped charge warhead intended for armoured targets. Seven of the Lancasters reached Gdynia, 950 miles from their base; in the haze, one pilot dropped his bomb by mistake in the harbour, on the estimated position of the German battleship *Gneisenau*, whilst another believed he had scored a direct hit on *Graf Zeppelin* (but no damage was ever reported). If these aircraft had managed to sink the *Graf Zeppelin*, this raid would have ranked as one of the bombing war's epics. No Lancasters were lost.

John's was one of the twelve Lancasters which flew the 950 miles from 106 Squadron's base at Coningsby to Gdynia. The plan was to attack from 6,000ft in brilliant moonlight; instead they found much haze and it seems that John's CS bomb landed the closest with his 'near miss'. As the Germans never did use the *Graf Zeppelin* as an aircraft carrier, it is possible that John's bomb did in fact do some damage.

YEAR 1942		AIRCRAFT		PILOT, OR 1ST PILOT	2ND PILOT, PUPIL OR PASSENGER	DUTY (INCLUDING RESULTS AND REMARKS)
MONTH	DATE	Type	No.			
—	—	—	—	—	—	TOTALS BROUGHT FORWARD
AUG.	31	LANCASTER	5731	SELF	6 CREW	N.F.T.
			for AUGUST	42	LANCASTER	
			"B" Flight 106 Sqdn.		2.	
			Date 1.9.42.		3.	
			Signature W. Hopgood F/Lt.		4.	
			Total wooldevale ... 96 and for w/c ---------------- w/c			
		"B" Flight Commander			O.C. 106 Sqdn.	
		No. 106 Squadron				
SEPT.	1	LANCASTER	5731	SELF	Sgt's BRENNAN, BATES, HOBSON, NEWMAN. f/Sgt's LEWIS, MERRICK.	OPERATIONS — SAARBRÜCKEN. 1 x 4,000 10 SBC's ON TARGET 9,000 f
SEPT	4	LANCASTER	5731	SELF	6 CREW	N.F.T.
SEPT	4	LANCASTER	5731	SELF	Sgt's BRENNAN, BATES, GIBSON, HOBSON, f/Sgt's LEWIS, MERRICK.	OPERATIONS — BREMEN. 1 x 4,000 10 SBC's ON TARGET. 13,000 PHOTO OF DOCKS.
SEPT.	6	LANCASTER	"R" 4118	SELF	1 CREW	TO - FROM SYERSTON.
SEPT.	7	LANCASTER	5731	SELF	6 CREW	N.F.T.
SEPT.	11	LANCASTER	QR."A"	SELF	—	FROM WOODHALL.
SEPT.	12	LANCASTER	4118	SELF	6 CREW	N.F.T.
				GRAND TOTAL [Cols. (1) to (10)] 661 Hrs. 10 Mins.		TOTALS CARRIED FORWARD

Here Guy Gibson's signature is missing from the wing commander slot

#SEPT 1ST: OPERATION SAARBRUCKEN
Bombs: 1 x 4,000, 10 SBCs, ON TARGET
In Avro Lanc R5731 ZN-M (B1)

Out of 231 aircraft that went, there was only one Lancaster (which was John's). Although his log shows 'on target' and the planes did in fact bomb accurately, the pathfinders had illuminated and marked a town which was actually Saarlouis, 13 miles to the north-west and situated in a similar bend of the River Saar. However, in Gibson's recommendation for Bar to DFC, he stated, '[Hopgood] has made several attacks on German targets and in September was one of a very small number of aircraft which bombed Saarbrucken, the primary, whilst others were bombing Saarlouis.' It has to be said that John's navigator Flight Sergeant Bill Bates deserved at least some of the credit. (Apparently this navigator, having completed a full tour of his thirty operations, was asked to join Hopgood for a 'special job', which was Operation Chastise, but his wife, sensibly in hindsight, had instructed him to decline the offer.)

John's 21st birthday on 29 August was celebrated in style: firstly a swim in the sea and then a grand party 'when the whole squadron turned out in force'. What does this tell us about the squadron's team spirit and John's popularity? It was just as well they cancelled his operations as this was to be his last ever birthday.

CONINGSBY
LINCS
2.9.42

My dearest Mother,

What a really lovely present [a bag of shaving equipment] – thank you so very much. Honestly it is just what I wanted. You say you thought I wanted something bigger – no, definitely not, as it would take up too much room in a case. Your telegram arrived ok and also the letters from David B and Richard Hope, as well as letters from U. Harold, Elliot, Marna and Betty and telegrams from O + C, as well as other telegrams – so it was very nice to receive all these on the same day.

My birthday started off with my being detailed for ops again, but fortunately they were scrubbed early on and we were able to go right ahead with the preparations and party. In the afternoon we went over to Skegness and bathed – it was grand. Then we came back here and all the boys gave me a grand party and dinner with plenty of champagne etc. The whole squadron turned out in force and we finished up with a very hilarious party.

Since I last wrote I have done 3 more trips – all very successful and enjoyable. The first one was in particular very satisfying as we shot down a FW 190, one of Germany's latest fighters. The target was a bit hazy and as we were circling around it dodging the flak etc and trying to make dead certain of our position, suddenly my rear gunner reported a fighter coming in to attack, and before much more had been said I could hear the old guns going and then 'Its ok skipper I've shot the b....... down'., and apparently he had as we saw the thing go down in flames and burn on the ground – so we are allowed to claim it as definitely destroyed. Then we eventually bombed the target ok from quite low down – got shot up a bit – just a few holes here and there but nothing vital, and got home ok. [How nonchalant John had become!]

The next trip [Gdynia] was a very long one [eight hours, fifty minutes, the Lancaster carrying a 'Capital Ship' bomb, their biggest bomb yet, and with a starboard engine not working]. After a few runs to make certain we bombed our target and all went well. Actually, after engine trouble before take off one of my engines more or less packed up on the way out and the turrets also but it wasn't bad enough to deter us from going or coming back ok.

The last one [Saarbrucken] was very ordinary and we managed to hit the target right in the centre from quite low down, in spite of a good deal of flak.

Last Sunday we went over to a large house and estate near here owned by some very charming people who invited us over any time to enjoy the garden and swim and play tennis. We had great fun and got some quite good tennis in. It was a great change to get away from the camp if only for an afternoon and evening. We hope to get over there as much as possible now.

Otherwise the news is just the same. Please tell Betty I am writing soon and longing to see and thank her for her present – I can't guess what it is.

Many many thanks once again for your lovely present – by the way the razor is just the sort I wanted – with much love to all,

Your loving Son.

John had not managed to get home for his birthday, but he had had four days break between operations, three days of which he did no flying. Guy Gibson, however, must have been temporarily absent and did not sign his log book this time.

SEPT 4th BREMEN
Bombs: 1 x 4,000, 10 SBCs, ON TARGET. PHOTO of DOCKS
In Avro Lanc R5731 ZN-M (B1)

Bremen in North West Germany was the receiver of ninety-nine attacks by the RAF in the Second World War, being as it was (and still is) an industrial city with a major port on the River Weser. Among the industrial buildings seriously hit on this night were the Weser aircraft works and the Atlas shipyard. Four dockside warehouses were destroyed and three oil-storage tanks were burnt out. Various public buildings, including seven schools and three hospitals, were hit.

Notice that John's operational flying time has dramatically increased to thirty-two hours, thirty minutes for August 1942. And look at September: it goes up to thirty-nine hours, thirty-five minutes. John clearly had a punishing schedule of operations at this time.

SEPT 13th BREMEN
Bombs: 1 x 4,000, 12 SBCs, ON TARGET

The Lloyd dynamo works was put out of action for two weeks and various parts of the Focke-Wulf factory, for from two to eight days.

YEAR 1942 MONTH	DATE	AIRCRAFT Type	No.	PILOT, OR 1ST PILOT	2ND PILOT, PUPIL OR PASSENGER	DUTY (INCLUDING RESULTS AND REMARKS)
—	—	—	–	—	—	— TOTALS BROUGHT FORWARD
SEPT.	13	LANCASTER	4118	SELF	Sgt's THOMAS, BATES, HOBSON, P/O MACKY, F/Sgt's LEWIS, MERRICK.	OPERATIONS — BREMEN. 1 x 4,000 12 SBC's ON TARGET 12,000ft
SEPT.	14	LANCASTER	5901	SELF	Sgt's BRENNAN, BATES, HOBSON, NEWMAN, F/Sgt's LEWIS MERRICK	OPERATIONS — WILHELMSHAVEN 1 x 4,000 10 SBC's ON TARGET 12,000ft PHOTO OF DOCKS.
SEPT.	16	LANCASTER	5731	SELF	6 CREW	N.F.T.
SEPT.	16	LANCASTER	5731	SELF	Sgt's BRENNAN, BATES, HOBSON, NEWMAN, F/Sgt's LEWIS, MERRICK.	OPERATIONS — ESSEN 1 x 4,000 12 SBC's ON TARGET 16,000ft FIGHTER ATTACK.
SEPT.	19	LANCASTER	5731	SELF	6 CREW	N.F.T.
SEPT.	19	LANCASTER	5731	SELF	Sgt's BRENNAN, Sgt BATES HOBSON, NEWMAN, F/Sgt's LEWIS, MERRICK.	OPERATIONS — MUNICH 1 x 4,000 6 SBC's ON TARGET 7,500 ft HYDRAULICS U/S HIT BY FLAK — Bomb Doors Open. JU.88 DAMAGED
SEPT.	23	LANCASTER	5731	SELF	6 CREW	N.F.T.
SEPT.	23	LANCASTER	5731	SELF	Sgt's BRENNAN, Sgt BATES HOBSON, CHRISTIE, F/Sgt's LEWIS, MERRICK.	OPERATIONS — WISMAR (JUNKERS FACTORY) 14 SBC's ON TARGET. 1,500 ft BOAT IN GUN + SUNK
SEPT.	27	LANCASTER	5731	SELF	7 CREW	H.L. BOMBING + FIGHTER AFFILIATION

Summary September 1942
Unit 'B' Flight 106 Sqn.
1.10.42.
W. Hopgood F/o

W. Hopgood F/Lt S/L
O.C. 'B' Flight 106 Sqn.

GRAND TOTAL [Cols. (1) to (10)]
694 Hrs. 35 Mins.

R. Gibson W/c
O.C. 106 Sqn.
TOTALS CARRIED FORWARD

} LANCASTER

Note the punishing schedule of operations

SEPT 14th WILHELMSHAVEN
Bombs: 1 x 4,000, 12 SBCs, ON TARGET. PHOTO of DOCKS

Overnight, 202 RAF bombers attack Wilhelmshaven, Germany, with accurate pathfinder marking (seventy-seven civilians were killed and more than fifty injured).

Despite having so much on his mind, John was still very concerned about his mother:

15 09 1942
Coningsby

My dearest Mother,

I am sorry I have not written for such a long time, but when I get a spot of time off in the evenings I usually feel far too tired to wade through correspondence, and so I am afraid I have been very slack lately about letter writing. Many thanks for your last letter – I'm not sure this bicycling of long distances is at all good for you – please don't go and overdo it.

Since I last wrote I have done 3 more trips [two to Bremen and one to Wilhelmshaven] – all successful and on two of them we got some good photographs of the docks and/or town area. They were all very ordinary – the usual flak and searchlights and nothing out of the ordinary happened to us.

A few days ago I went on another of these factory touring jobs – this time it took 3 days and was a very large one and I had to talk to 1500 workers – I couldn't see the end of the room. The next day I went to another factory which was considerably smaller where there were only about 300 workers to be talked to. However it was a great experience and of course very interesting. On the last night I happened to be near the aerodrome where my old first pilot is stationed so we had a very good party together.

I am expecting leave around the beginning of October – but it might be a week before (at the end of this month), or if not then, then later on about the middle of October. I will let you know as soon as I know definitely.

Much love to all,

Your loving Son.

Meanwhile John was in the thick of intensive operations, going out every two or three nights. Some of his sorties involved taking photos of the damage achieved; this was a very important aid, which informed future operations as to both strategy and target.

Below is the raid schedule showing who was to be in John's crew. Note that his petrol load was 1,660 gallons.

SEPT 16th: OPERATION ESSEN
Bombs: 1 x 4,000, 12 SBCs, ON TARGET FIGHTER ATTACK
In Avro Lanc R5731 ZN-M (B1)

Essen, another German industrial city, and a difficult target due to its heavy defence, was successfully bombed by 369 aircraft on this night. The Krupps works, famous for its steel production and for manufacture of ammunition and armaments, and in fact the largest company in Europe, was hit, not just by bombs but by a crashing bomber loaded with incendiaries.

SEPT 19th: OPERATION MUNICH
Bombs: 1 x 4,000, 6 SBCs, ON TARGET
HIT BY FLAK. HYDRAULICS U/S, JU 88 DAMAGED
In Avro Lanc R5731 ZN-M (B1)

A group of Lancasters (sixty-eight) and Stirlings (twenty-one) attacked Munich, and although most of the bombs fell within 3 miles of the centre of Munich, the bombing was not accurate enough to hit desired targets. John claims to have shot and badly damaged a Ju 88 on this trip. The Junkers Ju 88 was a German Luftwaffe twin-engine, multi-role aircraft and became one of the most versatile combat aircraft of the Second World War.

SEPT 23rd: OPERATION WISMAR (JUNKERS FACTORY)
14 SBCs, ON TARGET BEAT UP GUNS AND SEARCHLIGHTS
In Avro Lanc R5731 ZN-M (B1)

Wismar was a small German port, but it had a factory, called the Dornier factory, making Junker planes (see above). The operation was successful.

Life was anything but dull for John at the moment, but he arranged to be home on leave for his mother's birthday and wrote to her:

Coningsby
Lincs
26.9.42

My dearest Mother,

Many thanks for your last letter. It must be very dull for you at home without the 'children' around. Anyway I'm expecting leave around the middle of next month, October probably the 18th – so I shall be home for your birthday.

I have done another 3 trips since last writing. All of them were quite exciting. The first one to a very heavily defended place [Essen] in bad weather was very ordinary except that we were attacked by a fighter again. After an exchange of fire we saw no more of him and we claim him as damaged.

The next trip [Munich] was a long one in bright moonlight and clear weather – hence it was very pleasant flying. On the way out however we were again attacked by a fighter – a JU88. This time we exchanged quite a good bit of fire and we claim it as badly damaged – we could see our tracer going right into him.★ We received one or two small holes but no serious damage so carried on. The target was easy to find and we dropped our stuff right in the middle of it. However we got hit twice while doing the bombing run and collected some pretty big holes – so had to come all the way back with my bomb doors open, hydraulics unserviceable and 10 inches of flap still down.

The last trip [Wismar] was not so pleasant as regards weather but we managed to hit our target from a low level. Once again we were attacked by a fighter, but this time no shooting, as we outmanoeuvred him. **

I can't think of any more news as there is little else that we do here. I had dinner the other night and met Mrs Portal – wife of the big noise's brother. ***

Much love to all,

Your loving Son.

PS My wireless officer got a DFM a day or two ago.

★ Tracers are bullets built with a small pyrotechnic charge of magnesium or phosphorous in their base, making the projectile visible to the naked eye once ignited. It enables aiming corrections as the shooter watches its projectile.

** By corkscrewing?

*** Air Chief Marshal Sir Charles Portal; it was he who signalled from Washington on 14 May that Operation Chastise (Dambusters' Raid) should proceed.

At the end of September 1942 the Hampden aircraft was withdrawn from operations, and No. 5 Group was now unique in being the first all-Lancaster Group. But it was unable to deploy all its Lancasters due to fuel installation problems: only eighty out of two hundred were serviceable.

John now moved to Syerston with 106 Squadron, 61 Squadron and Wing Commander Guy Gibson. Whilst he continued to be fully immersed in operations, Betty started teacher training at the Charlotte Mason College in Ambleside, the Lake District, which put a large emphasis on 'Nature Study' and so really suited her. Of her experiences there, she says:

> It being war-time food was severely rationed. Feeling hungry was a common experience. Heating was another problem; there was little heat in any of the buildings so we resorted to warm cloaks or coats. Chilblains were a common complaint on toes and fingers. Clothes were rationed because of the war, and used up a lot of coupons, so my sister Joan had to contribute some of her coupons to get me dressed out for college!

OCT 1st: OPERATION WISMAR
Bombed Warnemunde. HAZY 14 SBCs Landed Kirmington
In Avro Lanc R5731 ZN-M (B1)

The RAF attacked this small port on the Baltic in Northern Germany with seventy-eight Lancasters of No. 5 Group. Bombing was scattered and two aircraft were lost.

YEAR 1942.		AIRCRAFT		PILOT, OR 1ST PILOT	2ND PILOT, PUPIL OR PASSENGER	DUTY (INCLUDING RESULTS AND REMARKS)
MONTH	DATE	Type	No.			
						106 Sqdn. SYERSTON.
—	—	—	—	—	—	— TOTALS BROUGHT FORWARD
OCT.	1	LANCASTER	5731	SELF	6 CREW	To SYERSTON WITH 106 Sqn.
OCT.	1	LANCASTER	5731	SELF	Sgt. BRENNAN P/O BATES	OPERATIONS — WISMAR. BOMBED
					HOBSON, NEWHAN,	WARNEMUNDE. HAZY. 5,000 ft.
					P/Sgt's LEWIS, MERRICK	14 SBC's LANDED KIRMINGTON
OCT.	2	LANCASTER	5731	SELF	6 CREW	To BASE.
OCT.	5	LANCASTER	5731	SELF	6 CREW	N.F.T.
OCT.	5	LANCASTER	5731	SELF	Sgt. BRENNAN, P/O. BATES	OPERATIONS — AACHEN
					HOBSON, P/Sgt's DAGG	1 x 4,000 12 SBC's. ON TARGET. 10,000
					LEWIS, MERRICK.	
OCT.	8	LANCASTER	5731	SELF	6 CREW	LOW-LEVEL FORMATION PRACTISE
OCT.	9	LANCASTER	5731	SELF	6 CREW	LOW-LEVEL FORMATION PRACTISE
OCT.	10	LANCASTER	5731	SELF	6 CREW	VERY LOW-LEVEL FORMATION PRACTISE
OCT.	11	LANCASTER	5731	SELF	7 CREW	VERY LOW-LEVEL FORMATION PRACTISE
OCT.	13	LANCASTER	5731	SELF	Sgt. BRENNAN, P/O. BATES,	OPERATIONS — KIEL.
					HOBSON, LEWIS,	1 x 4,000 9 SBC's ON TARGET. 12,000
					P/Sgt's LEWIS, MERRICK	PHOTO.
OCT.	15	LANCASTER	5731	SELF	Sgt. BRENNAN, P/O. BATES	OPERATIONS — COLOGNE
					HOBSON, LEWIS	1 x 4,000 12 SBC's ON TARGET. 11,000
					P/Sgt's LEWIS, MERRICK	Ju.88 DAMAGED
OCT.	17	LANCASTER	5731	SELF	Sgt. BRENNAN, P/O. BATES	OPERATIONS — LE CREUSOT (DAYLIGHT)
					HOBSON, LEWIS,	10 x 500. ON POWER STATION. 150 ft.
					P/Sgt. LEWIS, MERRICK.	A/c EXTENSIVELY DAMAGED BY BOMB BURSTS
						RETURNED ON 3 ENGINES. BURST TYRE. ALL
						PETROL TANKS HOLED. LANDED CROUGHTON
					GRAND TOTAL [Cols. (1) to (10)] 94 LANCASTERS IN FORMATION. FACTORY	TOTALS CARRIED FORWARD
					744 Hrs. 50 Mins.	

Note the mention of PHOTO on 13 October and formation flying

OCT 5th: OPERATION AACHEN
Bombs: 1 x 4,000 12 SBCs ON TARGET
In Avro Lanc R5731 ZN-M (B1)

Aachen was a small spa city on the highly defended western edge of Germany, part of the Siegfried Line; the Allies hoped to capture it to enable them to advance into the industrialised Ruhr Basin, which they eventually did. However on this smaller operation, 257 aircraft (including 74 Lancasters) attacked Aachen and most of the bombs fell off target. Six aircraft crashed in England, possibly in thunderstorms.

OCT 13th: OPERATION KIEL
Bombs: 1 x 4,000, 9 SBCs ON TARGET PHOTO
In Avro Lanc R5731 ZN-M (B1)

Kiel, the capital city of Northern Germany, was a major naval base and shipbuilding centre of the German Reich; it also produced submarines. On this raid, 288 aircraft (including 82 Lancasters) were employed, but a decoy fire site was operating and at least half of the bombing was drawn away into open countryside, although the rest of the attack fell on Kiel and its immediate surroundings.

Syerston
Notts
14th Oct 1942

My dearest Mother,

After a good many days we have at last got settled in here and it certainly is very pleasant. We are quite near to Nottingham now and of course have done one or two sorties into it. Our station commander is my old squadron commander. You remember the little bloke I used to tell you about – and he is incredibly good and kind to us all. In fact we are all very happy here and it should be great fun always.

Since I last wrote, rather a long time I'm afraid, I have done another three trips, two of them [Wismar and Kiel] very successful and the other [Aachen] due to appalling weather not so successful. Nothing much out of the ordinary happened on them, but they were all very interesting and on the last one we got a good photograph of the target area. ★

Leave is still not definitely fixed. It all depends on when a new flight commander comes. I have been 'acting' for some time now, but all being well he should arrive in another 2 or 3 days, in which case I shall get off on leave on the 20th until the 29th. Do by all means have Uncle Edwin to stay, why on earth not? I should like to see him again. I will wire you the exact date of my leave as soon as I know. It certainly will be a change to get a spot of leave, I've only had one week in nearly six months (instead of 6 weeks) in which time I have done about 30 trips.

Looking forward to seeing you,
Much love to all,
Your loving Son.

★ This involved the crew maintaining a straight and level run (the bombing run) for twenty to thirty seconds after they had dropped their weapons, waiting for a time delay flash bomb (released with their weapons) to detonate above their target and illuminate a time delay photograph. As bombing had previously been notoriously inaccurate, this encouraged crews to concentrate their efforts on the target and ensured the sortie being counted towards their total number of operations. Gibson had become very 'target photography' minded.

So John was 'Acting Flight Commander', awaiting the arrival of Sq Ld John Searby and Sq Ld Peter Ward-Hunt, both of whom were to make an indomitable trio with Guy Gibson.

The station commander mentioned, who came to Syerston in April 1942 and whom everyone loved, was Group Captain Gus Walker; he had previously been a bomber pilot and squadron commander of 50 Squadron (John's previous squadron) at RAF Syerston. Squadron Leader Gus Walker lost his right arm when he rushed, in a fire truck, from the control tower to a taxiing Lancaster Bomber which was on fire in an attempt to remove incendiary bombs with a rake from under the bomb bay to prevent a 4,000lb bomb from exploding. But it detonated. (This happened on 8 December 1942 whilst John was away from Syerston on a forty-eight-hour leave.) Returning to active service with an artificial arm, he was referred to by personnel as the one-armed bandit and was awarded the Croix de Guerre and Légion d'honneur; he later became Air Chief Marshal and received a knighthood.

OCT 15th: OPERATIONS – COLOGNE
Bombs: 1 x 4,000, 12 SBCs ON TARGET JU 88 damaged
In Avro Lanc R5731 ZN-M (B1)

During the Second World War, Cologne was one of the Military Area Command Headquarters in Germany; there were 262 air raids on this city during the war. However, this particular raid was not a successful one: winds were different from those forecast and the pathfinders had difficulty in establishing their position and marking the target sufficiently to attract the Main Force away from a large decoy fire site which received most of the bombs.

It was reported in the RCAF log:

> On the night of 15/16th October 1942, Lancaster 'M' was returning from target, Cologne, bombs having been dropped, flying at 15,000 feet, A.S.I. [Air Speed Indicator] 200 [mph] and losing height, when about 10 minutes from the Dutch coast it was attacked from a range of 150 yards from 200 feet below by a Ju.88 identified by both gunners and firing cannon and machine gun. Its fire was answered by the Rear Gunner (Flight Sergeant Merrick) … and the violent evasive action taken, by the pilot [Flt Lt Hopgood] on the third attack was so effective that the enemy aircraft did not open fire … Our gunners fired about 100 rounds per gun on each attack.★ … The Ju 88 is claimed as damaged.

★ As John was an excellent pilot, dauntless, and by this time completely at one with his Lancaster *M-Mother*, it is almost certain that this 'evasive action' he took was the 'corkscrewing', for which Lancaster Bombers were renowned and which became the standard action against a night fighter. Corkscrewing involved the pilot, throwing the Lancaster into violent dives to starboard, screaming through the air at up to 300mph, then jerking it upwards in a steep climb to port, often losing 1,000ft with each dive, until the attacker (Ju 88 in this case) had been evaded. Having no power controls or electronics, sheer strength in arms and legs was needed to operate flaps, ailerons and rudders, and the Lancaster would creak and groan; it was a testament to the strength of the pilot, and the manoeuvrability of this heavy bomber, that the Lancaster survived the strain of being flown like a stunt plane, even when it had a full bomb bay.

From 8–11 October John had been on intensive low-level flying and very low-level formation flying practice between operations. At first each squadron practised separately, then three squadrons would join up to form a wing and finally there was an elaborate exercise of No. 5 Group as a whole (all nine squadrons). Although not in tight formation, they were as compact as possible and flew across England as if on a mock operation. They were met by Fighter Command, who staged a dummy attack and found it very difficult to get out of the slipstream, then the formation turned and made for the Wainfleet Sands bombing range, opening out into an arc of some 25 miles before closing in again towards the target, where they dropped practice bombs. Very exciting. And think of the gut-vibrating roar of all those Lancasters; it must have been the mother of all air displays.

Unbeknown to John or any of the crews, they were practising for the daylight attack on the Schneider-Creusot work; John was one of the ninety-four Lancasters taking part, and the operation was codenamed 'Robinson' (Creusot was apt to be pronounced 'Crusoe' by the English.). Secrecy had been vital; the first fortnight in October saw several false alarms, when aircraft were loaded with bombs for this attack which was then cancelled.

#OCT 17th: OPERATIONS - LE CREUSOT (daylight)
Bombs: 10 x 500 ON POWER STATION 150ft.
94 LANCASTERS IN FORMATION Factory Destroyed
RETURNED ON 3 ENGINES, BURST TYRE, ALL PETROL TANKS HOLED,
LANDED CROUGHTON
In Avro Lanc R5731 ZN-M (B1)

This famous raid was carried out against the large Schneider factory at Le Creusot, situated more than 300 miles inside France. The factory (the French equivalent to Krupps) produced heavy-calibre guns, railway engines and possibly tanks and armoured cars. A large workers' housing estate was situated at one end of the factory. It was deemed the highest priority target in France. However, against Bomber Command's advice, Harris ordered an attack by day a very risky undertaking, to protect French civilian lives, at low level, to avoid anti-aircraft guns. For 300 miles the Lancasters flew at tree-top level across France, but once there, rose to a higher altitude and dropped nearly 140 tons of bombs. Eighty-eight aircraft bombed the Schneider factory; the other six attacked a nearby transformer station, which supplied the factory with electricity. The success of the attack, largely due to very accurate weather forecasting, was a remarkable feat of navigation and airmanship. Only one of the ninety-four Lancasters taking part was lost. Armament production was stopped for some time, and it took another two years before the power station was working again.

Wing Commander Guy Gibson's official report on the bombing of the Schneider Armament Factory at Le Creusot, France (after which John was awarded a Bar to his DFC), included the following:

> In addition to the main target, a formation of six aircraft were detailed to bomb the Montchanin Power Station – a vital target which, if hit, would cause chaos and confusion, cutting off all lights between the French Alps and Paris. In this formation, No 106 Squadron was represented by W/C G.P.Gibson DFC and F/L J.V.Hopgood DFC. The attack was made from 500 feet, each aircraft carrying 10 x 500lb bombs. Both crews claim that their bombs straddled the target – a claim which was justified by later reports which stated that the transformer house would take nearly two years to repair. Our two aircraft then circled the target and between them fired 1,000 rounds of ammunition into the transformers – a satisfactory and spectacular operation which brought forth vivid blue flashes each time a bullet hit a vital spot.
>
> All squadron aircraft returned safely and undamaged with the exception of W/C Gibson's (slightly holed) and F/L Hopgood's which was damaged by the blast of its own bombs, F/L Hopgood [incidentally this was the last trip of his tour] being a little too enthusiastic and bombing from below safety height.

John, having done so many raids without a break, was, it seems, becoming a little kamikaze; note he had gone down to 150ft on this operation. He wrote to Joan (his older half-sister) on 23 October 1942:

Dear Joan,

I have now completed 46* trips over Hunland, and much against my will have just been taken off for a few months rest. My last trip was the daylight to Le Creusot in France – very interesting, very exciting and great fun. Flying over France at nought feet, we could see all the panic that was going on. Cattle and sheep stampeded all over the place and completely spoilt the farmer's beautifully straight furrows, whilst the farmer waved frantically at us – I'm afraid he wasn't too friendly. However most people were very friendly and waved a great deal, others just stood still and gaped, whilst others picked up small children and ran for shelter misguidedly thinking we meant them harm I suppose. On one occasion 2 cattle jumped into a canal! The chateaux in the Loire district were *truly beautiful in the late afternoon shadows, and it seemed out of place to be tearing along to make war. Actually when we got there it was well worth it, and, although we suffered extensive damage while bombing and had to do one of those limping efforts home, I thoroughly enjoyed it and landed safely with no-one injured – though how I don't know as we had something like 100 holes, suffered from our own bomb bursts, and also a few flak holes from a solitary very rude machine gun. My crew were very thrilled especially the 2 Americans – it was very funny hearing them try to pronounce the French names!*

We have had a number of encounters with night fighters lately and as a result have one definitely destroyed and 2 Ju88s damaged. Our record therefore, which is painted on the side of my aircraft together with the number of trips done looks impressive. Above the record is a picture of Hoppity (the nearest cartoon figure name to my own), and our aircraft for no apparent reason is called Hoppity. Unfortunately after our last effort in it the machine will be some time before it sees service again.

Your brother John.

★ John's log book, however, records not forty-six but forty-seven trips/operations to date.

Indeed, for John, it was the end of that first *M-Mother*. However, according to RAF records, Lancaster R5731 was eventually lost raiding Hamburg on the night of 3/4 April 1943 (one of four lost that night).

Of course, this aircraft was called 'Hoppity' after his now confirmed nickname 'Hoppy'.

From October onwards No. 5 Group and Bomber Command concentrated on the Mediterranean offensive against Italy, and, by minelaying, on protecting the convoys travelling to invade North Africa against U-boats. German industrialised cities were relegated to second place in priority.

Hoppity

John, having now completed forty-seven operations in all (the normal tour of operations being thirty), was taken off operations at this point, and Wing Commander Guy Gibson and his comrades in 106 Squadron must have been worried about him and knew he was about to be decorated, so they sent him this telegram:

CONGRATULATIONS HOPPY GLAD TO KNOW YOU ARE COMPLETELY RESTED BUT YOU'LL SOON GET OUT OF THAT FEELING WHEN YOU ARE BACK HERE AND KNOW YOUR NEW JOB – WINGCO AND THE BOYS.

So John was about to be showered in glory.

YEAR		AIRCRAFT		PILOT, OR	2ND PILOT, PUPIL	DUTY
1942		Type	No.	1ST PILOT	OR PASSENGER	(INCLUDING RESULTS AND REMARKS)
MONTH	DATE					
—	—	—	—	—	—	— TOTALS BROUGHT FORWARD
OCT.	18	MANCHESTER	7434	S/L SEARBY SELF	7 CREW	FROM CROUGHTON
				OCTOBER 'B' flight 106 Sqd. 21. 10. 42.	42	LANCASTER
				OC. 'B' flight.		OC. 106 Sqn.
						A very fine operational tour. This officer has pressed home his attacks with great determination and he has shown himself to be one of the most outstanding captains of No 5 Group. DSO. DFC. OC 106.
					GRAND TOTAL [Cols. (1) to (10)] 745 Hrs 30 Mins	TOTALS CARRIED FORWARD

Here Guy Gibson writes that John is 'one of the most outstanding captains of No.5 Group' at the end of his operational tour

8

Per Ardua Ad Astra (Through Adversity, to the Stars)

The motto of the RAF aptly describes John's demanding pilot-journey to the stardom of his DFC awards.

On his return from his enforced leave he wrote the following 'thank you' postcard to his mother:

11.42

Address remains the same. Have a very good job (non-operational).

Had a grand leave thank you. Met and lunched with Uncle Mocar and had a very good time with my crew, needless to say. Sorry to miss Marna this leave.

Love to all, John

Joan (Marna and John's half-sister), who was a factory inspector (and when she retired in July 1965 received an MBE for her work), wrote to Grace on 10 November 1942 from Penn Road, Wolverhampton:

My dear Marna [Joan's name for Grace, her stepmother],

Your letter with all the family gave me much joy. It is splendid about John and I am enjoying a little reflected glory. I bet he deserved it too without taking into account Le Creusot. His letter giving a racey account of that effort arrived a few days before but he didn't mention the award though I expect he knew about it. I wonder if you'll go up to the palace?! I expect the village is also swelling with pride. ★ A boy in Crowbourne recently got one and that village looks upon it as their own!

I am glad that E is so happy and hope that she will qualify to stay on and finish the training.

M.J. (Marna Jane) seems to be seeing a life and will have a much better time and meet nicer people with her commission. In fact as far as I can see all the family seem to have landed on their feet.

I am really rather envious that I haven't been able to take advantage of war opportunities, as it were! However I expect I ought to feel glad that I can just go on doing my job which seems to get more complicated every day. Our last young man is going next Monday so I anticipate having to do more of heavier industries. Anyhow there do not seem to be many jobs from which women are now excluded, the majority of them are doing very good work (lighter side); jobs in which men felt that they had an unrestricted field. A lot of the male element are having to sit up and increase their output considerably to prevent themselves being outclassed. It 's jolly good for all of them!

We still farm quite hard and are now pulling and chopping beet, the latter is good fun but the former terribly back-aching! I can only manage Sundays and I usually get about 20 others to come out in the lorry and they are a good crowd and work well. All the others who looked upon it as 'a day in the country' have mercifully dropped out!

I hope to get a week end off before Christmas. If any of the young ones get any leave will you let me know as it seems so long since I saw any of them?

Much love Joan

★The village mentioned was Shere.

This letter is a marvellous statement, a triumph for the social history of women's emancipation. To quote Joan, 'Women are now doing jobs in which men felt that they had a restricted field', and she knew her stepmother (who was at heart a feminist) would be thinking the same. The war, though a dark cloud, had some silver linings, and one of those was to raise the profile of women in our society.

The 4 November 1942 saw the Second Battle of El Alamein, where Allied forces broke the Axis line and forced them all the way back to Tunisia. Winston Churchill said of this victory, 'Now this is not the end. It is not even the beginning of the end, but it is, perhaps, the end of the beginning.' After the war, he wrote, 'Before Alamein we never had a victory. After Alamein, we never had a defeat.' It was to pave the way towards victory for the Allies in North Africa, which would coincide with the Dams Raid. John expresses his delight at this success towards the end of his next letter.

John, returning from his two weeks enforced leave, was put onto testing the new Hercules-powered Mk II Lancasters and training new pilots.

RAF Syerston
10th Nov 1942

My dearest Mother,

Many thanks for your letter and also for enclosing all the others. I have had quite a number of others since including one from Wilfred Fison who is still up North but expecting to get to a squadron soon. My CO [Guy Gibson] wrote in my log book 'A very fine operational tour. This officer has pressed home his attacks with great determination and has shown himself to be one of the most outstanding captains in No 5 group.' Number 5 Group consists of 180 pilots or so.

I have a very nice job now, doing the job of a test pilot, testing out various new things etc. It's a very easy life and the best thing about it is that I am still on the same station with all my friends. The weather has been filthy lately so I have had little to do.

I went out to dinner the other night and met some very interesting people and heard some new things about the war and politicians. Isn't the news grand! At last it looks as if we made the first move and annoyed the Hun intensely. I hope the Russians are feeling a bit more pleased now. I should love to bomb Vichy. ★

I really did enjoy my leave and haven't eaten so much for a long time. Looking forward to Christmas. Much love to all,

Your loving Son.

★Vichy was the origin of 'Vichy France', a term which refers to a wartime government based in that city, south of Paris, and was later to be extensively criticised.

Marna wrote to John on 21 November from Officers' Mess, Drill Hall, Clay Cross, Derbyshire, delighted with his success:

My dearest little Brother,

I expect you have had thousands of pats on the back and perhaps one more from me could be accepted. I am thrilled to know that I shall be able to see you collect the old 'gong'. I hope you did receive a delayed telegram a week or so ago but I sent it to the old address.

I suppose you have had heaps of celebration parties, I can almost visualise a 'Worthington' standing in front of the King in the shoes of J.V.H.!! Aren't I rude?

If you have to send names up for the ceremony, you could attach my full title which no doubt would entitle us to the front row! I am still only Subaltern.

I was very annoyed to miss you on leave by 3 days but no amount of wangling could have got me off then so I didn't try it on – I had a lovely quiet time, sleeping and eating, walking and then sleeping again. It was a great change to the hectic existence I live here.

I am entirely on my own in this smutty mining village with a detachment of ATS – I like it on the whole but there are moments when I would give anything to see the sun clear and bright in a blue sky – the unit we are attached to is not too hot – RASC! ★ *However some of the officers are very nice, and they pull my leg unmercifully in the mess – I expect they are rather long suffering having me around!*

… Last night the ENSA people performed 'Arms and the Man', they had one or two west end actors in it so the result was a tip top show. ★★

… I hope the King doesn't require your presence on Dec 13th or round about, because I have an important engagement on which I couldn't miss – laugh if you like, but someone has written a sketch for me – he thinks I can act!

An offer of carting this to the letter box I can't refuse.

Please don't bother to answer but do send me a wire when you know the date, because I will get my stockings darned!

Good Luck,

Love Marna.

★ The Royal Army Service Corps.

★★ The ENSA was the Entertainments National Service Association, an organisation set up in 1939 to provide entertainment for British armed forces personnel during; Gracie Fields, of course, did a great deal for ENSA and brought her songs to so many servicemen and women in the Second World War.

Note that even though Marna was thrilled to bits for her brother, she didn't want his DFC presentation to interfere with her newly emerging theatrical interests.

John was still doing quite a bit of flying, testing fuel consumption and performance when using different fuels in the aircraft under different stresses. He was also training others, to keep up with the need for new pilots, and even flew over his home in Shere (see next letter) and saw someone in the garden.

106 Squadron in front of a Lancaster. John is seventh from left (note black shoes); Shannon is fourth from left

RAF Syerston
Lincs
21.11.42

My dearest Mother,

   Many thanks for your last letter. It must be very depressing for you all alone at home
without any of we 'children' around.

   There is not much news from here. My rear-gunner, a Yankee, has been awarded a
DFM for shooting down all our fighters. The King came here for a visit a few days ago
and was very impressed. He had a few words with me about my job, decoration, etc. He
looked very tired and haggard, but what impressed everybody, talked very naturally and
was full of laughter and good humour. I suppose I shall see him again soon, and you and
Marna as well.

   My job remains very interesting though the weather lately has been rather adverse. By the
way, did you notice me flying around in the Lancaster on Tuesday or Wednesday last I think
it was? I encircled several times and came down fairly low once. I saw someone in the garden.

   I am hoping to get a 48hr pass round about Dec 11th, as my old flight commander is
getting married then in Kent.★ So I should be able to get home for a night at least then.

   Lots of love to all,

   Yr loving Son.

★ John's old flight commander referred to here is John Wooldridge. John is shown third from
right (Dave Shannon is shown fifth from right) in the following picture taken at that wedding;
it is the last photo of John taken in his uniform.

The last picture of John in uniform

On 27 November 1942, to coincide with the exact time that Guy Gibson recommended John for a Bar to his DFC:

F/Lt. J.V. HOPGOOD, DFC 106 Sqdn
This officer has completed many successful operations since being awarded the DFC. One night in August he was detailed to bomb objectives at the port of Gdynia. His attack which was pressed home with the greatest determination, achieved excellent results. On another occasion in October, during the daylight attack on Le Creusot, Flt/Lt Hopgood participated in a particularly daring attack on the electrical transformer station, which was bombed effectively from a height of only 500 ft. In all his work with the squadron he has displayed the greatest keenness and devotion to duty.

CONFIDENTIAL

RECOMMENDATION FOR A NON-IMMEDIATE AWARD.

Christian Names … John Vere	Surname … HOPGOOD
Rank … Acting Flight Lieutenant	Number … 61281
Group … No.5 (Bomber)	Unit … No 106 Squadron

Total hours flown on operations … 269hr 50mn
Number of sorties flown … 45
Appointment held … Pilot
Recognition for which recommended … BAR TO DISTINGUISHED FLYING CROSS

Particulars of Meritorious Service:
Since being awarded the DFC after carrying out 32 successful bombing sorties, Flight Lieutenant Hopgood has gone on to complete another fourteen raids, all of which have been highly successful. His total flying time is 270 hours.

One night in August, he was detailed to attack a German capital ship lying in the Polish harbour of Gdynia.★ By pressing home his attack with great determination, his very large bomb is believed to have burst within thirty yards of its objective. He has made several attacks on German targets and in September was one of a very small number of aircraft which bombed Saarbrucken, the primary, whilst others were bombing Saarlouis.

On another occasion in October, Flight Lieutenant Hopgood was detailed to attack the Switch House and Transmitter Station at Le Creusot. So keen was he to hit his objective that he pressed home his attack from a height of only 500ft, his bombs bursting right across the objective and helping to destroy it completely.

He has brought his crew up to a state of high efficiency and has consistently brought back photos of the aiming point.

Flight Lieutenant Hopgood has been a Deputy Flight Commander in this Squadron for six months, and by always flying on most dangerous missions, he has set a standard which is still discussed and remembered by the aircrews of this Squadron.

Signed: Guy Gibson (Wing Commander, Commanding)   <u>Date: 27/11/42</u>
PAWheller (?) (Group Captain, No. 106 Squadron, RAF)

*This seems to be inaccurately stated: the boat was actually the *Graf Zeppelin* and the type of bomb was called a 'Capital Ship' (carried by John in Lanc AJ 5551, not *M-Mother*).

John's great-great-nephew, Ben, next to a bouncing bomb at Abbotsbury, Dorset

Now John was going from glory to more glory, and he was being recognised for his extreme courage and fortitude.

Meanwhile, still unbeknown to John, scientist Dr Barnes Wallis was about to trial his bouncing bomb on the fleet along the Chesil Bank in Dorset. He had been convinced for a while that the way to win the war was by destroying water supplies, or 'white coal' targets, i.e. dams which not only provided domestic water supplies but also the hydro-electricity that powered the factories making weapons and planes. Although Harris was extremely sceptical, his boss Portal was keen to give it a chance. Five bomb trials took place at Chesil Bank between 4 December 1942 and 13 February 1943.

Christmas 1942

During the Christmas of 1942 the Hopgood family were all scattered, and Grace knew that neither Marna nor John would be able to get leave home for Christmas.

> *RAF Syerston*
> *Nottingham*
> *22.12.42*

My dearest Mother,

Here's wishing you a very happy Christmas. I hope this will arrive in time for the day. I wish I could get home for the feast, but I am afraid it is quite out of the question.

I have been able to do nothing about presents yet. I have been busy every day lately and had no chance to do my shopping. I gather from blokes who have tried shopping that it is well nigh impossible to buy anything decent, so I think I will buy books all round unless anybody wants anything else in particular.

Perhaps you could let me know! I am not doing anything about other members of the family except the immediate ones, nor am I sending any Christmas cards, as I consider them an entirely unnecessary waste of paper; I hope people won't mind.

In case my Christmas wishes arrive late to others of the family will you please convey all my best wishes to any you may see.

Christmas here promises to be a gay affair. I am all set for 2 Christmas dinners, one in the mess at luncheon and one with some very charming people who have a lovely house near the 'drome in the evening and shall have to starve on the 23rd!!

As I said before I have been pretty busy lately with lots of flying – its been a great change from periods of idleness due to bad weather. 3 of my old crew have been granted commissions, and another refused one.* It's a small appreciation.

I went to a very good Army OCTU party the other night. Although it was a good party, there were a lot of Army types who completely fell into my general category of 'Brown jobs' as we call them.** However we were well treated and were the last to leave.

Must stop now – lots of love to all at home and best wishes for a happy Christmas,
Your loving Son.

★John was commended in his Bar to DFC as having brought up a highly efficient crew, and he
is pleased they have been commissioned, i.e. made officers.
★★John had clearly not entirely lost his family's judgemental attitudes.

Actually Betty did not go home for Christmas either; she stayed at the Charlotte
Mason College with mumps.

On 26 December, Boxing Day, Marna wrote:

My darling Mummy,
    … Poor mummy you must have had a very quiet Christmas with us all away, I think
without exception all the mess rang up their respective parents on Friday morning. My call
to you came through in under 5 minutes! I had a hectic day and only managed half the
church service! In the evening, we in the mess had our meal; we became very merry towards
the end of the evening and ended up dancing a peculiar variety of musical chairs!
    I had quite a nice collection of presents, thank you very much for the hood, it is perfectly
lovely. I am very tempted to wear it with my uniform, but I hardly think I could! A lovely
box of Cox's orange pippins arrived from Caterham, and two nice ties from Uncle Edwin.
I must show you Aunty Amy's little gift, I suspected the wrappings so did not open it in
the mess – it was a 17th century pink garter with a purse attached thereto!!! I suppose I
can now add letters to my name appertaining to the order of the garter! …
    Your ever-loving Daughter

Both Marna and John seem to have had a good Christmas, Marna commenting
that 'All the senior NCOs and the officers waited on the men at dinner, the spirit
of comradeship was terrific, we were just all boys and girls together full of the
Christmas feeling'.
    John had flown around on Christmas Eve, flying low over his home, Hurstcote,
and Shere village; it was his way of saying 'Happy Christmas' to his family and
friends. His mother had apparently noticed the low-flying plane, which one
could hardly miss as John didn't take a Tiger Moth but, it seems from his log
book, the Lancaster Bomber, with five crew. The low roar of this plane vibrating
through the village must have sounded like a tiger let loose on Shere; I should
think the villagers either cowered in fright or, if more inquisitive, came out to see
what it was all about. John's mother ran into the garden and was thrilled to see a
Lancaster, knowing it must be her son.
    John was, however, still very concerned about his mother's health.

OFFICERS MESS,
RAF SYERSTON,
NR NOTTINGHAM
1.1.43

My dearest Mother,

I do hope you got my telegram today all right bearing with it all my best wishes and love for 1943, as also does this letter.

I am very sorry to hear your ankles are giving trouble – please take everything easily and give yourself a good rest – even if you do feel so full of energy. Are you sure that there isn't a cure – at any rate I'm sure something can be done to get them better. How wretched for you.

Thank you so much for those photos – they make me want to get home on leave again all the sooner. They really have come out very well, and everybody looks fairly reasonable!

Yes, that was me flying around on Christmas Eve about lunchtime. I saw several people in the garden – but there's not more than a few split seconds to pick out faces at that speed! I had great fun that day flying around to each member of my crew's home and sort of sending Christmas wishes to all!

My leave is a very problematic affair at the moment, and, further than saying I am overdue for it and that I definitely intend to take it as soon as I can, I cannot say. My job here is, I think, nearly completed and so my movements are likely to be fairly uncertain while I am posted the question of leave is a difficult matter.

However I will see what I can do about it – but do not count on me being able to get it this month.

Poor Betty – I wrote her a long letter and received one from her today. She seems quite cheerful though it must be very dull for her all cooped up over Christmas and the holidays – as indeed it must have been for you all alone with none of the 'children' around.

Christmas here was of course a very gay affair. As is the age old custom we (the officers and NCO's) all served the airmen's lunch – and a jolly good one it was too. Then we had our own lunch (not quite so good) and settled down to a very gay party in our mess in the evening. Next day the weather was again very bad and so we were able to have another Christmas dinner with those local people I spoke about in my last letter. It really was a grand meal – champagne and lovely old port and then lovely hot rum punches. They really are extraordinarily kind to we RAF. They threw another enormous party last night (New Years Eve) and we all really had a grand time.

This might amuse you:– the new group captain put up a notice board to the effect that no dogs are to be allowed in the ante-room in future. (There are many dog-lovers in the mess and about ½ a dozen dogs of all sizes). So some wit promptly drew a very good picture of the ante-room scene round the fire-place with the dogs sitting in chairs smoking and drinking etc. while a group captain is drawn curled up on the floor in front of the fire.

YEAR 1943		AIRCRAFT		PILOT, OR	2ND PILOT, PUPIL	DUTY
MONTH	DATE	Type	No.	1ST PILOT	OR PASSENGER	(INCLUDING RESULTS AND REMARKS)
—	—	—	—	—	—	— TOTALS BROUGHT FORWARD
JAN	2	LANCASTER II	D.S.609	SELF	P/O LUND + CREW	INSTRUCTION
JAN	3	LANCASTER II	D.S.603	SELF	P/O LUND + CREW	INSTRUCTION
JAN	3	LANCASTER II	D.S.607	SELF	F/LT GILPIN + CREW	INSTRUCTION
JAN	4	LANCASTER II	D.S.610	SELF	F/LT DIERKES + CREW	INSTRUCTION
JAN	9	LANCASTER II	D.S.603	SELF	5 CREW	HEIGHT TESTS. LOADED — 22,500 ft. UNLOADED — 25,180 ft.
JAN	11	LANCASTER II	D.S.608	SELF	F/LT BURNS + CREW	INSTRUCTION
JAN	12	LANCASTER II	D.S.607	SELF	F/LT GILPIN + 6 CREW	HEIGHT TESTS. LOADED — 18,500 ft.
JAN	13	LANCASTER II	D.S.603	SELF	6 CREW	LOCAL
JAN	16	LANCASTER	QR."K"	SELF	3 CREW	FROM TANGMERE
JAN	16	LANCASTER	5637	SELF	P/O BATES. SGTS CASS, ROBERTSON, HOBSON, CRAWLER. F/SGT. SIMPSON	OPERATIONS — BERLIN. 14 SBC's ON TARGET. 19,500 ft. 1ST BIG RAID. PHOTO
JAN	18	LANCASTER II	D.S.603	SELF	4 CREW	HEIGHT TESTS. LOADED — 24,200 ft
JAN	20	LANCASTER II	D.S.603	SELF	5 CREW	LOCAL
JAN	21	LANCASTER II	D.S.603	SELF	6 CREW	LOCAL
JAN	24	LANCASTER II	D.S.603	SELF	6 CREW	X COUNTRY
JAN	25	LANCASTER II	D.S.603	SELF	6 CREW	LOCAL

SUMMARY FOR January 1943
UNIT SHQ. Syerston
DATE 25.1.43.
SIGNATURE W. Hopgood F/O.

AIRCRAFT TYPES
1. Lancaster I
2. Lancaster II
3.
4.

GRAND TOTAL [Cols. (1) to (10)]
873 Hrs. 05 Mins.

TOTALS CARRIED FORWARD

Except for the Berlin Operation, John is now instructing new pilots and testing out the new Lancaster Mk II planes fitted with British Hercules engines (due to a shortage of Merlin engines)

The biggest dog is saying to another 'Aren't all these group captains a damn nuisance, old boy!' This was also placed on the mess notice board!

Once again all my very best wishes and love for the New Year, and may this year be a victorious one, so that next year we may all think about, and enjoy, peace.

Much love,

Your loving Son.

John was awarded a Bar to his DFC on 11 January 1943.

Officers Mess,
RAF Syerston,
Nr Nottingham
12.1.43

My dearest Mother,

I saw in the paper the other day that a Sgt K.W.Y. Fison had been killed with a F/Lt Hillary, a famous RAF writer. ★ I fear this must be Wilfred – I do hope that it is not. If it is could you please let me know at once so that I may write to Uncle Kenneth and also make enquiries as to details at the aerodrome where it happened.

If you received my telegram you will have by now discovered I have been awarded a bar to my DFC – I enclose the citation [see pages 199 to 200].

Many thanks for your letters. It must be a great help for you to have Betty at home now and see a bit of Marna at week-ends. I do wish I could get home on leave soon – the chances I am afraid aren't too good at the moment – certainly not until the end of the month.

Just as I am writing your telegram has arrived. I am so sorry to hear about Wilfred – what a tragedy. I am sorry that I cannot get leave for the funeral. If you will let me know the aerodrome where he was stationed, I will fly over and get some details as to how it happened.

At the moment I am in the middle of a pretty important job and cannot break it off and take a 48 hrs pass. I am writing to Broadleaze at once – but don't know the name of his wife – another piece of information I need as soon as possible please. Wilfred's pilot was a very budding novelist and his one book is excellent of its kind – about the RAF. He was badly burned in a crash during the Battle of Britain and had just started flying again. Please express my deep sympathy to all when you go to the funeral.

The weather hasn't been so good lately – a good deal of snow – but that has cleared up a good deal now and I am able to get flying again.

Much love to all at home.

Your loving Son.

★ Flight Lieutenant Richard Hope Hillary, an Australian, died aged 23; he was a Battle of Britain pilot and wrote a book called *The Last Enemy* on his experiences in this battle. In September 1940, flying a Spitfire, he shot down a German Messerschmidt, but in the course of this, his aircraft was hit and caught on fire, causing him extensive burns to his face and hands. He bailed out into the North Sea where he was rescued by the Margate lifeboat and received plastic surgery, including new eyelids. He forced himself to return to flying and returned to service. However, it seems that due to his burn injuries, he was not really fit enough to fully control the aircraft and he crashed his Bristol Blenheim on 8 January 1943 during a night training flight and died with his radio operator-observer, Wilfred Fison, a distant cousin of John's, whom he had known from Marlborough College.

JAN 16th: OPERATION BERLIN
14 SBCs. ON TARGET. 1st BIG RAID

Although John was 'off' operations, it seems that he was needed and eager to go on the first operation to Berlin. It meant at least four hours of flying over heavily defended areas; its anti-aircraft defences were only equalled by those of the Ruhr as a whole, and the night fighter force would attack with their full force. Hence, due to their higher-flying ability, enabling them to be out of range of the flak, this raid used only Lancasters (and Pathfinder Halifaxes), an all four-engine bombing force. The bomber force was really still inadequate for the task but they managed to muster nearly 400 Lancasters. It was the first use of 'target indicators', the coloured flares used by the pathfinders, but Berlin was well beyond the range of GEE and so needed proper radar, which was not yet developed fully. Due to haze and snow, the actual aiming point was not detected but scattered damage hit some important factories and only one Lancaster was lost.

Officers Mess
RAF Syerston
Nr Nottingham
19.1.43

My dearest Mother,
Good News – I am getting a week's leave starting the 26th all being well. Marna wrote saying she would be on leave then; I hope Betty won't have gone back then? So I decided to try and coincide our leaves to help with cooking etc.

106 Squadron and Lancaster, 1942

After a lot of trouble and wangling, I managed to get me an aircraft the other night and did a trip to Berlin. It was a most enjoyable trip as trips go and we did pretty well. You have probably read all about the raid in the papers. Richard Dimbleby★ – the BBC reporter – flew from here – a most interesting man who has been everywhere in this war – Finland, Norway, Greece, Crete, Malta, Egypt, and Libya. I had my old navigator with me which was a great help as all the other chaps in my crew were new.★★

I do hope your ankles are not too painful – it must be horrid to have to sit around so much instead of running about like you used to.

I had a letter from Oliver a few days ago saying that he was expecting to have a week's leave starting 22nd – so he ought to be home when Marna and I are.

Much love to all,

Yr loving Son.

★ John has had an encounter with Richard Dimbleby, father of David Dimbleby, arguably one of the best BBC reporters of all time; he had flown on this raid to Berlin (although not in John's Lancaster) as an observer, doing an on-the-spot commentary, which was broadcast on the radio the following day.
★★ Hobson?

Then followed a week's leave at home in Shere. It seems John caught up with several friends and relations, witnessing some sad consequences of the war. He is still awaiting a date for his awards.

RAF Syverston
Feb 43

My dearest Mother,

What a grand leave and as usual what lovely rich food. Thank you for it. I had quite a good time in London – though the visit was rather depressing as she had just heard that her husband had been killed. Marna and I went to the Simpsons in the Strand and had a very good meal of hare, jugged in red wine sauce. I eventually caught my own train and arrived back to find everyone OK here.

I expect my investiture will take place about the middle of next month, as some chaps who were awarded 'gongs' the same time as myself are going up this month.

Do hope you have not been worried by too many alerts – it must be quite a change to hear the warning again! I have been doing a good deal of flying lately and think that we have nearly finished off our job here. I have been making enquiries and requests as to another job, and should hear something definite fairly soon.

There have been a lot of parties around here lately which have all been good fun. We have long discussions these days on education etc – you would love them – especially as these locals have all read the Beveridge Report and know quite a lot about it. ★

Well there never seems to be much, if any, news these days,

Much love to all,

Your loving Son.

★ William Beveridge, an economist, reported on 16 November 1942 identifying five 'Giant Evils' in society: squalor, ignorance, want, idleness and disease. He stated, 'Now, when the war is abolishing landmarks of every kind, is the opportunity for using experience in a clear field. A revolutionary moment in the world's history is a time for revolutions, not for patching.' (On 21 March 1943, Winston Churchill would urge the population to wait until after the war to make the big social reforms recommended in the Beveridge Report. In 1945 the social welfare reform began, leading to our 'Welfare State', including the National Health Service, National Insurance and the introduction of Family Allowance.)

John now moved to GTF (Gun Training Flight) Fulbeck, which is also sometimes referred to as B&G Flt. It is interesting to note that David Maltby (an ex-Marlborough College student) was on this flight for six months before going to 97 Squadron in March 1943.

John was working hard instructing new pilots, testing aircraft (see log book entry 7–24 March to see the different aircraft he flew which did not include Lancasters) and visiting a fighter squadron. You will also see listed some of the specific skills taught to trainees, for example 'Fighter Affiliation', which refers to

1485 G.T.F. FULBECK.

YEAR 1943		AIRCRAFT		PILOT, OR	2ND PILOT, PUPIL	DUTY
MONTH	DATE	Type	No.	1ST PILOT	OR PASSENGER	(INCLUDING RESULTS AND REMARKS)
—	—	—	—	—	—	—
						TOTALS BROUGHT FORWARD
MARCH	7	MANCHESTER	7524	SELF	1 CREW	AIR TEST
MARCH	7	MARTINET	321	SELF	—	LOCAL
MARCH	8	MANCHESTER	7401	SELF	F/LT LEONARD, OLIVER, INGHAM, BIRD + JOHNSON.	FIGHTER AFFILIATION
MARCH	8	MANCHESTER	7525	SELF	F/S. LEONARD, OLIVER, INGHAM, BIRD + JOHNSON.	FIGHTER AFFILIATION
MARCH	9	MANCHESTER	7492	SELF	5 CREW	FIGHTER AFFILIATION
MARCH	9	MANCHESTER	5791	SELF	6 CREW	FIGHTER AFFILIATION
MARCH	10	MANCHESTER	5839	SELF	P/LT OLIVER, BIRD, INGHAM, JOHNSON + CREW	FIGHTER AFFILIATION
MARCH	11	DEFIANT	1135	SELF	—	LOCAL
MARCH	11	MANCHESTER	7477	SELF	2 CREW	AIR TEST
MARCH	12	LYSANDER	2636	SELF	—	TO SYERSTON
MARCH	12	T. MOTH	5245	F/O NOCK, SELF	—	RETURN
MARCH	15	DEFIANT	1617	SELF	P/O TAYLOR	TO SYERSTON + RETURN
MARCH	16	LYSANDER	2636	SELF	F/LT MITCHAM	TO SWINDERBY + RETURN
MARCH	16	MARTINET	878	SELF	—	FIGHTER ATTACKS
MARCH	18	MARTINET	879	SELF	—	FIGHTER ATTACKS
MARCH	20	MANCHESTER	7484	SELF	P/O TAYLOR. T/SGT. EYRES. WEBER. T/O HOWARD + 3CREW	TO MIDDLETON ST. GEORGE + DALTON
MARCH	20	WELLINGTON III	727	P/SGT. EYRES	SELF	FROM DALTON
MARCH	21	MANCHESTER	7525	SELF	P/O JORDAN. P/O TAYLOR P/O BAKER. T/SGT'S EYRES WEBER + HURLEY. P/O JONES	TO DISHFORTH TOPCLIFFE DALTON + CROFT
MARCH	21	WELLINGTON III	3659	SELF	—	FROM CROFT
MARCH	22	MARTINET	880	SELF	S/L UNDERY	FIGHTER ATTACKS
MARCH	22	MARTINET	880	SELF	—	FIGHTER ATTACKS
MARCH	23	MARTINET	880	SELF	—	FIGHTER ATTACKS
MARCH	24	MANCHESTER	7524	SELF	P/O BAKER, T/SGT. EYRES	TO DISHFORTH
MARCH	24	WELLINGTON III	332	SELF	—	FROM DISHFORTH

GRAND TOTAL [Cols. (1) to (10)]

942 Hrs 45 Mins.

TOTALS CARRIED FORWARD

Note the variety of planes John is flying

a flight where a bomber would be intercepted by a friendly fighter, giving a trainee crew the chance to practise spotting (searching or 'sweeping the sky' in a methodical pattern) and tracking incoming fighters with their guns, and then for the pilots to train in evasive manoeuvres.

Unbeknown to John, Guy Gibson was at this very time choosing whom he wanted in a pick squadron to do a very special mission.

Officers Mess
RAF Syerston
Nr Nottingham
3.3.43

My dearest Mother,

   The reason I have been so long in writing is due to the fact that I have been away for a week and pretty busy rushing about in all directions.

   I went down to an aerodrome on the south coast to do some more tests. I had plenty to do, but also had a very good time and lovely weather. I met a very old friend who used to fly with me at Cranwell 2 years ago and whom I had not seen since then. He had been out in Malta and shot down quite a number. It was a great change and I am sorry I couldn't stay longer. It was a fighter aerodrome and the fighter boys certainly lead an easy life compared to ours. Whilst down south I went over to see Oliver and had lunch with him. I got back yesterday and am expecting a posting within a day or two − where I still don't know.

   Will drop you a PC as soon as I know to where I am being posted.

   Much love,

   Your loving Son.

At last John receives a provisional date for his investiture: it is to be on 6 April 1943 at Buckingham Palace.

Officers Mess
RAF Fulbeck
Nr Grantham
Lincs
15.3.43

My dearest Mother,

   My new address as above. I have just moved in here − it is a pretty isolated sort of place and just a lot of huts to live in. However it is quite near Syerston and I shall manage to keep in touch with the squadron as before. There is quite a good bunch of chaps here and we are only a small number − so that everyone knows everybody else in only a day or two. We do quite a good deal of flying here and train pupils in gunnery. I am flying a lot of new types of aircraft which makes flying very much more exciting.

   Yesterday I got a preliminary warning about my investiture − not yet official. It will be on April 6th at BP. I have managed to arrange for leave about then − probably starting on 29th of this month. When I get the official summons to attend I shall apply for two tickets − for you and Marna (if she can make it). Now I quite agree with you in keeping the lunch exceedingly small − just you, Marna, Betty (if it is worth getting her from college − she won't see anything at BP), Oliver, U Mocar, U Elliot and perhaps Aunty Sylvia and Celia (if she is fit).★ *That makes nine at the most. There will be plenty of time when I am on leave to arrange details so don't worry about them until I am home. I will write to Marna and Oliver about it. In the evening I rather want to have a celebration with my RAF friends in town and would stay the night there and go back to Fulbeck the next day. We could go to a show in the afternoon however.*

The squadron has collected a lot more awards lately – my best friend (Brian Oliver) got a bar to his DFC, the first gunner to win two awards so far, and my bomb-aimer a DFM. ★★ *That makes five of my old crew who have won awards – pretty good for a crew.*

Much love, looking forward to seeing you all soon,

Your loving Son.

★ Little did John know the determination of his mother and sisters, who managed to get Betty into Buckingham Palace despite not having a ticket.

★★ Brian Oliver was to write the following about John to his mother following the Dams Raid:

> I do not know how much he spoke about his work, so I feel I must tell you that right from early days, he did a magnificent job, continuously and uncomplainingly, and this most recent operation from which he is missing was the most splendid of them all. When I was on the Squadron with him, his example was such that all sought, but few were able to emulate it – it is not possible to assess how much we owe him.

Marna, getting a bit overexcited about her brother, wrote to John on 21 March 1943 from Derby:

My dearest Brother,

Oh boy, Oh boy, I bet you are getting excited, I am anyway – I am trying to get leave from Sat – Wed but whether this will work or not I don't know, it would be impossible to attempt getting my 7 days then so I shall simply ask for 48 hours and take about 96! His unit is very sticky about leave so I don't think my usual wangles will come off, but I shall have a shot at it. …

See you soon I hope,

Your loving Sister.

Officers Mess
RAF Station,
Fulbeck.
Nr Grantham,
Lincs
22 03 1943

My dearest Mother,

No definite confirmation of the investiture yet, but my leave is more or less fixed up. I intend to get home on the 31st, but I may spend a night in town with my old first pilot – Peter Smith – in which case I would not get home until the 1st.

Many thanks for your last letter. I have written to Marna, but as yet received no reply. I hope Elizabeth will be able to get to town for <u>the day</u>.

You don't say how your health is these days, so I take it you are better. Please don't go and overdo it and get worse again.

Life here is quite a change – flying is interesting. I am certainly not a test pilot – I merely have a good opportunity to fly different types of aircraft which I have not flown before.★ Running a 'Flight' gives me plenty to do and the work is certainly not boring. The chaps here are grand types – all ex-operational – and we have good parties and I play a lot of bridge. At the moment I am busy landing and taking off aircraft by control from the ground at night – a very dull job which comes along every 3 or 4 nights.

I will write a wire again as soon as I know dates of leave and investiture definitely. Looking forward to seeing you all,

Your loving Son.

★John's log book shows he flew the following aircraft in March: Manchester, Wellington III, Martinet, Defiant, Lysander and Tiger Moth.

When John's investiture date was announced, Grace wrote a letter to Miss Straubenzees, the principal of the Charlotte Mason College, to ask leave for Elizabeth to attend her brother's investiture at Buckingham Palace to receive the DFC and Bar from King George VI. Miss Straubenzees called Elizabeth to the drawing room and formally explained that she could not sanction leave for this in wartime. However, Grace, determined her daughter would attend, rung up the head to insist Betty be given permission to attend; Miss Straubenzees then sent a message to Elizabeth that, against her advice, she would release her, seeing that her mother had been so insistent.

Meanwhile, important things were afoot that would dictate John's future. On the afternoon of Sunday, 21 March Guy Gibson, and some administrative staff, arrived at Scampton to begin the new and as yet unnamed squadron, X Squadron. Gibson requested that the adjutant be changed to his old colleague from 106 Squadron, Flight Lieutenant Humphries. On 25 March the squadron was named the 617 Squadron.

The next day, 26 March, John visited Scampton for the first time (flying there in a Tiger Moth and landing on its then grass runways); this must have been the moment he realised that Wing Commander Guy Gibson wanted him for a very special squadron. Although surprisingly not logged in John's log book, it seems that at about this time, Gibson, knowing only that water and low flying at night were to be involved in his next very secret operation, decided to try out low flying for himself. Late in the day, he took John and Dinghy Young with him and went to the Derwent Reservoir in Derbyshire. They found low flying at dusk more difficult than expected because the water looked black and it was impossible to judge where the surface was, and they apparently narrowly avoided having an accident. This instigated the idea to use Aldis lamps to shine and converge on the surface of the water (though of course this only worked in moonlight when they would be mirrored on the surface).

John was on the brink of the next step towards his destiny, but for the moment, the most important event on the horizon for John was his investiture at Buckingham Palace.

9

A Special Squadron is Formed

On 14 January 1945, the *Sunday Express*, London, ran the following article:

How the world's finest bomber squadron planned
The greatest air feat of the war
By Wing-Commander
GUY GIBSON, V.C., D.S.O., D.F.C.

In March 1943, after I had done 173 sorties and was pretty tired, the A.O.C., Air Vice-Marshal the Hon. Ralph Cochrane, sent for me and said: 'How would you like the idea of doing one more trip?

'It will be a pretty important one, perhaps one of the most devastating of all time, but I can't tell you any more now. Do you want to do it?' I said I thought I did.

Nothing happened for two days. On the third he sent for me and said: 'I have got to warn you that this is no ordinary sortie, in fact it can't be done for at least two months.

'Moreover, the training is of such importance that the commander-in-chief has decided that a special squadron is to be formed for the job. I want you to form that squadron.

'As far as air crews are concerned, I want the best – you choose them.

'Now there's a lot of urgency. I want your aircraft flying in four days' time.

'And not a word to anyone. Secrecy is vital.'

It took me an hour to pick my pilots. I picked them because I honestly believed that they were the best bomber pilots available.

Next morning I went to the personnel officer to fix up the ground staff. Then to the W.A.A.F. officer for M.T. drivers and cooks.

And so by the end of two days the squadron was formed.

Next night I arrived in the mess at Scampton. In the hall were the boys. By their hands you could see that these were the aces of Bomber Command.

All in all, they probably knew more about the art of bombing than any squadron in the world.

Ready in three days

There were 21 crews which means 147 men – nearly all under 24, but all of them veterans.

My speech to them was short. I said: 'You're here as a crack squadron to carry out a raid which I am told will have startling results, some say it may even cut short the duration of the war. What the target is I can't tell you. All I can tell you is that you will have to practise low flying until you know how to do it with your eyes shut. Of all things security is the greatest factor.'

By the third day we were all set to begin training and we had been named the 617 Squadron.

It seems that the article above was actually written by a ghostwriter in Gibson's name and that there is some inaccuracy about Guy choosing all his pilots; however, it is consistently agreed that he did choose John.

John flew to Scampton in a Manchester on 30 March to be part of this new 617 Squadron, under Wing Commander Gibson, who knew him well from 106 Squadron. The next day John took a Lancaster on a local familiarisation flight with Flight Lieutenant Shannon, from the RAAF, the Royal Australian Air Force (who was to become pilot of Lancaster *L-Leather*, also in the first wave of Operation Chastise).

The log book shows a ten-day break (between 31 March and 11 April) which was John's leave to attend the investiture for his DFC and Bar. So whilst 617 Squadron had already begun training in earnest, John was on leave. Perhaps he had only accepted Guy Gibson's offer, or maybe order, to be in 617 Squadron on condition that he first took his leave for the investiture.

It is also interesting to note when checking his log book that Guy Gibson has no flights recorded between 11 March 1943 and 1 April 1943, when he must have been busy setting up his new squadron, journeying to and fro between Scampton and important people such as Barnes Wallis and Portal. Gibson was also testing out equipment, and on 28 March radio-telephone sets, already standard in Lancasters, were found only to be effective in daylight, at a height of 2,000ft, between two aircraft flying 40 miles apart. As this would not be adequate for the requirements of Operation Chastise, it was decided that VHF radio-telephones would be needed.

Guy Gibson by now had met Barnes Wallis, and on 8 April the first type 464 Provisioning Lancaster was delivered to Scampton (specially adapted to carry Barnes Wallis' bouncing bomb).

Gibson reports on this meeting as he continues in the *Sunday Express* article:

617 SQDN. SCAMPTON.

YEAR 1943		AIRCRAFT		PILOT, OR 1ST PILOT	2ND PILOT, PUPIL OR PASSENGER	DUTY (INCLUDING RESULTS AND REMARKS)
MONTH	DATE	Type	No.			
—	—	—	—	—	—	TOTALS BROUGHT FORWARD
MARCH	30	MANCHESTER	7524	SELF	P/O JONES	TO SCAMPTON
MARCH	31	LANCASTER	4926	SELF	P/T SHANNON	LOCAL.
APRIL	11	LANCASTER	735	SELF	CREW	LOW - LEVEL X. CTY.
APRIL	12	LANCASTER	309	SELF	CREW	LOW - LEVEL FORMATION X.CTY.
APRIL	13	LANCASTER	309	SELF	SGT. BRENNAN. P/O OSBORNE, P/O BURCHER, GREGORY, SGT. WHITE, MINCHIN	LOW - LEVEL X CTY. BOMBING & FIGHTER AFFILIATION
APRIL	14	LANCASTER	329	SELF	CREW	FIGHTER AFFILIATION - FORMATION
APRIL	14	LANCASTER	4926	SELF	CREW	N.F.T. & TO WICKENBY.
APRIL	14	LANCASTER	4926	SELF	CREW	X CTY. NIGHT. LOW-LEVEL (MOONLIGHT)
APRIL	15	LANCASTER	735	SELF	CREW	X CTY. LOW-LEVEL. SCOTLAND & IRELAND
APRIL	16	LANCASTER	309	SELF	CREW	X CTY. LOW-LEVEL FORMATION BOMBING
APRIL	16	LANCASTER	309	SELF	CREW	X CTY. NIGHT. LOW-LEVEL (MOONLIGHT)
APRIL	21	LANCASTER	437	SELF	SGT. BRENNAN. P/O OSBORNE. P/O BURCHER & GREGORY, F/SGT. FRASER. SGT. MINCHIN	X CTY. LOW-LEVEL. BOMBING.
APRIL	21	LANCASTER	309	SELF	CREW	DUSK LOW-LEVEL BOMBING.
APRIL	22	LANCASTER	309	SELF	CREW	LOW - LEVEL BOMBING.
APRIL	24	LANCASTER	735	SELF	CREW	X CTY. LOW-LEVEL. DARK GLASSES.
APRIL	25	LANCASTER	735	SELF	CREW	X CTY. LOW-LEVEL DARK GLASSES
APRIL	30	LANCASTER	735	SELF	CREW	X CTY. LOW-LEVEL DARK GLASSES
APRIL	30	LANCASTER	437	SELF	P/L MUNRO CREW	NIGHT LOW-LEVEL TACTICS

SUMMARY FOR APRIL 1943
UNIT "B" Flight 617 Sqn.
DATE 1. 5. 43.
SIGNATURE [signature] F/L.

AIRCRAFT TYPES
1. Lancaster.
2. Manchester.
3.
4.

[signature] O.C. 617 Sqn.

[signature] S/L
O.C. "B" Flight

GRAND TOTAL [Cols. (1) to (10)] 988 Hrs. 30 Mins.

O.C. 617 Sqn
TOTALS CARRIED FORWARD

Note the emphasis on low-level night flying (X CTY means cross country)

The military objectives needed a very high amount of explosive placed very accurately to shift them or blow them out. At first there was no airplane with a high enough performance to carry the required load at the required speed. The Lancaster Bomber solved this problem. Next the explosive would have to take the form of either a very large bomb or a very large mine, to be dropped within a few yards of the right spot from below 300ft. If they're dropped above that height then accuracy falls off and the job can't be done.

'Other snags are flak, balloons and the difficulty of flying over water at low level.'

'Over water?' I queried.

'Yes, over water at night or early morning with a lot of haze or fog all round.' … 'Now what I want to know from you is this: can you fly to the limits I want? These are roughly a speed of 240 miles an hour at 150 feet above smooth water, having pulled out of a dive from 2,000 feet, and then be able to drop a bomb accurately within a few yards?'

I said I thought it was a bit difficult but worth trying.

Artificial night

Next day I told my Squadron conference what I knew about the accuracy required and the height. Then came the problem. Dinghy began speaking. 'The first big snag will be to get practice in moonlight. I've heard that in America they've brought out a special form of synthetic night flying. All the windows of the aircraft are painted blue, and the crew wear yellow goggles inside.'

We got immediate priority to have three aircraft fitted up.

Meanwhile, back in Shere, John, Betty and Grace were relaxing in the garden at Hurstcote. The photos shown were taken the day before John's investiture, which was the last time he was to see his family.

John's last afternoon at home in Hurstcote garden with his mother

John's last leave

Betty, having managed to escape the clutches of her principal at Charlotte Mason College, Ambleside, remembers:

I caught a train from Windermere to Paddington to return to Hurstcote for the event.

John was at home. He looked pale and very drawn and was smoking heavily, his fingers yellow with nicotine stains. He spoke little of what he was doing (sworn to secrecy) and seemed to find comfort in playing Chopin and Mozart etc. on the piano which he did beautifully.

Mummy hired a car to drive us all up to London for the event. It was from 'Weller's' from the village (Shere). We drove right through the main entrance of Buckingham Palace. Then we had to show appointed tickets; we had been allotted only two so I knew I had to make myself scarce and meet Mummy and Marna afterwards. I managed to keep beside them until I was through the doors where the elderly gentleman usher waited for me to give him my ticket.

I was a bit overcome and confessed I hadn't got one! To our amazement he asked us to wait a minute and then beckoned all of us through to the long-seated room to await the ceremony. Our seats were almost in front of the King and the Beefeaters were standing in a line to the left and right of him. The band played 'God save the King' and we all stood, after which the long queue of about 300 service-men and women presented themselves to His Majesty King George VI for their medals. We were oh so proud of John, who looked so slim and young as he bowed and shook the King's hand. It was my last ever impression of him! … (And it was only to be a month afterwards that I knocked on Miss Straubenzees drawing room door at The Charlotte Mason College, to inform her that John had been killed in action; as you would expect she was lost for words and looked very sheepish!)

John Vere Hopgood

Flt Lt John Hopgood DFC + Bar

F/Lt. JOHN VERE HOPGOOD, D. F. C. & BAR
106 Squadron & 617 (Dambusters) Squadron
Shot down while bombing the Moehne Dam 16/17 May 1943

Then John returned to Scampton, where intensive specialist training in low-level flying was already under way. By 14 April, 617 Squadron was focusing on low-level flying at night and by 16 April, at night and in 'formation'.

On 13 April Upkeep (bouncing bomb) trials began off Reculver (Kent); it was a revolving depth charge bomb.

In his article, Guy Gibson continued:

> The maintenance people tell me that already a few aircraft have come back with leaves and tree branches stuck in their radiators. This means the boys are flying too low. You've got to stop this or else someone will kill themselves.

Notice that John's crew on 13 April included Sergeant Brennan, who was his flight engineer; Gregory, who was his front gunner; Minchin, who was his wireless operator; and Burcher (RAAF), who was his rear gunner. All of these men were to lose their lives alongside John at the Möhne Dam. Sergeant Charlie Brennan in particular would prove to be courageous, loyal and professional to the end.

Charlie qualified as a flight engineer in 106 Squadron on 20 June 1942. He then flew as John's flight engineer consistently from 14 August 1942, only doing three trips with different pilots, except when he was on an Elementary Flying Training Course on Oxfords at Waddington from 7 September 1942 for five days and on a conversion course to Lancasters from December 1942 until March 1943. This flying training is significant because, as a second pilot was no longer required due to pilot shortage, it was now necessary for the flight engineer not only to understand the mechanics of the aircraft but to be able to take over piloting duties in case of an emergency.

It is also interesting to note that in Charlie Brennan's log book there is a change of handwriting from 1 May until his death on 17 May, which matches identically that of the last line of John's log book, the only one *not* written by John himself. It is likely that the two log books were updated after their deaths by Harry Humphries, the adjutant.

Officers Mess
RAF Station
Scampton
Lincoln
20.4.43

My dearest Mother,
I am sorry I have been such a long time in writing but there has been so much to do by day and night that I put letter-writing aside.
As soon as I got back here and assembled my crew I immediately tackled all the work we have to do and have been extremely busy since then as I said before.

I like my new crew – all very experienced types and damn good chaps as well.
My flight engineer is my old one, but all the rest are new faces, except my rear-gunner
[Burcher], an Australian, who was on my last squadron though not in my crew. There are
3 officers besides myself, which is much better than an all sergeant crew which I had before.
Will write again soon,
Love to all,
Your loving Son.

This revelation is significant in that John's crew were changed comparatively late. A pilot's crew became his family and had to work as a close-knit team with loyalty, trust, expertise and mutual responsibility; it was wonderful how in such a short space of time these qualities could be, and indeed were, forged so effectively in *M-Mother*. John still showed the influence of his upbringing by preferring those of his own class (officers). Or was he just trying to fit into the Hopgood mould in his letters to reassure his mother that he was mixing with the right people? He was, after all, 'a good squadron type' and therefore, unlike what we hear of Guy Gibson, able to socialise with all types of people.

On 21 April Flight Sergeant Fraser from RCAF (the Royal Canadian Air Force), replacing White, joined John's crew as his bomb aimer.

On 24 April Gibson agreed to height of release of upkeep bomb being lowered from 150ft to 60ft.

The 25 April was Easter Sunday. John's log book records that on that day he was piloting Lancaster 735 (not *M-Mother* but presumably one of the three fitted with blue Perspex windscreens to simulate night flying), with the same crew which would accompany him to the Möhne Dam (except that his navigator was Osborne); it was a daytime cross-country trip, using 'dark glasses', the yellow goggles. This was also the first day that Prime Minister Winston Churchill had allowed church bells to ring, there being no more danger of an invasion. The bells of Lincoln Cathedral, and in all the nearby towns and villages, would have rung out on this Easter Day if they could muster a band in these difficult wartime days; just imagine the cacophony of sounds, with the joyous, too-long-silenced bells mixed with those deep-throated Merlin engines.

Guy Gibson continued:

We [Gibson, Hoppy* and Young] were on our way in my faithful G for George towards a reservoir near Sheffield. This lake is surrounded by high ground with just enough industrial haze blowing over it to make it ideal for the job. We came screaming down at the right airspeed to pull out as near 150 ft. as we could judge, and released a missile – it fell short. After several more tries we found it fairly easy.

Dangerous

That night at dusk we tried again, but it wasn't so good. The water, blue by day, was now black – we nearly hit that black water.

Even Spam said, 'Christ, this is bloody dangerous,' which means it was.

The next day the A.O.C. sent for me, and I noted three large packing cases in his office. 'There are models of your targets,' he said. 'Now I'm not going to tell you where they are, but Jeff [Barnes Wallis] has told me that you won't be able to train your squadron unless you know. You have got to be the only man in the squadron who can possibly know the target until the day before the attack is to be made.'

The three models were of three very large dams – perfect to the smallest tree.

[Barnes Wallis then updates Guy]: … 'As you know, the Ruhr Valley is the most highly industrialised area of the whole of Germany. One great snag is the lack of water supply. So in 1911 the Germans built a mighty barrage dam blocking the Möhne Valley through which the River Ruhr flowed.

'The Germans are very proud of this dam. It is rather beautifully built, Gothic and all that. It is some 850yds long and 140ft thick and as high as it is thick, and the lake it holds back is about 12 miles long, holding 140 million tons of water.

'At the same time they built another dam nearby called the Sorpe, very much smaller and of earthen construction.

'If they were to be breached the resultant shortage of water for both drinking and industrial purposes might be disastrous. Of course the floods would result in more damage than has ever happened in this war.

'The third dam is the Eder some 60 miles away, which supplies a lot of hydro-electric power. This holds back 202,000,000 tons of water.

Vital Feet

'But to breach these things is not as easy as it looks. You'll have to plan a special method of attack within a month.'

'Why the urgency?'

'Because dams can only be attacked when they are full of water. At the moment the water is 12 feet from the top, but we can only attack them when the water is four feet.

'Your projectiles will have to fall so that they sink into the water, actually touching the dam wall itself about 40 feet down and if they are not touching it'll be useless. Then when the mine explodes by a hydrostatic fuse, I have calculated that a crack will appear just as it did in the models. More mines in exactly the same spot will shift this wall backwards until it rolls over.'

'So the attack would have to be carried out at a dead height within a foot or so of 150ft., at an accurate speed and aiming had got to be perfect, over black water, in bad visibility …

I was completely bewildered. It seemed almost impossible.

One fine day in April, a wing commander came up to see me. He was the sighting expert. His idea was a very simple bomb-sight using the age-old range-finding principles. Within half an hour the instrument section had knocked up the prototype. It cost less than the price of a postage stamp.

Soon extraordinary accuracy was being achieved in practice bombing.

Now it was time to plan our route to the target.

We went down to see Charles Pickard of F for Freddie fame who probably knew more about the flak defences of Holland and Belgium than any other man living. He showed me how to get through the gaps.

Then we sat down to imitate this winding journey, if possible, over England. It was easier than we expected. For the River Rhine we had the River Trent, for the Ruhr Hills we had the Cotswolds, for the Möhne lake we had Uppingham Reservoir, though it was much smaller.

How the Germans would have liked to know about all this. So security measures were far-reaching and efficient. All our telephone wires were tapped, all conversation was checked. All our letters were censored.

Some say that even the barmaid in the nearby pub was given three months holiday.

★This may be an inaccuracy by the ghostwriter, as Hoppy probably did not go on this trip; it seems to coincide with when Hoppy was on leave for his investiture and, although cited in several books since, it is not noted in his own log book.

On 28 April the exhausted crews of 617 squadron were given two days off by their wing commander, Guy Gibson, giving them a chance to refresh but stressing the need for absolute secrecy. Hoppy's crew was no exception, and it gave John Fraser, *M-Mother*'s new Canadian bomb aimer, a chance to marry his English sweetheart, Doris, in a quiet country church. It seems that Hoppy visited an old doctor friend, from Coningsby, and his wife in his two days off, and they had a 'terrific party'; he may have been nursing hangover the following morning, and what with two new crew and a new aircraft to test out, he would have had very little extra time. (See Hoppy's last letter.)

On 30 April, six new Avro Lancasters were delivered to 617 Squadron at Scampton aerodrome; one of them was Hoppy's ED925 *M-Mother* referred to in his last letter to his mother. (It was to fly a total of seventeen hours before being shot down and exploding into the hillside near the Möhne Dam.)

On this 30 April Hoppy honed his crew's skills by doing two hours of low-level flying practice, cross-country again, with 'dark glasses' to simulate night flying. Later, when it became dark, this time accompanied by Flight Lieutenant Munro, they took a second trip to practise more night low-level tactical flying.

Officers Mess
RAF Station
Scampton
Lincoln.
3.5.43

My dearest Mother,

Am just sending off a telegram to say I cannot make the wings for Victory Parade & speech-making on May 5th. Definitely I am much too busy + even a day off is out of the question at the moment. It's a pity — but it can't be helped. I hope you collect plenty of cash & that the occasion goes off according to plan. I see little chance of my getting leave until June — probably not until about the middle (N's birthday).

I am very sorry to hear about Mrs Bray — however the fact that the family were expecting it must have softened the shock somewhat. Please give my sincere sympathy to Edmund Bray & Margaret.

We are all much more settled in now though there is plenty of work still. We had a terrific inspection the other day — inspections are always a mistake I think as it means nobody does any work for two days except clean up the most impossible places. And as soon as the inspection is over out come all the untidy & illegal objects and nobody or nothing really benefits from it.

I have made two alterations in my crew just recently — a new Navigator & a new Bombardier. My old Nav. went sick, and my old Bombardier proved unsatisfactory.

The replacements are grand chaps — both Canadians who have been flying together for a long time. My aircraft letter is once again an "M" and I am having my old crest painted on.

We had a very enjoyable evening recently when we all went over to see an old Doctor & wife friends at a local town whom we used to know when we were at Coningsby It developed into a terrific party. Now that they know we are about again we have had invitations from several of our old friends in that District, so when the weather gets warmer we should get quite a lot of tennis + swimming.

Sorry I can't make the 5th pity it can't be postponed until June,

love
much to all,

yr. loving Son.

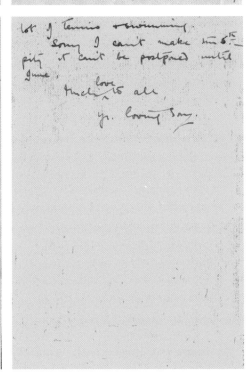

Last letter received by John's mother

Munro was to become first pilot of Lancaster *W-Willie* in the second wave of Operation Chastise.

On 1 May 1943 Flight Officer Earnshaw (also RCAF) became John's navigator. Both Earnshaw and Fraser had come from 50 Squadron but Hoppy had been there before them, and their times had not overlapped.

Hoppy had had several last-minute changes, which meant having to run extra tests and do extra training: firstly his new and just-married bomb aimer Fraser, secondly his even newer navigator, Earnshaw, and thirdly, after it had been checked over by the Scampton ground engineers, his brand-new *M-Mother* Lancaster. He was busy! It is likely that Hoppy would have still found time to down a beer in the squadron bar with his good friend Guy Gibson, and it is said (although I wonder if it is a legend built on fiction from the 1952 film rather than fact, knowing the Hopgood reticence with dogs) that he bought the odd beer for Gibson's trusty dog, even furnishing him with a cigarette in his doggy jowls! It would seem far more true to John's character that he would have drummed out a jazzy tune on the mess piano (but possibly he had too many cares for that now).

On 1 May the first full-size Upkeep was dropped and Gibson told Wallis he was confident of success.

On 3 May Hoppy did his first flight in the new *M-Mother*, with Flight Lieutenant Hay (presumably as second pilot to help him check it out) and described his plane as 'A Honey' in his log book. All was well. And he wrote this letter, which was to be the last that his 'dearest Mother' would ever receive:

Officers Mess,
RAF Scampton
Lincoln
3.5.43

My dearest Mother,

Am just sending off a telegram to say I cannot make the Wings for Victory Parade and speech making on May 5th. Definitely I am much too busy and even a day off is out of the question at the moment. It's a pity – but it can't be helped. I hope you collect plenty of cash and that the occasion goes off according to plan. I see little chance of my getting leave until June – probably not until about the middle (M's birthday).

We are all much more settled in now though there is plenty of work still. We had a terrific inspection the other day. Inspections are always a mistake I think as it means nobody does any work for two days except clean up the most impossible places. And as soon as the inspection is over out come all the untidy and illegal objects and nobody or nothing really benefits from it.

I have made two alterations in my crew just recently – a new Navigator and a new Bombardier. My old Navigator went sick and my old Bombardier proved unsatisfactory. ★

The replacements are grand chaps – both Canadians who have been flying together for a long time. My aircraft letter is once again an 'M' and I am having my old crest painted on.

We had a very enjoyable evening recently when we all went over to see an old Doctor and wife friends at a local town whom we used to know when we were at Coningsby. It developed into a terrific party. Now that they know we are about again we have had an invitation from several of our old friends in that district, so when the weather gets warmer we should get quite a lot of tennis and swimming.

Sorry I can't make the 5th – pity it can't be postponed until June,

Much love to all,

Your loving Son.

* Notice Hoppy is using an Americanism 'Bombardier' instead of the English 'bomb aimer', which must be because his new bomb aimer was the Canadian John Fraser (who had replaced the previous 'unsatisfactory' one).

Grace had been hoping that John would get back to Shere for the 'Wings For Victory Week', a national UK fund-raising event from 1–8 May 1943 to fund new aircraft.

Instead of returning to Shere, John did not miss out completely and joined in locally, noting in his log book, 'Wings for Victory "Beat-up" at Horncastle, Formation Bombing, low level'. To appear in the log book they must have been given permission to do this as a one off; it must have been both a thrill and a fright for the residents and very memorable.

The signatures here are Mickey Martin's and Dave Maltby's. Mickey was pilot of *P-Popsie* and Dave was pilot of *J-Johnny* and both were in the first wave of Lancasters on, and survivors of, Operation Chastise. Martin survived the war but Maltby was killed in action only four months later in the raid on the Dortmund–Ems Canal.

On 5 May the Air Ministry at Washington decided 26 May as the last date for Operation Chastise; this was later changed to 19 May.

On 6 May John piloted his first proper flight in *M-Mother* on a two-hour daytime excursion to Manston in Kent, in low-level formation, presumably as a practice for flying low over water on The Wash off Reculver. This is what Guy Gibson was referring to when he wrote of Hoppy in *Enemy Coast Ahead*:

Once when training for this raid we had gone down to RAF Manston [a fighter station in the Second World War] in Kent, and had shot up the field with wings inside tail planes, and even the fighter boys had to admit it was the best they had ever seen. I should say Hoppy was probably the best pilot in the squadron.

On 11 and 12 May, 617 Squadron crews dropped practice Upkeeps off Reculver at 60ft, and one Lancaster was damaged beyond repair. John once again logged flying to Manston and back in *M-Mother* and this time in formation with Wing Commander Gibson for VHF (i.e. radio) tests; he logs dropping stores at 60ft, which may have been the practice Upkeeps. John had completed 1,000 hours of flying on this day.

On 13 May the first live and armed Upkeep was successfully dropped off Broadstairs. *M-Mother* (and its crew) was involved in bombing and tactical practice on this day, although John's log does not state where. *M-Mother* also practised cross-country moonlight tactics once darkness fell: very poignant for three days later.

This date also saw the end of the North Africa Campaign and the defeat of the Axis forces in Tunisia who surrendered yielding over 275,000 prisoners of war; this huge loss of experienced troops greatly reduced the military capacity of the Axis powers. (This, followed by the success of Operation Chastise, provided a huge morale boost for the British and Allied forces, and was a turning point of the war.)

On 14 May Chiefs of Staff agreed to mount Operation Chastise (the Dambusters' Raid). John in *M-Mother* did two sorties with his crew, both after dark: the first undergoing night flying tests, and the second practising low-level moonlight tactics.

The next photo is a rare one because most of the 617 squadron photos were taken after Operation Chastise; as it was of the highest secrecy there were few

Guy Gibson explains the route

taken before the raid. There was, however, a full squadron photo taken on 15 May, just before the raid.

On 15 May the second live and armed Upkeep was dropped off Broadstairs, without spinning, to test for resistance to violent impact. It was successful. The AOC (Air Officer Commanding) came over and told Guy Gibson that the next night was the night. As he left, Barnes Wallis arrived in a white plane to check all was ready. Key 617 Squadron personnel were given their preliminary briefing. Guy Gibson said:

> Hoppy was now told the target, as were Dinghy, and Henry as well as Bob. And that night Hoppy saved our lives. The route the SASO [Senior Air Staff Officer] and I had planned between us had taken us over Huls – a well-defended rubber factory on the edge of the Ruhr, which wasn't marked on the flak map. He happened to know all this, and suggested that we should go a little farther north.

Bronze of Guy Gibson and Nigger, at Scampton

Guy's last comment refers to the fact that John had been on an operation to the Huls Rubber factory in October 1941. There was an atmosphere of nervous expectation, everyone knowing that the big night was about to happen; the medics often issued those due to take part in operations with sleeping tablets, but there is mixed information as to whether sleeping tablets were given to those taking part in Operation Chastise.

That evening nobody drank alcohol at the bar, except perhaps Gibson's Labrador, Nigger. It was later this same evening that Nigger was tragically killed by a car, and indeed the word 'Nigger' was that very night the codename for the dam breaching.

George Gregory, who was to be front gunner in *M-Mother*, was particularly agitated, so much so that Adjutant Harry Humphries, who shared digs with him, took him out for a stroll around the mess to calm him down. This is significant in hindsight because Gregory met his death even before reaching the Möhne Dam, at the same time as enemy flak hit *M-Mother*, wounding Hoppy and crippling a port engine. Ken Earnshaw, *M-Mother*'s navigator, predicted that eight aircraft would not return; he proved to be absolutely and uncannily correct.

On 16 May full and final briefings were given and Operation Chastise went ahead.

Betty tells how impressed John had always been with the many RAF ground crews, and not just those in 617 Squadron; he had often remarked that they didn't receive enough accolades for their vital work. John may have been brought up a snob but now most of his pretention and arrogance were gone; for him class distinctions had blurred and disappeared as he had matured and become more involved in the fellowship of flying and fighting. This was apparently not the same story for John's now close friend, Guy Gibson, who was still living much of the time in his ivory public school tower.

Most of the crew, including Gibson, had had a lie-in that morning. But of course in the hangars, workshops and offices of RAF Scampton the many ground crew were frantically busy. They loaded the bombs onto the Lancasters, using cranes and trolleys, loaded tracer bullets into the machine guns in the front and rear gun turrets, adjusted the compasses, which were affected greatly by the Upkeep bomb, and did 101 other preparatory duties. John himself would have been methodically doing more than 200 checks on *M-Mother* and making last-minute adjustments; his crew would also be checking guns, instruments, equipment etc. Still none but the crew knew for certain that this wasn't just another, though more sophisticated, 'night flying programme', as they had been led to believe. Secrecy was at its utmost.

The medics issued those taking part with cod liver oil and tablets to keep them awake, 'wakey, wakey' pills. These turned out to be caffeine and benzidine tablets (since found to be carcinogenic). The crews then headed to the mess for their treat of bacon with two eggs, only given before an operation, and then there was a time when all they could do was wait for the go ahead, often pacing up and down, and with nerves jangling. Apparently John's *M-Mother* crew played a friendly game of cricket whilst waiting, all but Burcher and Fraser, who just sat by *M-Mother* and mused over what was to come; little did they know that they were to be her only survivors that night.

It seems that John wrote a 'last letter' that evening, and then had second thoughts about it being sent. After all, there had been a huge build-up to this operation and, as W.J. Lawrence writes in his book *No 5 Group, RAF*, even on a routine operation 'to be a bomber crew required persistent fortitude at a time when the stoutest mind and heart would have every excuse to show a natural and normal weakness'. Almost certainly John had had a moment of absolute panic, being gripped with fear and sure that now his time was up. Unusually for him, he may have allowed himself an outpouring of the pent-up emotion and raw fear in this letter, almost certainly written to his mother. John was only 21 years old, and deputy for this raid, ready to take over from Guy Gibson should anything happen to him; he was incredibly young to be shouldering such formidable responsibility.

Pilot of *L-Leather*, the Australian Flight Lieutenant David Shannon was not yet even 21 years old. John and Dave were walking out to their aircraft together, and it seems John was justifiably concerned about this trip: as they paused behind a hangar for a last cigarette, John said, prophetically, 'I think this is going to be a tough one, and I don't think I am coming back, Dave.' This shook Shannon, who responded, 'Come off it, Hoppy, you'll beat these bastards; you've beaten them for so long, you're not going to get whipped tonight.'

John asked his friend Dave to seek out his 'last letter' and destroy it if he did not return. He must have worried about the impact it might have had on his mother, who took great pride in her family, and particularly in her only son, being related to those dauntless and intrepid earls of Oxford. John would not have wanted his dear mother to remember him as weak and gutless, which would, after all, have smacked of Low Moral Fibre!

However, from the moment Flt Lt John Vere Hopgood, DFC + Bar entered his Lancaster AJM 925/G (*M-Mother*) that evening, he was back in professional and excellent pilot-mode and was to show extreme 'Courage Beyond Fear'.

The last paragraph of Guy Gibson's *Sunday Express* article reads:

Off for Germany

On May 16th, reconnaissance aircraft reported that the water level of the dam was just right for the attack. It was a great moment when the public address system on the station said: 'All crews of No 617 Squadron report to the briefing rooms immediately.'

The boys came in hushed.

I let the scientist tell them all about it.

I shall never forget the final briefing. [Barnes Wallis] was very worried, because he felt personally responsible for their lives.

He said to me: 'I hope they all come back.' I said, 'It won't be your fault if they don't.'

The A.O.C. gave a pep talk. Then I explained the attack again, although they knew it backwards. I spoke for just over an hour.

Standing around before the take-off everyone was tense and no-one said very much.

I said to Hoppy: 'Hoppy, tonight's the night; tomorrow we will get drunk.'

Then someone at the control caravan waved a flag. I opened the throttles and we were off for Germany.

M-Mother crew for Operation Chastise

Hymn No 7
Marlborough College Hymn Book 'Courage' by J.L. Steiner (1688–1761):

Courage, brother! Do not stumble,
Though the path be dark as night;
There's a star to guide the humble:
Trust in God, and do the right.

YEAR 1943		AIRCRAFT		PILOT, OR 1ST PILOT	2ND PILOT, PUPIL OR PASSENGER	DUTY (INCLUDING RESULTS AND REMARKS)
MONTH	DATE	Type	No.			
—	—	—	—	—	—	— TOTALS BROUGHT FORWARD
MAY	1	LANCASTER	437	SELF	SGT. BRENNAN SGT. MINCHIN P/O EARNSHAW F/SGT. FRASER P/O GREGORY P/O BURCHER	WINGS FOR VICTORY "BEAT UP" AT HORNCASTLE. FORMATION BOMBING — LOW-LEVEL.
MAY	2	LANCASTER	437	SELF	CREW	AIR TO AIR FIRING
MAY	3	LANCASTER	925/G	SELF	F/L HAY + CREW	BOMBING + TEST. — (A HONEY)
MAY	4	LANCASTER	909	SELF	CREW	TEST.
MAY	4	LANCASTER	437	SELF	P/O KNIGHT + CREW	NIGHT LOW-LEVEL TACTICS
MAY	6	LANCASTER	925	SELF	P/O EARNSHAW P/O SPAFFORD + CREW	TO + FROM MANSTON. LOW-LEVEL FORMATION.
MAY	9	LANCASTER	925	SELF	CREW	LOW-LEVEL X CTY. TACTICAL PRACTISE
MAY	9	LANCASTER	925	SELF	CREW	LOW-LEVEL X CTY. TACTICAL PRACTISE
MAY	11	LANCASTER	925	SELF	CREW	TO + FROM MANSTON. LOW-LEVEL FORMATION WITH WING/CO. V.H.F. TESTS
MAY	11	LANCASTER	925	SELF	CREW	STORE DROPPING. 60'. 220 IAS.
MAY	13	LANCASTER	925	SELF	CREW	BOMBING + TACTICAL PRACTISE
MAY	13	LANCASTER	925	SELF	CREW	X CTY. LOW-LEVEL (MOONLIGHT) + TACTICS
MAY	14	LANCASTER	925	SELF	CREW	NFT. + BOMBING
MAY	14	LANCASTER	925	SELF	CREW	FORMATION EXERCISE. LOW-LEVEL (MOONLIGHT)
MAY	16	LANCASTER	925	SELF	CREW	OPERATIONS — MOHNE DAM MISSING

SUMMARY FOR MAY 1943
UNIT B.FLT. 617 SQDN
DATE 1.5.43
SIGNATURE

AIRCRAFT TYPES
1 LANCASTER
2
3
4

F/LT.
OC B.FLT.

GRAND TOTAL [Cols. (1) to (10)]
1009 Hrs. 25 Mins.

S/L W/CR OC B.FLT.
TOTALS CARRIED FORWARD
617 SQDN.

At 2139★ hours on 16 May, coincidentally the day after Mothering Sunday in Germany, they took off from Scampton (following the second group, who were flying to the Sorpe Dam). Wing Commander Guy Gibson led the first wave in *G-George*, followed by Flight Lieutenant John 'Hoppy' Hopgood, DFC and Bar, in *M-Mother*, John being Guy's second in command.

★There is an inconsistency in the various records of the take-offs by some eleven minutes; clocks were operating on Double Summer Time in the Second World War.

SINGLE-ENGINE AIRCRAFT				MULTI-ENGINE AIRCRAFT						PASS-ENGER	INSTR/CLOUD FLYING [Incl. in cols. (1) to (10)]	
DAY		NIGHT		DAY			NIGHT					
DUAL	PILOT	DUAL	PILOT	DUAL	1ST PILOT	2ND PILOT	DUAL	1ST PILOT	2ND PILOT		DUAL	PILOT
(1)	(2)	(3)	(4)	(5)	(6)	(7)	(8)	(9)	(10)	(11)	(12)	(13)
21.45	42.20			28.10	443.10	113.20	3.35	225.25	111.35	7.55	23.40	9.15
					1.50							
					1.10							
					.55							
					.20							
								1.50				
					2.00							
					1.10							
								1.50				
1,000 hrs. flying completed					2.10							
					.35							
					1.25							
								2.30				
					.50							
								1.30				
DEATH PRESUMED												
21.45	42.20			28.10	455.35	113.20	3.35	233.05	111.35	7.55	23.40	9.15
(1)	(2)	(3)	(4)	(5)	(6)	(7)	(8)	(9)	(10)	(11)	(12)	(13)

CENTRAL DEPOSITORY
★ JAN 1947 ★
ROYAL AIR FORCE

These last two pages in John's log book show his WINGS FOR VICTORY 'BEAT UP' AT HORNCASTLE, his trips to Manston to test the Upkeep bomb, rigorous night-time low-level flying across the country (X CTY LOW LEVEL MOONLIGHT) leading up to Operation Chastise. Finally is the one line John was unable to enter himself, and therefore is in another's handwriting (that of Harry Humphries, the 617 Squadron Adjutant), stating in red letters: MAY 16 LANCASTER 925 SELF CREW OPERATIONS – MOHNE DAM MISSING. Also note the recognition of completing 1,000 hours of flying and the rectangular stamp mark: DEATH PRESUMED. The signatures at the bottom of the page are those of Mickey Martin (pilot of P–Popsie) and David Maltby (Old Marlburian and pilot of J–Johnny)

10

'Courage Beyond Fear'

Let us now imagine the scene inside *M-Mother* on that legendary night. Please note that John Hopgood, the pilot, will be referred to as 'Hoppy', there being two other Johns in his crew (John Minchin and John Fraser).

M-Mother set out at 9.28 p.m., two minutes before a particularly beautiful sunset, prompted by the green Aldis light flashing on the Scampton runway control. In formation with Martin's *P-Popsie* and Gibson's *G-George*, and with its four Merlin Rolls-Royce engines thundering into a crescendo, it took off from the grass runway, carrying its heavy and uniquely adapted load. Once in the sky, the engine note changing slightly as the rpm was reduced, *M-Mother* roared over the darkening Lincolnshire countryside with its elegant landmark of the cathedral. In the spherical glass cockpit, Hoppy, the pilot, was sitting to the left in a raised and padded seat with arm rests; he was using all the muscles in his left hand to fly the machine and in his right to reset the gyro and other instruments. His eyes were checking the compass, the airspeed indicator, the horizon, the ground, and the blind-flying panel where the instruments were winking. Hoppy was determined to do the best possible job, and his mind was totally focused on the mission ahead. Anyone flying a Lancaster had to be tough and gutsy.

On this audacious mission it was crucial that there was effective communication between the pilots, and so higher frequency radios (VHFs) from fighter planes had been strapped on to the Lancasters (on Gibson's and Hopgood's there was a second radio in reserve in case of malfunction). Hoppy was ready to take over the leadership from Gibson if his plane was shot down.

His trusty flight engineer, Charlie Brennan, who was also a mechanic, sat on Hoppy's right on a collapsible seat (known as a 'second dicky seat'), with the fuel selectors and gauges on a panel to his right behind him. It was his job to nurse the fuel levels, swap to another tank when the level became low and ensure there was enough diesel to get home; he also controlled the airspeed with the throttle and boost controls. Both Hoppy and Charlie knew that the panel above the cockpit could be used as their emergency exit.

Position of crew in a Lancaster

Behind the pilot and flight engineer, and behind a curtain fitted to allow him to use light to work, sat the navigator, Ken Earnshaw. His position faced to port beside a chart table with a map on rollers, and a panel mounted to the side on the fuselage to check the airspeed. Once over the sea, he would throw out a flame float for the rear gunner to estimate drift. On this occasion he couldn't refer to his altimeter as they were flying too low, so he was in charge of the spotlights, standard Aldis lamps, mounted under the nose of the aircraft and to the rear of the bomb bay. They were angled to the right for ease of observation, and it was Ken's job to watch them, passing on his observations to the pilot, Hoppy, who adjusted his height accordingly.

Way up in front in a turret, ready for anything and poised to shoot, was George Gregory, the expert front gunner, his feet in stirrups to hold him up above the bomb aimer. To the rear of the turret was the side crew door, on the starboard side of the fuselage. This was the main entrance to the aircraft and also could be used as an emergency exit. Beneath George, and lying flat, his chest on a padded rest in the nose of the plane, was John Fraser, the bomb aimer (or bombardier). Here he had access to the bombsight controls, the bombsight computer and bomb release selectors on the right. Whereas some of the other Lancasters in the first wave would be using chinagraph markings on the cupola to judge the correct distance from the dam at which to drop their bomb, John had a simple Y-shaped bomb-aiming gadget, the original Dann version. There was a flattened section of the cupola on which he could rest this bomb-sight when needed, but for now he needed a clear view out of the large transparent Perspex nose cupola to assist the

navigator with map reading; he was pleased to see that it had been cleaned of the
dead insects which often accumulated there.

The wireless operator, John Minchin, sat on a seat at the front of the main spar,
facing forwards, with his radios mounted on the left-hand end of the chart table,
facing the rear of the aircraft. On his left was a window, and above him was the
astrodome, used for visual signalling and by the navigator for celestial navigation.
On this mission he was responsible for activating the hydraulic motor to impart
backspin to the bomb ten minutes before delivery, controlling the weapon
speed to 500rpm. Behind John Minchin were the two spars for the wing, which
created a major obstacle for crew members moving down the fuselage even on
the ground. At the end of the bomb bay the floor dropped down and had been
adapted to hold the massive cylindrical Upkeep, or bouncing bomb.

Right at the tail end of the fuselage, over the spars for the tail plane, and the Elsan
chemical toilet, and therefore about 10m behind the others, was the rear gunner Tony
Burcher; he sat in his exposed position in the tail turret, which was entered through
a small hatch in the rear of the fuselage. It was probably the most uncomfortable
and coldest seat, and so cramped that Tony would have hung his parachute on a
hook inside the fuselage, near the turret doors. Not being heated, he would have
been wearing an electrically heated suit to prevent hypothermia and frostbite. The
centre section of Perspex had probably been removed from the turret to improve
visibility, as the transparencies were difficult to see through at night. Tony's escape
route would involve rotating his turret to the side and dropping out backwards
through the two rear turret doors. This rear turret was the best defensive section and
so Tony was equipped with four Browning machine guns, each with 2,500 rounds of
ammunition; George, in the front turret, had two such machine guns.

The night was clear and lit by the full moon. The sea, despite the unexpected
slight north-easterly wind, seemed calm like glass. The crew was silent. The
four Merlin engines purred loudly. The atmosphere was loaded with challenge,
expectation and realism but no doubt hope also. Although fully alert to the task
in hand, this may have been the one time Hoppy may have fleetingly been able to
think of his mother, Grace, his home in Shere, his sisters Marna and Betty, and his
pleasure at being back on operations with the thrill of action; after that moment
he would have had to divert all of his attention to the challenging job in hand.

As they crossed the Dutch coast, Hoppy skilfully and steadily dropped
M-Mother to an altitude of about 50ft to avoid radar and searchlight detection and
flew in perfect formation with the other Lancasters. Any previous forebodings
had probably by then been obliterated from his mind as his professionalism took
over and he refocused on the mission ahead.

There seemed to be no night fighters to warn the others about, so Tony
Burcher concentrated on looking for searchlights and flak guns at which to shoot.
Suddenly, they nearly hit high-tension cables; Tony remembered afterwards that,

although Gibson and Martin's Lancasters rose over them, he was suddenly aware of his plane, *M-Mother*, dropping, and then he saw the cables passing above him. They avoided a great number of searchlights by dodging behind trees.

Keeping in perfect formation until the Rhine was in sight, Hoppy suddenly saw Gibson, in *G-George*, take a very sharp turn as he was 6 miles off course and heading for the heavily defended Duisburg. For the next couple of minutes *M-Mother* and *P-Popsie* both lost contact but picked him up again, flying along the Rhine under heavy fire from barges.

A little after this, about twenty minutes before reaching the Möhne Dam, they flew over an unexpected aerodrome near Dorsten, which was heavily defended and had not been marked on their combat charts. Immediately all three of the Lancasters in front (*G-George*, *M-Mother* and *P-Popsie*) were picked up by the searchlights and illuminated brightly. Tony managed to shoot out some of the searchlights and almost immediately *M-Mother* was hit by flak; a shell burst in the cockpit area, damaging a port engine, and we know that at this point shrapnel killed or mortally wounded George Gregory, the front gunner (he never subsequently answered the internal radio/telephone), scratched rear gunner Tony's stomach and lower leg, and wounded Hoppy on the forehead. Now just south-west of Dülmen, the flak was still coming at them. John Minchin, the wireless operator, may have been hit then or later on at the dam.

Once *M-Mother* was no longer being bombarded by flak, Hoppy said, 'Right well what do you think? Should we go on? I intend to go on because we have only got a few minutes left. We've come this far. It's no good taking this thing back with us. The aircraft is completely manageable. I can handle it OK. Any objections?' It seems that Charlie Brennan, sitting right beside Hoppy at the time, was the only one to voice any objection, saying, 'What about your face? It's bleeding like …' and Hoppy interrupted him saying, 'Just hold a handkerchief over it.' In hindsight, the consensus seems to be that anyone else would have turned around at that point and headed for home, but not Hoppy – that was the type of man he was.

So they continued. The port outer engine was working on reduced revs, so the propeller did not yet need to be feathered (tilted away from air current to reduce drag), and there was a glycol leak, but somehow Hoppy kept it going despite the loss of power. They did not inform their Wing Commander Guy Gibson of the damage to their aircraft or of their injuries; they took the decision to continue themselves. And they took a pride in stifling their fear, no man wanted to admit they couldn't handle it if their injured pilot could handle it. Charlie Brennan had left his 'dickie seat' and was standing over Hoppy, holding a handkerchief to his head to stop the flow of blood clouding his eyesight; it was, of course, important the pilot could see clearly. By now the Gee navigation had also been jammed by the enemy. But still they would, against all odds, complete the enormous and special task they had started, and for which they had intensively trained; this was 'courage beyond fear'.

Twenty minutes later, *M-Mother*, along with the first wave of Lancasters, reached the Möhne Dam, arriving at about midnight. The dam looked, in Gibson's words, 'like a battleship, guns were firing, as well as from the power house just below the dam, but there were no searchlights. The bursting shells and the tracer were reflected in the water, so that there seemed twice as much …' It was camouflaged with pine-tree cut-outs along its wall, there were torpedo nets in front of it. (Less than twelve hours earlier, and by a rather disconcerting coincidence, this dam had been the setting for German families to celebrate Mother's Day, peacefully picnicking alongside the clear blue Möhnesee.)

Defending on the dam wall, Unteroffizier Karl Schutte and his men were taken by surprise. Gibson's plane took up position and, flying at 225mph, switched on his lights as he came over the lake, shining them on the water to intersect and confirm his height at 60ft. All the way over enemy territory his bomb aimer had been studying the rolled map of their journey, but having arrived, his focus had been on his Y-shaped bomb sights, aligning them with two towers on the dam. The flight engineer started the motor up to rotate the bomb, and at split-second timing the bomb aimer released the bomb. Although there was plenty of gunfire, the gun placements, taken by surprise, were pointing in random directions. The bomb bounced on top or the water as planned, sunk as it reached the dam, and exploded releasing a 500m fountain of water, appearing white in the moonlight. But the dam was not breached. The throb of the bomber revved into an accelerated roar and rose from its position into the sky and away from the dam.

Hoppy's bomb aimer, John Fraser, recalls Gibson calling, 'It's a piece of cake!', after his *G-George* had dropped the first bomb. This, of course, was far from true.

Now it was Hoppy's turn, and the picture had changed. The Germans now knew where to aim and all the guns were poised. *M-Mother* had had a two-minute wait to allow the waves to calm down and ensure target accuracy and was in communication with Gibson on his higher frequency fighter radio. But Gibson was clear and gave Hoppy the signal to go, 'Hello, "M-Mother". You may attack now. Good luck.' 'OK. Attacking.' Came Hoppy's reply. The turbulent waters of the lake above the dam had subsided. *M-Mother* turned in for her bombing run on three and a bit engines. The enemy was ready and *M-Mother* didn't stand a chance.

In the cockpit Ken Earnshaw, the navigator, switched on the two searchlights to allow the pilot to fly at 60ft above the water. They shone out of the aircraft's belly. He peered out of the starboard side to talk his pilot down to the correct height. To Hopgood's right stood his flight engineer, Charlie Brennan, who, having dressed Hoppy's head wound as well as possible, stopped his ministrations and was now nursing the throttle of the three and a bit remaining engines to achieve the correct speed. They emerged from their hiding place, and faced the dam. Mounted on the tops of the dam's sluice towers, the approaching Lancaster would have appeared as a near stationary target to Karl Schutte and his gunners. They were ready for their prey.

They had had time to manoeuvre the guns and, in the 2,000m and seventeen and a half seconds available for *M-Mother* to take up position to drop the bomb, they subjected the illuminated Lancaster to prolonged and intensive flak. They had failed to hit Gibson's aircraft, but this time they were prepared and determined, and they quickly struck Hoppy's machine, firing at *M-Mother* relentlessly. Even without the loss of the front gunner, *M-Mother* would have had no means of suppressing the incoming fire. Soon another engine was struck and disabled, and a fuel tank in the wing ignited.

There was no time for fear: all John's training and instinct was focused on positioning the Lancaster at 60ft altitude on a straight course for the dam and to hold it long enough for the bomb to be released. There was no question of acknowledging his injuries, and his plane was struggling with both port engines now either useless or damaged; all his skill and effort was needed to keep on course. Charlie Brennan set the motor to revolve the bomb while Ken Earnshaw was watching the lamps on the water and instructing Hoppy as to his altitude: 'Down, down, down, steady, up a little, hold it there, down a little, dead on!'

Bomb Aimer John Fraser was lying prone in the nose of the aircraft, holding his bombsight; he talked his pilot onto the correct heading for the attack and peered at his rudimentary bombsight lining up his nails with the two sluice towers. At the correct range he would release their 4-ton Upkeep bomb, which shook the aircraft as it revolved at 500rpm, suspended beneath the bomber's belly. *M-Mother* hit a wall of fire and was juddering as flak ricocheted off from all angles. Fraser knew the split-second accuracy had not quite happened, and he was about to tell Hopgood to abort the attack and circle for another attempt when flames shot past him. He afterwards recalled, 'We overshot our mark and were going to call it a dummy run when flak hit.' He knew there would be no second attempt. Word came to unload. He released the bomb, which hurtled across the dam between the towers, clearing the dam parapet and hitting the powerhouse below.

By this time *M-Mother* was beyond salvation and John Fraser thought their time was up. The nose emergency hatch (only 22in by 26.5in) was beneath him and it would be a real struggle to exit through whilst wearing a parachute, besides they were too low to stand a chance of a parachute inflating.

Meanwhile, in his rear turret Tony Burcher could see flak shooting past, so he had the turret poised on the beam waiting until the guns came within his range; he could only go to a right angle of the aircraft's axis, but with all the flames and flak, suddenly his turret jammed (the damaged port outer engine must have packed up completely at this point, for it was this engine that supplied the hydraulics to the rear turret). At this point either John Minchin or Charlie Brennan shouted, 'Christ! The engine's on fire!' Charlie tried to quell the blaze but without success. Hoppy, however, remained calm, and as if it was an exercise, he said, 'Feather it. Press the extinguisher.' No panic, no rush. The flames grew stronger and Hoppy said, 'Right prepare to abandon aircraft.'

Not long after, Hoppy ordered, still in a calm and relaxed manner, 'Right everybody get out.'

Tony Burcher hurriedly hand-cranked the turret back, and, disobeying his training routine, kept his helmet on so as to keep in contact with the pilot, as he crawled back into the fuselage to get his parachute and put it on. Then he radioed, 'I am abandoning aircraft', at which point Hoppy shouted, 'For Christ's sake get out!' Tony was about to jump when he saw John Minchin crawling along the floor with his leg dragging uselessly behind him; in a hell of a state, he had somehow struggled towards the back and over the main spar of the aircraft, trailing his parachute in one hand. Tony put his parachute on him but by now he had lost consciousness, so all Tony could do was to pull the parachute's D ring, breaking the parachute open, and push him out. He did not survive.

Against all odds, Hoppy, in one last tremendous surge, powered his disintegrating Lancaster, rearing up in a roaring rage of pain and with no port engines and the port wing a mass of flames, into a steep climbing turn to starboard (the only direction possible with the two dead port engines and the drag caused by the wing). He managed to gain another 200ft to enable his remaining crew to take their chances and escape at 300ft, the lowest possible height for any parachute to inflate. At this point, Tony, squatting on the step by the door, pulled his own

'Courage Beyond Fear' by Lenz Krenzler (in collaboration with Shere Fraser)

D ring (normally not recommended before leaving an aircraft), felt a sudden gush of rising hot air from the burning plane, which threw him up against the tail-fin of the Lancaster, dragging his parachute out after him. He was jerked into the air and then immediately hit the ground.

John Fraser afterwards recalled, 'The rear gunner, Tony Burcher, and I were both above escape hatches, and dumped out as the plane started coming apart.' He noticed that 'the trees looked awful damned close'. He realised he had no chance of survival if he jumped and then pulled the ripcord, so he pulled it before jumping, and luckily the silken parachute billowed out in front of him pulling him from the aircraft. He noticed 'The tail wheel whizzed past my ear', and then in the two or three seconds whilst he was still in the air, he saw the aircraft crash. 'I landed near the wreckage in a wheat field adjoining a railway line, totally unhurt.'

M-Mother's fuel tanks had exploded and its port wing just fell off. Hoppy had had no thought for his own life, and Charlie Brennan had stayed with his pilot, devoted to the end. They had both given their lives for their crew; Ken Earnshaw had also failed to escape from the blazing aircraft.

Tony Burcher had landed in a ploughed field, having broken his back on the tail-fin and his knee-cap on landing but surviving probably the lowest free-fall parachute jump in history.

Gibson described Hoppy's attack as follows:

Hoppy, the Englishman, casual, but very efficient, keen now on only one thing, which was war. He began his attack. He began going down over the trees where I had come from a few moments before. We could see his spotlights quite clearly, slowly closing together as he ran across the water. We saw him approach. The flak by now had got an idea from which direction the attack was coming, and they let him have it. When he was about 100 yards away someone said hoarsely over the R/T, 'Hell! He's been hit.' M.Mother was on fire – an unlucky shot had got him in one of the inboard petrol tanks and a log jet of flame was beginning to stream out. I saw him drop his mine, but his bomb-aimer must have been wounded, because it fell straight on to the powerhouse on the other side of the dam. But Hoppy staggered on, trying to gain altitude so that his crew could bail out. When he had got up to about 500 feet there was a livid flash in the sky and one wing fell off. His aircraft disintegrated and fell to the ground in cascading, flaming fragments. There it began to burn in a field some three miles beyond the dam. Someone said, 'Poor old Hoppy.' And another said, 'We'll get those bastards for this.' The time was 34 minutes past midnight.

A furious rage surged up inside my own crew, and one said, 'Let's go in and murder those gunners.' As he spoke, Hoppy's mine went up. It went up behind the powerhouse with a tremendous yellow explosion and left in the air a great ball of black smoke.

Power station, Möhne Dam, 1943

However, *M-Mother's* attack had not been in vain. The explosion of his bomb on the power station not only destroyed the power station, with its seven transformers and 2,700 gallons of oil, but the energy from the gigantic flash dislodged the southern (left) anti-aircraft gun from its mounting, putting it out of action. The blast of their bomb also threw the gunners on the dam to the ground injuring several and so significantly reducing the gunfire potential against the next Lancasters. (The picture, taken pre 1943 and now presented on an information board at the Möhne Dam, shows the power station in its original position, below and central to the dam; it was not rebuilt until 1953, and then positioned where it now stands, to one side of the dam.)

Karl Schutte remembered really laying into the second aircraft, '*Endlich, nach langer zeit, darf man schie en!*', their success at hitting it '*Die Schüsse liegen gut!*' and flames coming out of it, '*eine Flamme herausschlägt*'. Then came the explosion from *M-Mother's* bomb on the power station and he reported a massive explosion '*eine fürchterliche Detonation!*', dust taking their breath away, '*Staub nimmt uns fast den Atem!*', stones flying at them '*Steinewirbeln umher*' and a huge impact throwing him to the floor '*ein Starker Schlag wirft mich zu Boden*'.

So now, with much less resistance from the German gunners, thanks to *M-Mother's* bomb disabling more than half the guns, Operation Chastise could continue.

It was Martin's turn next in *P-Popsie*. Gibson flew on Martin's right to draw the enemy fire. His bomb exploded near the left (south) tower. But the dam was not breached. Then came Young in *A-Apple*. Gibson flew over and around the dam whilst Martin flew on Young's right to draw the enemy fire. His bomb succeeded in producing a small breach. (Incidentally *A-Apple* was subsequently shot down near Amsterdam at 0258 that same morning on its way home.)

Finally, with the last bomb, came Maltby (the other Old Marlburian) in *J-Johnny*. Gibson flew on Maltby's right and Martin on his left to shield him. The gun on the north tower jammed. The bomb bounced, sunk, exploded and the dam was breached. Mission successful. Gibson radioed back to England the prearranged code word, 'Nigger' (after his beloved dog), indicating that the dam had been breached. As each of these aircraft pulled away from the dam, the crews would have seen, just 3 miles below, the flames and glow from *M-Mother* over the hillside where it had finally come to rest.

The entry in red at the end of Hoppy's log book was presumably updated by Adjutant Harry Humphries when Hoppy did not return:

MAY 16 LANCASTER 925 SELF CREW OPERATIONS–MOHNE DAM MISSING

And, in red in a square box:

DEATH PRESUMED

Eight of the nineteen Lancasters that set out had failed to return, 53 men out of 133 had lost their lives, and three were captive (two of them from *M-Mother*). The Möhne and Eder dams had been breached and the Sorpe Dam had been damaged. Gibson was awarded a VC for his leadership of the raid. Thirty-three other survivors also received awards for bravery (43 per cent of the survivors). Not one of the fifty-six men who did not return was posthumously recognised: Churchill did not want to dwell on its dead because the Dambusters' Raid had served as a huge morale boost to the British Nation.

FOR OUR TOMORROW THEY GAVE THEIR TODAY!

AJ-M 'Mother'
Flight Lieutenant John 'Hoppy' Hopgood   R.I.P.
Flying Officer Ken Earnshaw   R.I.P.
Sergeant Charles Brennan   R.I.P.
Sergeant John Minchin   R.I.P.
Pilot Officer George Gregory   R.I.P.

John Maxwell Edmonds

11

Après Moi Le Déluge

Following the fateful but legendary night of 16/17 May 1943, the 617 Squadron adopted its now well-known motto: *Après Moi le Déluge*.

This Dambuster motto was originally attributed to the King of France, Louis XV (1710–74) or to his most famous lover, Madame de Pompadour (1721–64). If read literally, it means 'After Me the Flood'; *le déluge* can also mean chaos. Both these would be very appropriate for 617 Squadron, which, having breached the Möhne and Eder dams, left a trail of destruction in its wake. But a second meaning could be, 'I've had my time (fun) and after me the world can go to hell for all I care,' indeed this is what Karl Marx★ believed was the basis of capitalism, i.e. 'I'll make money now and I don't care if the country goes to pieces after I've gone.' In that sense it is not such a good postscript (in fact quite the opposite) for John Hopgood, who was an idealist and would have wanted his sacrifice, and those of his peers, to be for the greater good of the nation, freeing it from the tyranny of the Nazis and, indeed, Karl Marx's communism.

Squadron badge

The Air Ministry Communique broadcast by BBC morning of 17 May 1943 was as follows:

In the early hours of this morning a force of Lancasters led by Wing Commander G P Gibson DSO DFC attacked with mines the dams of the Möhne and Sorpe reservoirs. These control two-thirds of the water storage capacity of the Ruhr basin.

Reconnaissance later established that the Möhne Dam had been breached over a length of 100 yards and that the power station below had been swept away by the resulting floods.

The Eder Dam, which controls the head waters of the Weser and Fulda Valleys and operates several power stations, was also attacked and was reported as breached. Photographs show the river below in full flood.

The attacks were pressed home from a very low level with great determination and coolness and in the face of fierce resistance. Eight of the Lancasters are missing.

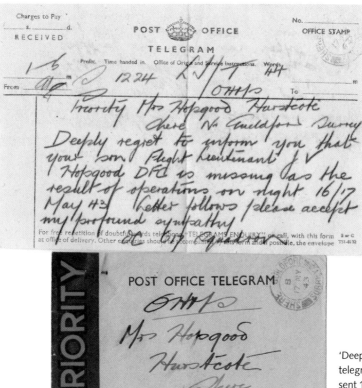

'Deeply regret' telegram sent 17 May 1943 from Scampton

On that 17 May morning, following the attack on the Möhne Dam, John's mother received this telegram, probably written by adjutant of 617, Harry Humphries. Grace wrote:

> Thank God, Marna was here – indeed she answered the door-bell & took the telegram from the Postmaster who brought it up himself & said he 'was v. sorry to have to bring bad news', so Marna opened it and called me – but somehow I felt it had come.

Wing Commander Guy Gibson wrote immediately to Grace, emphasising John's extreme courage, saying:

> *It is with deep regret that I write to confirm my telegram advising you that your son, Flight Lieutenant J. V. Hopgood DFC., is missing as a result of operations on the night of 16/17th May 1943.*
>
> *John has been with me for over a year and we have done many operations together, and it is with the deepest regret that I now say that I am alone. He was a great personal friend and was quite the finest pilot I have ever known.*
>
> *The circumstances which led to his not coming back are most unlucky. When attacking the Möhne Dam, his aircraft was subjected to intense light flak fire and his port outer engine caught fire. I watched him climb up to 1000 ft to enable his crew to bale out, and although I am quite certain that some of them got away I would not like to raise your hopes too high until we know for certain. John would always be the last to leave his aircraft, and this is but one of the many small things that made him one of the finest pilots in Bomber Command.*
>
> *If, as is possible, your son was able to abandon his aircraft and land safely in enemy territory, news will reach you direct from the International Red Cross Committee within the next six weeks.*
>
> *Please accept my sincere sympathy during this anxious period of waiting.*
>
> *I have arranged for his personal effects to be taken care of by the Committee of Adjustment Officer at this Station, and they will be forwarded to you through normal channels in due course. If there is any way in which I can help you please let me know.*
>
> *Yours Very Sincerely Guy P Gibson*

What is particularly significant are the words 'I am now alone. He was a great personal friend.' It has been said that Guy Gibson was an authoritarian figure, with few friends. It seems that, sharing a similar background, and having an easy sociable empathy with people in general, John had achieved a level of friendship possibly not experienced by Wing Commander Guy Gibson before, one without which he was to feel genuinely lost.

As for John's bravery, flying and piloting skills, there is no doubting Guy Gibson's admiration; John was the 'best pilot Guy Gibson had ever known'.

On Tuesday, 18 May, the headline of the *Daily Express* read:

Waterspouts shot 1,000 ft. up as Lancasters swooped with sea mines on giant dams.

Escaping torrents devastate vast war producing area, wreck railways and bridges.

FLOODS ROAR DOWN RUHR VALLEY

Fliers see 30ft wave LIKE A NEW INLAND SEA – AND STILL SPREADING FAST

And in *The Times* on the same day:

RUHR DAMS BREACHED: DARING LOW-LEVEL ATTACK BY LANCASTERS: WALLS BLASTED OUT WITH 1,500LB. MINES: VAST DAMAGE BY FLOODS.

However, the German High Command's report of the raid was extremely understated:

Weak British air forces last night penetrated into German Territory and dropped a small number of high-explosive bombs on some places.★ Two dams were damaged, and heavy casualties were caused among the civilian population by the resulting floods.

★ Weak indeed!

Meanwhile, up in the Lake District, John's sister Betty was blissfully unaware of her brother's plight, training to be a PNEU teacher in the Charlotte Mason College, Ambleside. She was absorbed in her love of nature, out in the fresh air, painting flowers and noting details of 'All things bright and beautiful, All creatures great and small' in her notebook.

Walking into her college library she does, however, remember seeing, slung on a table, a picture of a burst dam on the front page of the *Telegraph* for 17 May, but she had no idea that it was in any way connected to her brother John. Betty only found out about John by chance when half-sister Joan wrote her a letter on 18 May 1943, saying, 'Oliver has just rung me up to tell me the sad news about John. Don't worry too much.'

Betty wrote in her diary for Thursday, 20 May, 'Climb the Langdale Pikes. Yesterday heard that John was missing from the Möhne dam raid. It is awful.

Betty, unaware of John's plight,
paints Lousewort

On return from Langdale Climb, I fall off my bike. I have quite a jar and sleep the night in the sick room.'

Betty knew no more of what had happened and so just awaited the next communication. Such was war!

Her mother had immediately written to her the following letter, but it seems she did not post it, hoping perhaps for some better news to tell her youngest daughter, who was away from home alone. She starts the letter below with the noncontroversial subject of the weather, before broaching the subject of the real sad message:

TUES MAY 18. 1943
HURSTCOTE,
SHERE, SURREY

My darling Bets,

Marna came home on Friday afternoon for a week & has got in for a spell of lovely sunny weather. We both wondered what you were doing in the Lakes on Sat afternoon & Sunday, if you had same weather.

Now, darling, I have to tell you that there is bad news of John — We had a telegram on Monday lunch time from his C.O. saying he was 'missing from operations night of 16/17 May'. Of course he was one of the picked crew to do this marvellous raid on the Ruhr Dams — Wing Co. Gibson who led the raid was J's C.O. — You will of course have read the accounts in the newspapers or heard them on the wireless — I shall not send this letter to you until I have received a letter from Wing Co. Gibson — so that you may have all the information I can get. I wired Oliver immediately asking him to try & get details *from John's station. Oliver phoned me yesterday evening; he says a <u>large</u> percentage of men escape from their planes when hit. But, seeing the nature of the work to be done & the awful floods caused in the district for miles and miles around, I can't feel very hopeful. It is some comfort to know that John was chosen for such a highly important piece of work – he will have loved the idea of it – the bursting of such large Dams, from the air, is so novel & so spectacular that, as the report of it says, it is one that will go down in the history of aerial warfare – it may prove to have results which will affect the war on the Continent.*

In our anxiety – even in our possible loss – we can feel proud that our John was skilful & courageous enough to be chosen to take part in such a piece of work.

I wish you did not have to receive this news while away from home – it is so much harder to have none of the circle to talk to about him. The blow falls heaviest on our dear Marna who has been John's <u>almost</u> twin – so little difference in their ages – I know what my brother Elliot meant to me as a girl (& also now). I feel it is harder for both John's sisters than for me & you will know that Mummy is thinking & praying for <u>all</u> her children. This world seems such chaos as we see it 'through a glass darkly', but there is a God of love above it all. One day <u>we</u> may hope to see clearly.

Yr loving Mummy.

What a heroic mother Grace was, no wonder she had such a heroic son. Thank goodness her strong faith in God upheld her, alongside her pride in knowing that her son, still only 21 years old, had not only been chosen for an elite squadron but had excelled himself as a pilot and shown courage beyond fear for a hugely prestigious cause.

The letter Betty did eventually receive from her mother quoted Guy Gibson's letter and continued:

<u>I</u> <u>don't</u> think this looks very hopeful as John would be the last to leave, & anyway <u>what</u> a territory to come down in – floods & dislocation for more than 100 miles round.

We all prayed especially for John in Church yesterday. The Rector made an announcement from the Chancel Steps calling J. 'Gallant and Brave'. Everyone is so sympathetic & so upset by the news.

I have so much to write so no more today my darling little daughter.

Uncle Elliot was with us for W/E. We went to Cinema on Saturday to please Marna, but as it was showery and quite a good film, it was a good thing to do. John is not out of our thoughts for an instant but it doesn't do for mummys to give way – If he comes back after the War, he may need all the cheerfulness & strength that we can muster – if he doesn't, others will.

You shall have any more news good or bad, as soon as I get it.

Marna sends love, & has written.

Yr V. Loving Mummy.

So back in Surrey, Hoppy's mother was keeping a very stiff upper lip and, alongside her deep and meaningful faith in God, which assured her that everything was for a higher purpose, she found comfort in words such as 'gallant' and 'brave' and was magnificently supported by her brother Elliot, the rector at Shere church, and all of the Shere village community.

Kind-hearted Marna, with true Hopgood grit, and despite her intense grief over John, returned to her ATS work after her week's leave, which she continued until the end of the war.

Trying to be hopeful and positive for her mother's sake, she wrote from Markeaton Park, Derby on 6 June 1943:

My darling Mummy,

I don't know where to start in commenting on your letter there were so many bits of news. First and foremost I hope with all my heart that John got out of that plane at a reasonable height and was able to make the landing safely. I rather feel from the first accounts we had that this may be quite possible.

I paid a visit to the Red X depot here and asked for details of sending things to prisoners, they told me this: the next of kin can send 4 personal parcels in a year containing clothes, books etc. through the Red X. Also they will send a parcel of food, cigs and chocolate to a prisoner every month as soon as you can give them the name and address of camp, this is done free, but no doubt one would contribute towards the expense. Then from the post office you obtain special letter cards at 2½ d each which you send as often as you like, I enclose one so that if we get good news there will be no delay in getting a line off.

And from Woodbine House, Smedley Street, Matlock, on 4 July 1943, Marna wrote, 'When are we going to hear about John? I am still hopeful.'

However, all hopes were finally dashed when Grace received this telegram, dated 6 July:

(NO CHARGE FOR DELIVERY)
Immediate Mrs Hopgood   Hurstcote, Shere, Guildford

Immediate from air ministry Kingsway P.C. 672 6/7 Deeply Regret to advise you that according to information received through the International Red Cross Committee, your son, Flight Lieutenant John Vere Hopgood DFC and bar is believed to have lost his life as the result of air operations on night of sixteenth/17th May 1943; the air council express their profound sympathy. Letter confirming this telegram follows. His uncle E.R. Fison Esq [Elliot] is being informed 061051B.

On 6 July Marna sent the following letter to her mother:

My darling of darling Mummys,

I got your letter today. As soon as I saw it I knew the worst because I never get a letter at this end of the week from you. I just don't know what to write because I feel so much and all sorts of thoughts keep rushing into my mind. Yes your fears were right and at the time of the first news I felt it would be the end, but I was not going to give that impression because it would have just upset both of us, so I put into operation the old drill of self discipline in the face of trouble. Perhaps you thought I took it rather with a light heart and I hope I gave that impression because I must be a better actress than I thought.

It's no good writing all my conclusions, thoughts and fears for the past 6 months but I have one outstanding memory and that is a very beautiful one. As our darling said goodbye to us after the investiture party, I took a long look at him thinking how perfectly built he was, full of life, handsome and courageous with a sweet smile on his face that made you want to smile back because it laughed at the world and was happy and I thought, that is how I shall always remember him if my fears do come true; did you see it too?

I expect we both noticed quite a number of things and were both silent about them because one does not want anyone else to believe it could possibly be true.

You are wonderful, the most wonderful mother that anyone could wish to have but I feel it would not be wise for me to come home just now, we should be too sympathetic to each other and everything would hurt so much more – I will wait for my leave and by then we shall I hope enjoy talking about him and will get some comfort from it.

I feel so sorry for dear little Betty because she really did love him in a strong quiet way and no-one seemed to notice it because they all thought I was his favourite, but I don't think that was right, we were all three very fond of each other and there was no degree of fondness between any one of us.

If you do want me please do say so and I will endeavour to get some compassionate leave, but honestly I agree with you, the war effort must come first and we must work doubly hard now to avenge it.

Don't worry about me because I have some very kind people round me here, I get all the sympathy I can put up with, but it is you that I am worried about. I am going to bed now as I have not slept for the last two nights, somehow I felt there was something in the air,

Your ever loving little

Daughter.

Although Marna bravely soldiered on following the telegram, for Grace the stiff upper lip was now no more, and she unloaded to her daughter Betty in a real outpouring of grief and emotion:

July 6th 1943

My darling little Bets,

I do wish I need not write this letter to you when you are so busy – At first I thought I would write to you so that you would get this at College – But in case anyone glanced at the Casualty lists, or any of the family wrote to you thinking you knew about John, I feel I must not delay any longer.

Our dear dear John has consciously and willingly given up his Earthly Life for the sake of his crew who were also his friends. John has conquered Sin & Conquered Death – he has passed into such Joys as are past man's understanding.

I do not say this glibly, I got the news on Sat morning & everything turned <u>BLACK</u> – at last, on Monday, I wretchedly asked God to help me to <u>understand.</u> Gradually & very wonderfully, the light came & I see now & can be thankful for John & not in the <u>least</u> sorry for myself. I <u>know</u> that John we loved, & laughed at, & admired is now as much more wonderful & beautiful as the butterfly is more splendid than the grub.

When you get away from your work, you will think out about John for yourself & I pray that God will <u>help</u> you as he has helped me.

Whatever you do, don't worry about <u>me.</u> I feel absolutely certain that God has got John safe from all EVIL, & I know He is with me, teaching me many things comforting me.

It is rather touching that their mother compares John's life and death to a caterpillar metamorphosing into a beautiful butterfly for Betty's sake, since she was always so wrapped up in nature. Grace herself, consumed by religious fervour,

No. 617 Squadron,
R.A.F., Station, Scampton,
Lincoln.

8th July 1943.

My dear Mrs Hopgood,

It is with deepest regret that I now have to write to confirm the telegram you have received, that your son Flight Lieutenant J.V.Hopgood was killed in action on the night of 16/17th May 1943.

Please accept my sincere and heartfelt sympathy and that of the Officers and airmen of the Squadron, in the sad loss which you have sustained.

Yours Very Sincerely,

Guy P. Gibson

Mrs. Hopgood,
"Hurstcote",
Shere, Surrey.

DO/4/43.

Guy Gibson's letter to Mrs Hopgood

her personal way of coping with her grief, showed a remarkable, undaunted and very moving faith in God.

Two days later Wing Commander Guy Gibson confirmed John's death by writing from 617 Squadron:

My dear Mrs Hopgood,
  It is with deepest regret that I now have to write to confirm the telegram you have received, that your son Flight Lieutenant JV Hopgood was killed in action on the night of 16/17th May 1943.
  Please accept my sincere and heartfelt sympathy and that of the officers and airmen of the Squadron, in the sad loss you have sustained.
  Yours very Sincerely,
  Guy Gibson.

And Grace received an acknowledgement of sympathy, signed by King George VI.

Betty's older half-brother Oliver wrote to Grace from the Lake District, saying:

The news about John is a shock to us all, but I am sure that he would not want us to mourn for him. I shall always remember him as one who put all his energy into doing his duty, who enjoyed life to the full and who would go out of his way to be kind to anyone he met. Let us try to follow his example.

Betty, who was now very busy doing her teaching practice in Ambleside, wrote to her mother, saying:

My darling Mummy
  Thank you for letting me know about John. It's sad that he has been taken from us, I find it hard to realise that it is so.

The letter continues with her daily tasks with the children, concluding with, 'I don't like teaching Children at desks'!

And what of Guy Gibson, *M-Mother*, and its crew?

On 23 May 1943, Wing Commander Guy Gibson was quite rightly awarded the VC for his role and extreme bravery in Operation Chastise; he had tried to draw fire away from the planes attacking the dams after *M-Mother* with absolutely no regard for his own safety. Just over a year later, on the night of 19 September 1944, he went missing whilst returning from an operation attacking the German town of Rheijdt. Gibson was later confirmed dead, aged 26, after his crashed Mosquito aircraft was found near Steenbergen in the Netherlands; it may have had a fault with the fuel gauge and simply run out of fuel, but it is said that Guy was never the same after the Dams Raid, suffering a kind of breakdown, possibly in part due to the losses of brave men he witnessed and in particular that of his good friend Flt Lt John Vere Hopgood.

After his death, Winston Churchill justly described Gibson as 'the glorious Dam-buster'. In the future Gibson came to be known as the first 'Master Bomber' as he had pioneered a 'chaperoning' role at the Möhne Dam by courageously and selflessly flying alongside *M-Mother* and the other aircraft making their attacks, to draw the enemy fire.

M-Mother crashed close to Ostönnen, on a meadow with the peculiar name of Heaven's Gate. The parachute of John Minchin did not open completely; his body was found in a field between Haarhöhe and the site of the crash. The burial of the five dead airmen took place at 12.30 p.m. on 20 May 1943 at Soest East Cemetery, with full military honours. Their remains lay in compartment twenty in three grave sites until they were moved on 14 August 1947 to the British Military Cemetery at Rheinberg.

Rear Gunner Tony Burcher sent a letter to John's mother by '*Kriegsgefangenen-post*' from the prisoner-of-war camp Stalag Luft 3. Although it was written on 5 June 1943, after censorship it must have been delayed, perhaps on account of its contents, and then only forwarded from Gomshall PO on 20 July to her at Wellington Hotel, Seaford, Sussex:

Dear Mrs Hopgood,

I was the rear gunner of the aircraft in which your son lost his life and I wish to express my deepest sympathy. I can honestly say John was about the bravest man I have met and I was proud and honoured to have flown in his aircraft. I had the occasion to return to the aircraft after the accident and it was quite evident that any Captains death was instantaneous. He was given a decent burial with full German military honours. Although I am rather handicapped at the moment, if there is anything I can do for you please don't hesitate to ask me and I would be only too pleased to oblige. I will if I may, visit you when I return to England.

Sincerely Yours,

Tony Burcher.

In later years, Tony Burcher recalled, to his grandchildren, his escape from the disintegrating *M-Mother*. He remembered that, having pushed John Minchin, who had been blocking his way, out of the plane after pulling his D ring, he squatted on the step by the rear door of *M-Mother* and then:

Suddenly there was a great rush of air [upwards] and the next thing I felt was a hell of a belt across my back. I had hit the top of the Lancaster's tail fin. That was one of the things that saved me that night, because my parachute must have been dragged out after me. I had pulled the D ring before I left the Lancaster. Normally that was a stupid thing to do. The Lancaster was in a banking turn to starboard, I suppose that's why I hit her fin. The next thing I knew I was being jerked in the air and hit the ground at the same time.

It seems it was this 'jerk' which saved his broken back from snapping completely, as it would surely have done had he hit the ground normally. He also broke his knee-cap.

Landing in the middle of a newly ploughed field also helped to save me as it cushioned my fall rather well, and, where I landed was in a bit of a valley, so that must have given me extra height. If John had flown the Lancaster straight ahead I would have landed in the path of the flood waters, and would have almost definitely drowned in them. John Hopgood and Charlie Brennan had to know they were never going to escape from the aircraft in that kind of situation and still give the aircrew a chance to get out. So they stayed to the end and I am alive because of that.

Tony recalled crossing a field and crawling under a culvert, not realising that he had a broken back. There were rats in the culvert, and he thought he could hear a train (undoubtedly the roar of the flood waters from the dam), which gave him the hope of escape. He thought that he had stayed there for three days in a state of semi-consciousness but eventually left the culvert to escape the rats. He crawled across a road, only to be spotted by an English-speaking boy, a Hitler Youth, pushing a bicycle. The boy and a passing policeman, also on a bike, carried him between their two bicycles on some fence posts, to the local police station. Tony withstood questioning and torture without giving much away and was eventually taken to a German hospital, where he received excellent medical treatment.

Despite his broken back, Tony Burcher survived in a prisoner of war camp until the end of the war and seemingly never divulged that he had been part of Operation Chastise. Apparently, after he'd been picked up (and kicked by a Hitler Youth), Tony's request for a glass of water was met with incredulity '*Vasser, vasser?* We have no *vasser*; your lot saw to that!' They connected all English prisoners as responsible for their lack of drinking water. Tony did, however, receive good treatment from the German medics, though his back and knee troubled him to the end of his days.

Flt Sergeant John Fraser, John's bomb aimer, also wrote to Grace after the raid, saying, 'We can wait and hope and pray, not only for our own dear ones, but for all those others in distress and in our waiting, we may be able to learn some lesson God is trying to teach us.'

He had landed uninjured 1,500ft from the wreckage of the Lancaster *M-Mother*, in a wheat field. Hiding his parachute in a culvert, Fraser had, as the dawn chorus began to sound, walked back towards the dam to cross on a causeway thinking he was on the wrong side of the river; the position of the dam having been drilled into his memory. From a hiding place in the woods he watched hundreds of inquisitive Germans drive up on horseback to watch as Burcher was captured; then a tight cordon was thrown around the area.

John Fraser filtered through the cordon and evaded capture.

As a trained navigator, he followed the stars and travelled by night, surviving by eating turnips and potatoes from farmers' fields. He journeyed 200 miles north-west between Hamm and Dortmund and west along the Lippe Canal. Here, 8 miles from Wesel on the Rhine, and only 30 miles from the 'safety' of occupied Holland, after approximately ten days on the run, and heavily fatigued, he was caught during the day by a policeman on a bicycle near the Dutch border and became a prisoner of war.

He spent two weary years in four prisoner-of-war camps, where he was moved up ranks from flight sergeant to flight lieutenant and when liberated by the Russians from his last camp at Luckenwalde, south of Potsdam, emerged a commissioned officer. He took part in the 'Great Escape' and recalled being among 1,200 prisoners of war landed back in the UK. His wife, Doris, had stayed on in England during his imprisonment and they met again in May 1945, when they moved to Canada.

After repatriation John Fraser travelled to the quiet Surrey village of Shere to inform Hopgood's mother of the courage and skill of her son that gave him the chance of life. To mark the debt that he felt he owed to his pilot, when he returned to Canada he named a son John Vere and a daughter Shere, after the peaceful Surrey village where John Hopgood had grown up.

In the village of Shere, a memorial service for John Hopgood and his crew was held on what would have been John's 22nd birthday, 29 August 1943. The final hymn was:

Hymn 293: O Valiant Hearts

O valiant hearts, who to your glory came,
Through dust of conflict and through battle flame;
Tranquil you lie, your knightly virtue proved,
Your memory hallowed in the land you loved.

Proudly you gathered, rank on rank, to war,
As who had heard God's message from afar;

All you had hoped for, all you had, you gave
To save mankind – yourself you scorned to save.

John and his four crew are lined up together at the Rheinberg Cemetery, still kept in immaculate order by the War Graves Commission, a band who remain as loyally together as on the night they died, hopefully never to be disturbed.

It is fitting to end this patchwork of John's life with the well-known 'Ode of Remembrance', taken from Laurence Binyon's poem 'For the Fallen', which was first published in *The Times* in September 1914:

They shall grow not old, as we that are left grow old;
Age shall not weary them, nor the years condemn.
At the going down of the sun and in the morning
We will remember them.

The first verse of the same, which is not so well known, is also particularly appropriate for Grace and her son John:

With proud thanksgiving, a mother for her children,
England mourns for her dead across the sea.
Flesh of her flesh they were, spirit of her spirit,
Fallen in the cause of the free.

On 7 September 1968, John's dear mother, Grace Hopgood (née Fison), died in Marlborough, shortly before her 80th year. She is seen here in her last passport photo, proudly wearing the silver brooch of the 'RAF Wings', still resolutely remembering her son. From the window of her room, she could see Marlborough College, thus right until her last breath she had been 'keeping guard' over her dear son John's spirit.

Grace Hopgood aged 79 years wearing RAF wings brooch

Postscript

In May 2013, I, Jenny Elmes, niece of John, daughter of Betty and granddaughter of Grace, had the privilege, along with other members of our family, of attending the 70th anniversary of the Dambusters' Raid in Lincolnshire. It proved a truly glorious, memorable and humbling experience, where we met, among others, Mary Stopes-Rowe, Barnes Wallis' daughter; Les Munro, pilot of *W-Willie*; and Bomb Aimer 'Johnny' Johnson from Joe McCarthy's *T-Tommy* crew. (John Hopgood's log book showed that 'Johnny' Johnson was one of his crew in a Manchester on 8 March 1943 at GTF Fulbeck, practising 'Fighter Affiliation' and that on 30 April 1943 Flight Lieutenant Les Munro was part of Hoppy's crew on a low-level night flight to practise tactics.)

Betty and George 'Johnny' Johnson, 70th Anniversary, Lincolnshire (courtesy Josh Thorpe)

Betty and Barnes Wallis' daughter, Mary Stopes-Rowe, 70th Anniversary

However, the most poignant trip for me was when, between 16 and 19 May 1993, I had the amazing experience of accompanying Marna to Germany for the 50th Anniversary Tour of the Dambusters (with Major and Mrs Holt's Battlefield Tours Ltd). That trip was the spark that fired the tinderbox of my compiling and writing this book.

Crossing the Channel from the white cliffs of Dover, we journeyed by coach with 500 other Dambuster admirers, all of whom were wonderful people, and many, like ourselves, having special connections to the raid: Alan Cooper, who wrote *The Men Who Breached the Dams*; Bob North, the archivist for 617 Squadron; the son of Eric Coates, who wrote the music 'Dambuster March'; and Syd Jones, an ex-617 squadron pilot.

The itinerary of the tour involved visiting Steenbergen churchyard to visit the grave, and nearby crash site, of Wing Commander Guy Gibson, the three dams Eder, Sorpe and Möhne, and two cemeteries (Reichswald Forest CWGC and Rheinberg CWGC) where most of the men killed on the Dams Raid, including John, were buried with a small ceremony of remembrance (including the placing of a wreath on the Cross of Sacrifice in each ceremony, as well as putting personal crosses on John and his crew's graves).

Probably the most significant day for me was when, on 17 May, we visited the Möhne Dam, the same date the dam was attacked and, in 1993, a Monday just as in 1943. It had been rebuilt by 5,000 workers within four months of Operation Chastise. In the middle of the special commemoration, organised by the German veterans, the mayor and other local dignitaries, we were introduced to Karl Schutte; it was he who had shot down *M-Mother* and, notably, had been

M-Mother crew graves at Rheinberg Cemetery

John Hopgood   John Minchin   Charlie Brennan

George Gregory   Ken Earnshaw

awarded the Iron Cross for his bravery on that fateful night. What an ordeal for him to meet us, knowing he had been responsible for a close relative's death; he faced this ordeal by being a little over-oiled with alcohol. And who could blame him. We shook hands with Karl and were interviewed by a German newspaper, *Möhnesee*. Marna was quoted as saying to Karl, 'You were only doing your job to the best of your ability, just as my brother was doing his job to the best of his ability.' I was proud of her. After the trip she wrote, 'To have met some of the Germans who took part in this last war was a union of forgiveness and respect. Both sides were fighting for the honour of their country.'

We were presented with a twisted piece of aluminium, labelled and found with

Karl Schutte with his Iron Cross (and RAF badge presented that day)

Karl Schutte with another flak gunman

a metal detector, by Horst A. Münter, a teacher and aeronautical archivist. It is horrific to think that such pieces are all that is left of *M-Mother*, but in a way it was a blessing that the explosion must have been so mighty that John's death would have been instantaneous.

Helmuth Euler, who had been a young boy when the dam had burst and remembered the roar coming down the valley, introduced himself to us and signed his book *Wasserkrieg*, which he had compiled to mark the 50th anniversary. His book shows pictures of the unimaginable destruction as the waters surged down across 90km of the Ruhr localities: dead bodies of humans and animals, farms, roads, bridges and factories washed away, twisted railway lines and submerged houses – and also this picture of the crashed *M-Mother*.

We visited graveyards of villages washed away by the floods, with children's graves and carvings on ruined churches depicting the burst dam. At Himmelpforten we saw the memorial to a priest who, having been woken by the noise of the planes and the bursting dam, drowned whilst ringing his church bell to warn villagers the water was coming; most moved up to higher ground in time but some perished along with 749 foreign workers in a labour camp. In all over 1,300 innocent people had lost their lives below the dam.

M-Mother crash remnants (including RAF button)

Crashed *M-Mother* Ostonnen, Germany (courtesy Euler)

Marna and Jenny
at crash site

I am sure John would have been beside himself with grief if he had lived to know, in later life, the effects of the Dambusters' Raid and other operations.

On this 50th anniversary tour Marna and I were treated with great sensitivity and allowed to pay private tributes and lay crosses at John's grave in Rheinberg ahead of the crowd. I remember the beautiful misty May morning we were there, and the immaculately kept graves, and the last post being played reverently with an ex-RAF officer lowering the flag. It was all very moving indeed.

John's crash site, with a damaged marker, was also in a very peaceful spot. The farmer who owns this land has a small museum in which he exhibits parts of the mangled wreckage of *M-Mother* and is knowledgeable and sensitive to the plight of the plane and her crew. Now the busy A44 autobahn forms a raised backdrop to the marker post and plaque, and modern wind turbines add a timeless continuity to the scene.

Bibliography

Bishop, Patrick, *Bomber Boys* (Harper Press, 2007)

Churchill, Sir Winston, *The History of the Second World War* (W&N, 2015)

Cooper, Alan, *The Men Who Breached the Dams* (William Kimber, 1982)

Euler, Helmuth, *Wasserkrieg* (Fotostudio Euler, 1992)

Gibson, Guy, *Enemy Coast Ahead: Uncensored* (Crecy, 2006)

Holland, James, *Dam Busters: The Race to Smash the Dams 1943* (Corgi, 2013)

Lawrence, W.J., *No. 5 Bomber Group, RAF* (Faber and Faber, 1951)

Acknowledgements

There are many people who have helped me and encouraged me along the way in producing this book: one of my mainstays has been jumbo-jet pilot Andy Bailey, who has helped me unstintingly with technical aviation terms and RAF interpretations. Of course members of my extended family, in particular Annabel Young (Marna's daughter), James Hopgood (Oliver's son), and my dear mother Betty Bell (John's sister) have all been open to my using the family documents and happy to add any memories of their own. Others I wish to acknowledge include: my husband Graham Elmes, Josh Thorpe, John Villers, Keith Fleming, John Newth, Charles Foster, James Holland, Shere Fraser, RAF Scampton, The National Archives at Kew, and RAF Hendon.

Index

INDEX

If you enjoyed this book, you may also be interested in …

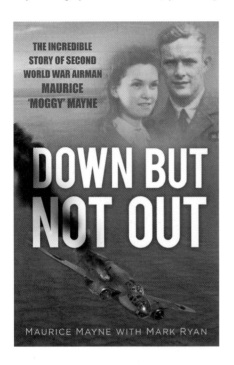

9780750952064

£17.99

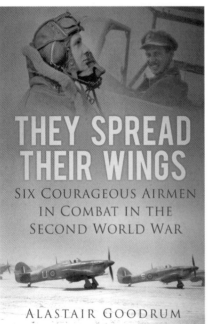

9780752487588

£14.99